C000285864

BATMAN

A CELEBRATION OF THE CLASSIC TV SERIES

BOB GARCIA AND JOE DESRIS

Batman: A Celebration of the Classic TV Series
ISBN: 9781781167885
Limited Edition ISBN: 9781785655128

Published by Titan Books
A division of Titan Publishing Group Ltd.
144 Southwark St.
London
SE1 0UP

First edition: 2016

10 9 8 7 6 5 4 3 2 1

Copyright © 2016 DC Comics.
BATMAN and all related characters and elements are © & ™ DC
Comics.
DC LOGO: ™ & © DC Comics.
WB SHIELD: ™ & © WBEI. (s16)
TIB032549

Batman created by Bob Kane and Bill Finger.

BRUCE LEE® is the registered trademark of Bruce Lee Enterprises, LLC. The Bruce Lee name,
image, likeness and all related indicia are intellectual property of Bruce Lee Enterprises, LLC. All
Rights Reserved. www.brucelee.com.

Liberace likeness used with permission of the Liberace Foundation for the Performing and
Creative Arts. www.liberace.org

Excerpts from Frank Gorshin and William Dozier interviews with Kevin Burns are Copyright 1989,
2015 Kevin Burns, Courtesy of Prometheus Entertainment. All rights reserved.

Original 1966 Yamaha "Batcycle" (page 206) (credit: Teddy Pieper ©2012 Courtesy of RM
Sotheby's).

Batmobile pictures (page 74-75) courtesy of Mark Racop, Fiberglass Freaks, officially licensed
sellers of 1966 Batmobile replicas.

Excerpts from William Dozier, Frank Gorshin, Cesar Romero interviews with Kevin Burns are
Copyright 1989, 2016 Kevin Burns, Courtesy of Prometheus Entertainment. All rights reserved.

Titan Books would like to thank everyone involved with putting this marvelous book together.
Bob and Joe, for all their knowledge, passion and hard work. Adam West and Fred Westbrook for
their support, and the many people who agreed to their image use. And of course huge thanks
to Josh Anderson and Amy Weingartner, without whom this book would not have been possible.

To receive advance information, news, competitions, and exclusive offers online, please sign
up for the Titan newsletter on our website: www.titanbooks.com

Did you enjoy this book? We love to hear from our readers. Please e-mail us at:
readerfeedback@titanemail.com or write to Reader Feedback at the above address.

No part of this publication may be reproduced, stored in a retrieval system, or transmitted,
in any form or by any means without the prior written permission of the publisher, nor be
otherwise circulated in any form of binding or cover other than that in which it is published and
without a similar condition being imposed on the subsequent purchaser.

Every effort has been made to source and contact copyright holders and those requiring
likeness approvals. If any omissions do occur, the publisher will be happy to give full credit in
subsequent reprints and editions.

A CIP catalogue record for this title is available from the British Library.

Printed and bound in China.

CONTENTS

A CELEBRATION OF BATMAN

You've done it. You've done it, Super Batfans. Your love for the classic *Batman* has enabled me to celebrate over forty years of the same kind of regard or affection. It never occurred to me, all those years ago, that I was creating a character for the screen that would withstand the test of time, one that would become an "evergreen." Your affection for my Batman has not dimmed. For that I am grateful. You've made me an icon. That's what I am told. What that means is that I can enjoy the spoils of success. For that I thank you. There have been so many wonderful Batman fan encounters, and I am constantly reminded of the influences our show had on viewers young and old. So many of you grew up with us. Now you watch with your young families because you took us seriously as kids and enjoyed the fantasy and adventure while being fed ethics and morality lessons; perhaps we did some good. As you became adults you became aware that our *Batman* was an absurd comedy- adventure. We brought you laughs. It always amazes me that so many of you remember lines and situations from our shows.

I see many of you playing dress-up as Batman and Robin or our spectacular villains ("trick or treat"). Our villains were memorable and quite Shakespearean in dimension.

Some of the most well-known and celebrated actors in the world knocked at the Batcave clamoring to be part of the show. I am reminded of the late Frank Gorshin as the Riddler in our first show. He set the bar quite high, and his work in the role really informed those who followed what was expected. I loved working with Frank. He had a manic intensity and really immersed himself in the character. It is good to play scenes with actors who push the limits and are "off the wall." It has been written that a television series will continue for many years in reruns and other forms if the audience has an affection for the leading characters. That is positively reflected in the fact that Gorshin and other great *Batman* characters

continue to get considerable fan mail even after they are no longer with us. Certain of their progeny must find some joy in this. Frankly, speaking for myself I would rather not dwell on fan mail after death.

Cesar Romero is gone, too. But his Joker characterization still generates comments wherever I travel. Cesar played with great energy. He was always thoroughly prepared and ready to blow your socks off. He had an athlete's way of refreshing and pacing himself. Between setups he would be found fast asleep in his canvas-backed chair. He was a quiet napper, but his mustache would quiver through his white-painted face as he breathed. It was noticeably funny. However, when called for a shot he was instantly alive and quick and funny. The old pro was a great additive to our mix. And he insisted on keeping his mustache. He believed that it played an important part in his being known. He was convinced that it was his mustache that was partly responsible for all of his earlier movie successes.

As I write and remember these wonderful performers, I see Burgess Meredith waddling forward with his delightful rendering of the Penguin. I will never forget his nasal quack-like laugh and salacious expression as he spoke his lines and blew smoke while holding that long cigarette holder. The smoke drifted slowly under Batman's cowl. I'm sure it gave Batman more reasons to resent the Penguin's nefarious capers even more.

There were so many great stars in guest leads in *Batman*. I think of the wonderful Vincent Price as Egghead. Vincent was a wit and a raconteur. And he was a well-known collector of fine art. We had many laughs and his love of art was contagious. I've been painting for many years and he was kind and enthusiastic when he saw my stacks of work about my studio. I am fortunate that my artwork has been purchased by a number of collectors. Thanks for the inspiration, Mr. Price.

As a young actor, I had the opportunity of playing scenes with more guest stars than most people who ever

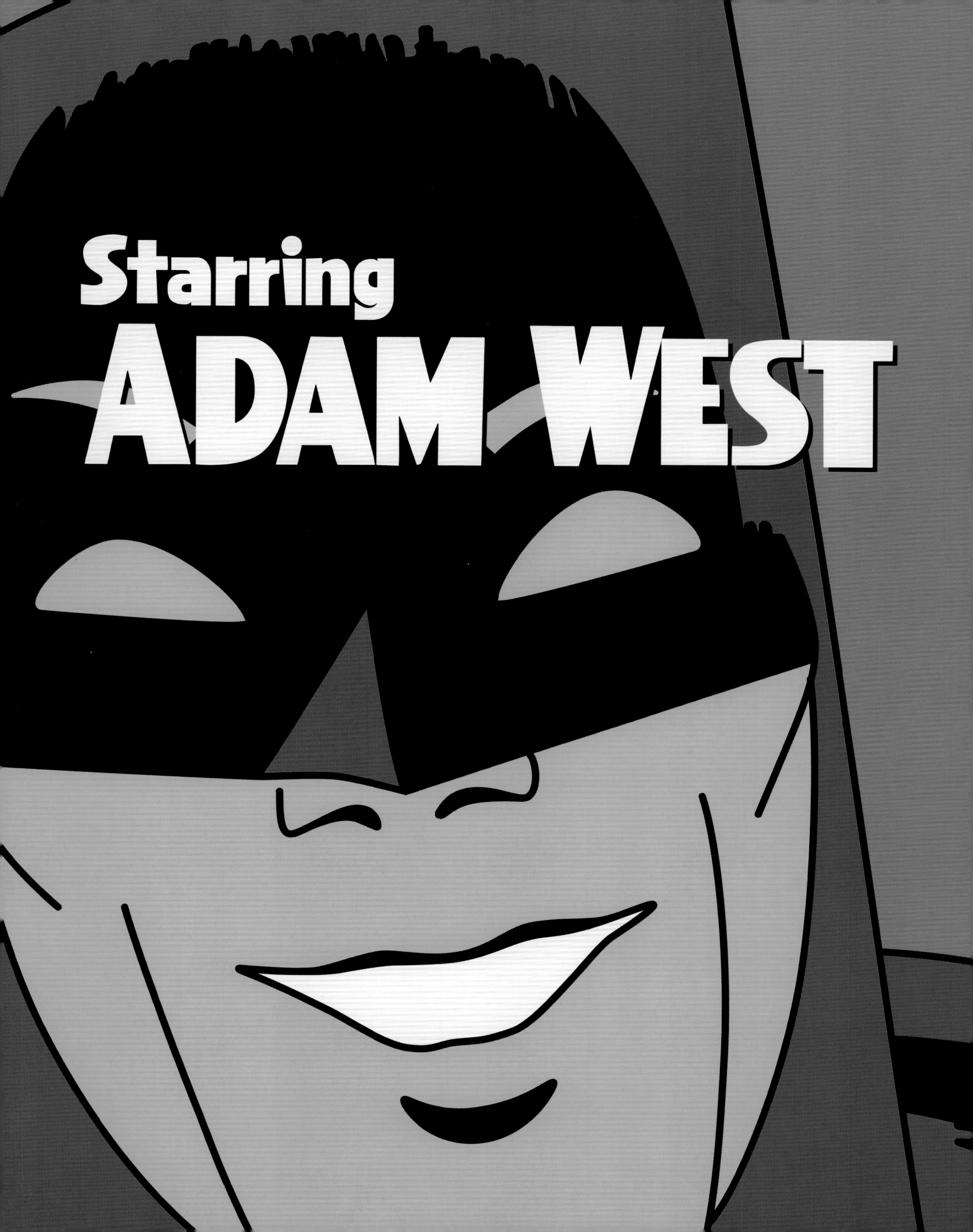
Starring
ADAM WEST

worked in Hollywood. They were celebrated names like Van Johnson, Ida Lupino, Milton Berle, Jerry Lewis, Dick Clark, Tallulah Bankhead, Jill St. John, George Sanders, Anne Baxter, Roddy McDowall, Shelley Winters, Cliff Robertson and Eli Wallach, just to name a famous few. The ladies who played Catwoman with such intensity gave my Batman a chance to react with a comedic confusion and subtle moments of desire, if not downright lust, behind that pointy-eared cowl of his. "You give me a curious stirring in my Utility Belt, Catwoman." Julie Newmar was our first Catwoman. Lee Ann Meriwether, a former Miss America, was our feature film Catwoman and the formidable chanteuse, Eartha Kitt, was our season three Catwoman. I'm sure you can understand why Batman was envied by so many virile young men in the audience. Three Catwomen at nine lives each was a bit much for even Batman to handle. But, I can assure you it was far from unpleasant.

As the years fly by, I've kept a respectful and friendly relationship with these fine actors. Of course I am sad to say, Eartha Kitt has passed on. Julie is writing books and has an award-winning garden. Lee Ann is still performing and has co-starred in several TV series projects post-*Batman* work. My life and work after *Batman* has been a bumpy and interesting road. You are all aware of the trap of typecasting. Yes, it happened to me big time. The reasons for this are simple. One cannot run around in the restrictions of costume playing a legendary character each week without being profoundly identified with the character. When one dominates the screen in that manner, and when people respond with great affection, it is difficult for some to think of the actor in other ways. It is especially difficult for those who do the casting.

There have been some basic advantages in this accepting attitude. I have had the challenge of elevating what seemed like pretty ordinary material, and I have worked so much in so many different projects, that I feel it has certainly sharpened my abilities. That is a plus, not a negative in a career. It might be called seasoning. Here I must be honest in giving the most important reason that I'm there when they call. I have had a large family to support. More than career, this has been my most important goal in life. I've been gifted with a wonderful wife of over forty years and our six children. They still laugh at my jokes and my goofing around. So you see I have much to celebrate these days. *Batman* has been a wonderful ride with twists and turns and many surprises. Because you love Batman I have learned to love Batman and overall it has been very good to me. Our Batman always seems to make people happy. In this troubled world it is good to make people happy and to make them laugh. I meet so many of you with great Batman memories. This makes me feel that all my career perambulations have been worthwhile. My connection to Batman has been reinvigorated with the Warner Bros. release of all 120 *Batman* episodes on Blu-ray. You've asked for this and it has finally happened. And I'm delighted that I also play Batman in the voice-over for the video game, *Lego Batman 3: Beyond Gotham*. There are also a number of toys, statues and other things with my likeness being produced from Warner Bros., DC Comics and others. There are comic books based on our 60s series. There is even an Adam West comic book in the bookstores.

Our Batman is enjoying quite an up-surge. With all the other work coming my way, one might say that this actor's position in pop culture is quite secure. I can only feel gratitude for my good fortune. And it is your love for Batman that made it happen. Thank you. Please have fun with this new *Batman* book. Let's celebrate!

Adam West
August 2015

THE COMMAND AT ABC: BATMAN ON TV

"Batman? Are you guys out of your mind?"

Executive Producer William Dozier's reaction to ABC execs asking him to produce the TV show

"And within three months it was called *William Dozier's Batman*."

Edgar J. Scherick, ABC Vice President of Programming, interview in 1993 by Bob Garcia

 There were three ABC executives who brought Batman to television. Yale Udoff, the Director of Night-Time Development, came up with the idea of doing a show based on the comic-book character Batman. Douglas S. Cramer, Vice President of Program Planning, thought it was a great idea, and did the majority of the heavy lifting to get the show made. He was a collector of modern art, especially Roy Lichtenstein, and a fan of Batman (as a kid he played in a Batman costume, with a friend dressed as Robin). The third man was their boss, Vice President of Programming Edgar J. Scherick, who actually bought the show and fought hard for it in the corporation. These three "wise men" saw the potential to do something quite different on TV. Different was good at ABC.

In early 1965, ABC was the third-rated network (out of three) and had a problem. They only had two top-ten shows in the 7.30 p.m. EST time slot in the previous eleven years – *Disneyland* (during 1954–1956) and *Combat!* (during 1964–1965) – and they were looking to

break that streak. ABC TV President Thomas Moore kept pushing experimental shows in other time slots (i.e. *Peyton Place*, *The Addams Family*, *Bewitched*) hoping to capture a younger audience. For the 7.30 p.m. time slot he needed to hit the youngest members of the American families, the kids. It was important to get kids to tune in to these shows because in 1965 most households only had one television and no remote control for fast channel changing. The channel being watched early in the evening usually stayed on for the rest of the night.

ABC's Vice President of Programming Daniel Melnick and Cramer wanted to imitate the success of the James Bond films. "Nobody had seen anything like the first couple of Bond movies," said Cramer. "It was larger than life. It wasn't real. It took large jumps in narrative, and the audiences stuck with it. We really wanted to do something in that vein." They had talked about it throughout 1964 and when Melnick left ABC to create the production company Talent Associates with Leonard Stern and David Susskind, the first thing he created was his spy series, *Get Smart*. That show became a successful spoof under the guidance of writers Mel Brooks and Buck Henry. When Melnick offered it to ABC, it was rejected with the comment that it was "un-American." In response, he took the show to rival NBC and although the network had officially closed its production slate for the 1965–1966 season, it opened a slot for *Get Smart*. "With the sting of that," said Cramer, "everyone agreed 'let's go out and find a show.'"

"We knew that cartoons had an audience in the early evening (ABC had *The Flintstones* and *Johnny Quest*), so we knew that if we could find the right cartoon, we could make it work," Cramer said. "But to do it with real live action would do more than just get kids, we would get a strong adult audience." ABC tried to acquire the rights to Milton Caniff's *Terry and the Pirates* and couldn't get them. Harve Bennett, ABC's Director of Network Program Development, who oversaw the network's television show development at all Los Angeles studios, suggested *Dick Tracy*, though he was thinking of a standard cartoon

show. Again, they lost out as the Tribune Syndicate which owned the strip refused the deal.

At the time, Dick Tracy was a very popular character, with cartoons on TV, licensing and a successful newspaper strip. The news shook up the Programming Department in New York, which had been confident it would get the show. Yale Udoff remembered the day he heard the news: "We thought we had the rights to *Dick Tracy*, and [then] lost them to NBC, and everyone was in an uproar." But he thought of a solution: his favorite childhood hero, Batman. "When I was a kid I used to read *Batman* comics," he continued. "I remembered this and went down [to a newsstand] and got a copy of a *Batman* comic and read it. I thought, 'This could do it,' but when I first told [Edgar J.] Scherick, he thought it was ridiculous."

Scherick remembered in a 1993 interview with Bob Garcia: "Udoff came in and said we ought to do *Batman*. We threw him out of the office, but he persisted, and we decided to look into it." Udoff wrote up a formal proposal. Cramer backed it, and Scherick decided to

Bottom left: Douglas S. Cramer, Vice President of Program Planning, ABC Television Network

YALE M. UDOFF
ABC Director of Night-Time Development

Yale Udoff worked briefly for ABC in the 1960s, and went on to make a career as a screenwriter and playwright. His television credits include episodes for *Tales from the Crypt*, *Against the Law*, *The Survivors*, and *Man from U.N.C.L.E.* He wrote the screenplays for the feature films *Eve of Destruction* and *Bad Timing: A Sensual Obsession*. He has written several plays including *The Little Gentleman*. Udoff's twenty-page outline entitled *Rembrandt The Third Meets His Master* was approved in April 1966 as a story for *Batman's* second season, however it was cut off at story level and did not go into production.

BATCOMPUTER OUTPUT END . . .

buy it. He took it to network head, Thomas Moore. "Eventually we convinced [Moore]," said Udoff. "Suddenly, all these executives were flying back to New York from L.A. reading *Batman* comic books hidden in their *Fortune* magazines so they could get an idea of what was happening. Eventually it got on the air."

From that point on, the show was in Cramer and Bennett's bailiwick. "ABC instigated the entire developmental process, which was very much the custom then," Bennett said in a 1993 interview with Bob Garciase. "In-house development was the rule rather than outside material coming to a television network."

Cramer went to see *Batman* creator Bob Kane about the show. "I met Kane to enlist his support and bolster his enthusiasm for the project," recalled Cramer. "I wanted the man who created it to support the show." It was the beginning of a long friendship between Cramer

and Kane, with the two men eventually working on several series and movie ideas.

After Cramer had recruited Kane, ABC lawyers and the company that owned all rights to *Batman*, National Periodical Publications (which later became DC Comics), hashed out a deal. On June 9, 1965, ABC and NPP signed an agreement for "a series of television motion pictures based upon and incorporating the literary property owned by National entitled *Batman*." Cramer then contacted the head of television production at 20th Century Fox, William Self, to handle the production of the show. "Fox had the best of everyone in production departments on their lot," said Cramer. "They managed to do quality productions on television that were on a feature level. That's one of the reasons we brought the show to Fox."

It was more than staffing; ABC had done several shows at the studio. "We had a very, very chummy relationship

Below: Adam West (Batman), Bob Kane and Frank Gorshin (Riddler) meet off-stage during filming of a first season Riddler episode.

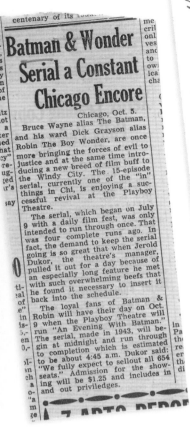

Batman & Wonder Serial a Constant Chicago Encore

Chicago, Oct. 5. Bruce Wayne alias The Batman, and his ward Dick Grayson alias Robin The Boy Wonder, are once more bringing the forces of evil to justice and at the same time introducing a new breed of film buff to the Windy City. The 15-episode serial, currently one of the "in" things in Chi, is enjoying a successful revival at the Playboy Theatre.

The serial, which began on July 9 with a daily film fest, was only intended to run through once. That was four complete runs ago. In fact, the demand to keep the serial going is so great that when Jerold Dukor, the theatre's manager, pulled it out for a day because of an especially long feature he met with such overwhelming beefs that he found it necessary to insert it back into the schedule.

The loyal fans of Batman & Robin will have their day on Oct. 9 when the Playboy Theatre will run "An Evening With Batman." The serial, made in 1943, will begin at midnight and run through to completion which is estimated to be about 4:45 a.m. Dukor said: "We fully expect to sellout all 654 seats." Admission for the showing will be $1.25 and includes in and out priviledges.

Right: Robert Dozier (left) writer of Ep#5–6 and son of series Executive Producer William Dozier (right).

Above: This clipping from the October 6, 1965 issue of Weekly Variety accompanied Bill Dozier's concerned note to Doug Cramer in New York, asking "Is this good or bad?" Cramer's reply attempted to assure Dozier that his version would "be above any comparison."

with Fox," noted Harve Bennett. "They had come through for us. They had done some pioneer programming [for us], *Peyton Place*, etc." William Self was a bit of a legend. He was hired to head up television production in 1959, and oversaw a boom with profitable series like *Voyage to the Bottom of the Sea*, *Lost in Space*, *Peyton Place*, and other 1960s classics. Richard Zanuck was quoted in Self's *Los Angeles Times* obituary: "I credit the whole television success to Bill. My contribution really was appointing Bill and letting him run with the ball. I had great confidence in him."

"One of the main reasons ABC came to us with a project like *Batman*," Self said, "was that they knew a studio of our size could handle the costs." 20th Century Fox handled finances, facilities, crews and other physical necessities of production, and various smaller companies handled the job of making shows. In *Batman*'s case, Self decided that William Dozier's Greenway Productions, which was shooting Rod Serling's western series *The Loner* on the Fox lot, should handle day-to-day operations. Dozier had given Self his first job in television and the two had maintained a friendship over the years. "Bill was a very capable guy," remembered Self. "He was a good executive, because you'd get an immediate answer out of Bill Dozier. In that sense, he was in my judgment a very good, tough executive."

Cramer had been pushing for Dozier to be involved. "Bill was one of my mentors in the world of television," explained Cramer, a young man of twenty-five at the time. "[Dozier was big] in the Hollywood social world, which I was fascinated by. Whenever I came to L.A., I was often at his parties. Bill actually introduced me to the woman I married, who was a gossip columnist for the *Los Angeles Times*, Joyce Haber. [Stars] came to his parties. They came to his screenings. He had one of the best screening rooms in town. His beach parties were fabulous. So I knew him well. When *Batman* came up, I wanted him to do it." Dozier had been trying to sell Cramer a Bruce Lee vehicle, *Number One Son*, a Charlie Chan spin-off with Lee as a secret agent. Dozier met Lee and became friends with the martial artist. The two wanted to work together and Dozier had a story treatment written by Lorenzo Semple Jr., but unfortunately ABC's top brass shot it down.

Scherick and Cramer called and discussed *Batman* with William Self. When they got together in L.A., Self brought in Dozier, who was flabbergasted that they wanted him to produce it. "I had never heard of Batman," Dozier said in a 1989 film interview with Kevin Burns at 20th Century Fox. "I never read comic books when I was a kid; my parents wouldn't allow me to. I had never seen a *Batman* comic book. Naturally I didn't admit any of this. I said, 'Well, let me think about it.'" Cramer left a small stack of comics with Dozier and set a date to meet him a few days later in New York. Dozier and his wife Ann would be there on the first leg of a vacation, which would take them to New York and Europe during May 1965.

"The very first conversation was in Bill's office in California where he wasn't convinced," said Cramer. "He was heading east, and I met him a few days later for dinner. I had gone back to Bob Kane and he gave me [comic] books with important stories in Batman's history. After dinner I gave Bill the books and more of a push." Dozier left for Europe not committing to the series. Back in April, Dozier had made arrangements to meet Semple in Spain on this vacation. Semple had recently moved

to Torremolinos in the south of Spain. Dozier was going to Madrid and wanted to meet the writer at the Ritz Hotel. The two had worked on several projects together including a December 1964 pilot script for *You're Only Young Twice*, another December 1964 pilot script for a half-hour comedy entitled *Heaven Help Us* which was produced but did not sell, and a science fiction pilot entitled *Mr. Zero* (no relationship to Batman's comic book nemesis). They were to discuss *Mr. Zero*. During that evening, Dozier had mentioned *Batman* and handed Semple one of the *Batman* comics.

"Bill said, 'I am extremely embarrassed to even show you this thing, but this is what ABC has given

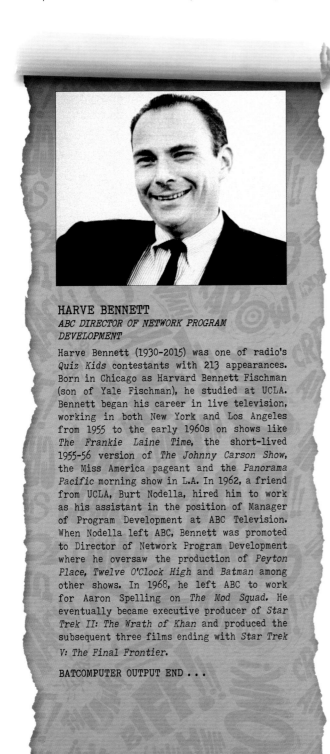

HARVE BENNETT
ABC DIRECTOR OF NETWORK PROGRAM DEVELOPMENT

Harve Bennett (1930-2015) was one of radio's *Quiz Kids* contestants with 213 appearances. Born in Chicago as Harvard Bennett Fischman (son of Yale Fischman), he studied at UCLA. Bennett began his career in live television, working in both New York and Los Angeles from 1955 to the early 1960s on shows like *The Frankie Laine Time*, the short-lived 1955-56 version of *The Johnny Carson Show*, the Miss America pageant and the *Panorama Pacific* morning show in L.A. In 1962, a friend from UCLA, Burt Nodella, hired him to work as his assistant in the position of Manager of Program Development at ABC Television. When Nodella left ABC, Bennett was promoted to Director of Network Program Development where he oversaw the production of *Peyton Place*, *Twelve O'Clock High* and *Batman* among other shows. In 1968, he left ABC to work for Aaron Spelling on *The Mod Squad*. He eventually became executive producer of *Star Trek II: The Wrath of Khan* and produced the subsequent three films ending with *Star Trek V: The Final Frontier*.

BATCOMPUTER OUTPUT END . . .

us,'" remembered Semple in a 1993 interview with Bob Garcia. "And he handed me a copy of a *Batman* comic. I thought it was sensational. I said, 'Don't worry about it.' He asked, 'How're you going to do it?' I said, 'Don't worry about it.' We didn't talk any further than that. We had dinner and he went home... It seemed to me that this would be fun."

"I always assumed it was a comedy," Semple said. "The word 'camp' was around but we didn't say we were going to make this campy. [Ours] was an approach done very straight. The concept of these grown people dressing up in these silly costumes, with butlers and Commissioner Gordon and Bat Signals and all that stuff, by definition, it's silly. That's the fun

of it. It seemed to be obvious that it was comic."

It wasn't that obvious to Dozier. In interviews, he often described how he figured out how to do the show on the plane trip home. Ann Dozier remembered that plane trip well. "The funniest thing was when he was first going to do it," she said, "he had never heard of Batman. He wasn't a comic-book reader. So we got on the plane and he had a lapful of comic books. He had his nose in them, and this stewardess came down to see if we wanted anything to drink. She looked at him. [Then] she looked at me with this 'Oh, you poor soul' look because he's sitting there with his nose in these stupid color comic books. By the time we got [off the plane], he looked at me and said, 'There's no way

Opposite right: Lorenzo Semple Jr.

Right: (From left) Burt Ward, Adam West and William Dozier.

WILLIAM DOZIER
EXECUTIVE PRODUCER

William Dozier (1908-1991) began working in movies in the early 1940s. He began as a writer's agent for Erle Stanley Gardner, F. Scott Fitzgerald and Dalton Trumbo at the Berg-Allenberg talent agency. In 1942, Dozier became head of Paramount's writing department, overseeing screenwriters Billy Wilder and Preston Sturges among others. In 1944, he moved on to RKO Radio Pictures, where he supervised production of *The Spiral Staircase*, *Notorious*, and *Crossfire*. In 1948, Dozier and his second wife Joan Fontaine created Rampart Productions to produce her films *Letter from an Unknown Woman* and *You Gotta Stay Happy*, which were distributed by Universal. He eventually divorced Joan and married actress Ann Rutherford in 1953. Dozier moved into television in 1950. The next year he began working in programming for CBS New York and then transferred back to CBS California. In 1959, he became the head of Screen Gems until 1964 when he founded his own company, Greenway Productions, where he would go on to work on *Batman*. William Self remembered him as a witty, sophisticated man who was a fantastic host of very large parties and great fun to be with.

BATCOMPUTER OUTPUT END . . .

you could do this straight. You've got to camp it.'"

Dozier drafted a letter to Semple on June 16 saying "something may be brewing on this," and sent him four more *Batman* comic books with a recommendation that he pay "special attention to" *Batman* 171 (May 1965). That issue marked the Riddler's first appearance since 1948, and was only the villain's third comic-book appearance. Neither Dozier nor Semple were aware that the Riddler had been a very minor character, but that would soon change since they had chosen that story to provide the basis for the pilot. The final script used elements of that story but was not a strict adaptation.

Harve Bennett remembered having the approval

meeting in Dozier's office with Ed Scherick, Douglas Cramer and himself. Dozier outlined how they wanted to do the show. He said, "We want to send it up. We want to do a gentle kind of spoof that comes out of the whole POW, BANG, WOW, SOCKO, and make it just a kind of a fun show." Bennett also believed that was the only way it would work. Dozier told them he wanted Semple to write the pilot. Within days of that meeting, on June 18, Dozier asked Fox's Director of Business Affairs Emmet Lavery Jr. to contact Semple's agent and make arrangements for "The Bat Man."

It's clear from correspondence between Dozier and Semple over the next few months that the two

Bottom left: The Mr. Zero referred to in the below letter was a completely different project with coincidentally the same name as the villain in Ep#7–8.

Bottom right: Frank Gorshin's Riddler in the pilot episode.

GREENWAY PRODUCTIONS, INC.

20TH CENTURY · FOX STUDIOS · 10201 WEST PICO BOULEVARD · LOS ANGELES 35, CALIFORNIA · CRESTVIEW 6-2211

WILLIAM DOZIER
President

June 16, 1965

Mr. Lorenzo Semple, Jr.
Molino Alto del Rosario
Torremolinos, Malaga, SPAIN

Dear Lorenzo:

      I assume you have read the one BATMAN episode I left with you. Herewith four others. Please force yourself through them, with special attention to the one marked, the one about The Riddler.

      Something may be brewing on this, quite apart from and in addition to MR. ZERO. If it does, and I'll know in a few days, I may ask you to pop over to New York (at our expense, of course)' and meet with me and then with me and some network chaps. We can try to find some M.de Ristal in Manhattan, or an unreasonable facsimile.

      Best,

abp
Enclosures

- NOs. 159, 169, 171 *(The Riddler)*
  Nov. Feb. May
Detective Comics - Apr. No. 290

Lee: Seles/on
Via Mgs.

EDGAR J. SCHERICK
ABC VICE PRESIDENT OF PROGRAMMING

Edgar J. Scherick (1924–2002) had come to ABC as the creator of *Wide World of Sports*. There he developed some of the network's highest Nielsen-rated shows: *Peyton Place*, *Bewitched* and *The Hollywood Palace*. Scherick was the one to make the decision to buy *Batman* at ABC. After leaving the network, he went on to produce Woody Allen's *Take the Money and Run*, Anthony Schaffer's *Sleuth*, Joseph Sargent's *The Taking of Pelham One-Two-Three*, and Bryan Forbes' *The Stepford Wives*. He also produced a slew of TV movies, including *The Raid on Entebbe*, *Siege at Ruby Ridge*, and *Path to War*.

BATCOMPUTER OUTPUT END . . .

WILLIAM SELF
VICE PRESIDENT OF TV PRODUCTION 20th CENTURY FOX

William Self (1921-2010) had started out as an actor in director Howard Hawks' recurring cast of characters, with parts in many of the director's movies including *The Thing from Another World*. Self was in thirty-three movies altogether. He moved into TV production during the 1950s working as the producer's assistant on *China Smith*. He was associate producer and eventually producer on 208 episodes of *Schlitz Playhouse of Stars*, which was an anthology series featuring stars like James Dean and Anthony Quinn, among others. William Dozier brought Self to CBS where he helped develop *The Twilight Zone* pilot, along with others. By 1965, Self had been at 20th Century Fox Television for six years, successfully overseeing *Batman*, *Voyage to the Bottom of the Sea*, *Daniel Boone*, *Peyton Place* and many more series. He left Fox with forty-four TV shows to his credit. He went on to produce the feature film *The Shootist* and various Hallmark Hall of Fame movies. As an interesting aside, he was a huge fan and collector of Annie Oakley, with his collection donated to the Buffalo Bill Historical Center after his death.

BATCOMPUTER OUTPUT END . . .

William Self – Vice President of TV Production 20th Century Fox

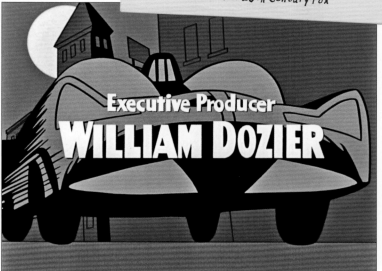

men developed the show's style together. Semple masterminded the details of storytelling, and Dozier knew what was needed on a television series. The letters flying back and forth between them showed a great camaraderie and friendship.

During a lunch at the 20th Century Fox commissary, Dozier brought his right-hand man Charles FitzSimons in on the deal. Dozier asked what he knew about *Batman*. Since FitzSimons had grown up in Ireland, and the comic wasn't very popular there, he was starting at ground zero, much like Dozier. He was a bit skeptical about the project, thinking that *The Flintstones* had been on since 1960 but had not even made it into the Nielsen Top 30 for the last two seasons. He believed that cartoon shows were on the way out. Dozier explained they didn't want to do *Batman* as a cartoon. "He wanted to do it with live actors," said FitzSimons in a 1993 interview with Bob Garcia. "I got goose bumps... I thought, 'My god, what a fantastic idea!' I studied the comics and Lorenzo was

hired to write the pilot."

The idea of camping it up didn't faze FitzSimons; when the two men had been at CBS, both had thought there was a place for camp comedy (even though Dozier loathed the term "camp"). FitzSimons had tried to get such a series based upon Erle Stanley Gardner's con man detective Lester Leith into production. They received no interest, but *Batman* now seemed a perfect opportunity.

A trip to New York to sell the idea to National Periodical Publications and ABC brass was arranged. On Monday, June 28, 1965, Dozier and Semple met privately in the morning to discuss *Batman*, then in the afternoon with National's Executive VP Irwin Donenfeld and Mort Weisinger, who had worked as story editor on the 1950s TV series *Adventures of Superman*. Weisinger is best known as editor of NPP's *Superman* titles, but he was also Vice President of Public Relations and both men were officers of the company. Donenfeld recalled National's first impression in an interview with

Top: Zowie, Howie! Producer Howie Horwitz in the Batcave. Dozier's copy of "The Curse Of Tut" script is on the desk. The exact purpose of the "Zowie" sign has been lost to history, although it may have been part of a magazine photo shoot.

Cinefantastique: "We had a big meeting. They were just beginning to get the idea on how to put the *Batman* program on. [Dozier] wanted to do it tongue-in-cheek. We weren't tongue-in-cheek type people, but we helped him out. We [even brought back] Alfred for him (Alfred had been killed the year before in *Detective Comics* 328 [June 1964])... Everything they did went against my grain. Our Batman was a brooding figure, up in the darkness with the cape around him, and theirs was this nut-head."

At 10 a.m. the next day, June 29, Dozier and Semple were well prepared for their meeting with the full board of ABC. After meeting with National, the two seemed to have worked out a pilot plot with enough panache to win over the board. Scherick recalled Lorenzo's pitch with a chuckle. "We had him explain it to the management of the company," he said. "I remember the meeting at the boardroom in New York with [ABC-Paramount President] Leonard Goldenson and everybody sitting there, and Lorenzo with a little butt of a cigarette in his mouth tee-hee-ing as he told this ridiculous plot to these guys... They thought we were out of our minds, thoroughly bereft of our reason. But we weren't gambling the whole network on this show, and they had enough respect for the people that they put in charge to give them a certain rein with their judgment... ABC was the place to take a chance with things. So I took a chance with it and it worked."

Filming *Batman* in color was one of the first decisions made by the network. A color TV show about a comic-book character would seem a no-brainer today, except when you take into account that almost 90% of US households did not have a color TV in 1965. However, that year ABC and other networks began switching the bulk of their programming to color so that by the fall of 1966, most shows were in color. People were very excited by this quick transition to color (buying color televisions at a record rate), and ABC wanted to make as big a splash as possible with *Batman*.

Batman was run from Greenway Productions' offices in the Lasky Building at Fox Studios. Dozier, FitzSimons and

also served as secretary; she was the wife of director William Graham, who directed the False Face episodes. FitzSimons was the point man on the *Batman* pilot. He worked with Fox on financial, facilities and scheduling matters. He worked with each studio department head, set up screen tests, and even handled rental agreements with vehicle suppliers.

Dozier continued working on the script with Semple, while dealing with the network, studio honchos, the show's publicity, and casting the pilot. He was in on every production meeting, and all major decisions crossed his desk.

Together they made ABC's *Batman* a reality.

Top: Burt Ward, Adam West and Neil Hamilton (Commissioner Gordon)

Opposite: Howie Horwitz (Producer) and William Dozier (Executive Producer) visit the Batcave.

SEMPLE WRITING BATMAN: AS ONLY HE CAN

> "I conceive this whole thing being so gorgeously square that it's hip; so far Out that it's In. No necessity to make it modern by using teenage slang and what not, indeed on the contrary."

Lorenzo Semple Jr. on writing *Batman* in a July 1965 letter to William Dozier

Lorenzo Semple Jr. worked from Spain at a time when there was no Internet or Federal Express. This meant that everything had to be done by airmail, telegram and on the phone. "European post offices were very fast," remembered Semple. "A little guy came to the door on his bicycle, rang the bell and said 'here's a letter'. It was amazing."

After leaving New York following the late-June 1965 meetings, Semple stopped in London where he shipped off a roughish story outline to Greenway on July 9. Entitled *The Bat Man*, Dozier received it July 13, 1965 and sent the synopsis around to network and Fox decision makers. Notes were returned to Semple July 23 with a comment from Dozier: "...first I must tell you that, without a single exception, everyone is enthusiastic about the outline generally and about what it promises in terms of the pilot and the series." Which, of course, was followed by fourteen detailed suggestions, typed single-space across four pages, regarding script changes. But it was good enough for the network to commit to a pilot

deal with Fox on July 28, 1965.

Dozier became concerned that Bruce Wayne was not normal enough for the audience. Semple assuaged his fears in a July 29 reply, where he wrote, "I quite understand what you mean by 'normalizing' Bruce, but I'm not worried by it. The way I see him, he is so ineffably square that he has a sort of *sui generis* normality strictly his own."

In that same letter he went on to discuss Robin: "I think it's important to think of him as essentially 15+ rather than 16+, if you see what I mean. He's a very big boy rather than a very young adult. Teenage girls swoon for him all right, but his mental processes (if any) are boyish and not mannish. I see him as Jack Armstrong, not that odious parking-lot attendant in old *77 Sunset Strip*."

Dozier accepted both characterizations, and continued to work with Semple on refining Batman and Robin throughout the months of preproduction. Their final decisions were incorporated in the show's "Bat Notes for Writers."

On August 9, Dozier received a first draft of the pilot while Semple's cover letter arrived August 10: "I'm intensely pleased with it," Semple wrote, "which I hope isn't too rotten an omen. It's sixty pages long, admittedly highly packed, but I consider length in no way unreasonable for a pilot. I have unprecedentedly found myself actually chuckling out loud over some of the dialogue. I don't think there's anything in it absurdly unshootable, and I can tell you that we've created one absolutely guaranteed new TV star: The Batmobile... I've tried to polish and tighten it until it shines and grunts, and in general I look on it as finished."

After a few days of discussion, copies of the script were sent by Air Mail Special Delivery to Douglas Cramer in New York on August 12. Harve Bennett received his own copy in Los Angeles. He remembered: "Every one of us fell down on the floor, laughing. It was *funny*."

The final script was turned in on September 3, 1965, with changes made over the next month. Bennett sent two pages of last-minute suggestions and changes in a letter dated October 14. Everything was finalized days before principal photography began on October 20.

Below: Burt Ward, Adam West and Neil Hamilton (Commissioner Gordon).

DOUGLAS S. CRAMER
ABC VICE PRESIDENT OF PROGRAM PLANNING

Douglas S. Cramer (1931-) is a well-known collector of modern art, and sits on the board of several museums. He began his career in the 1950s at Procter & Gamble in the TV department, then went to Ogilvy & Mather in 1959. He moved to ABC Programming in late 1962, and then to Fox Television working under William Self from 1966-1968, where he worked on *Batman*. He took over Paramount Television as Executive Vice President of Television from 1968-1972. In 1972, Cramer left Paramount to become an independent producer making the first TV mini-series *QB VII*, a multi-Emmy winner, and over 100 made-for-TV movies. He also began developing and producing for Warner Bros. Television a series of movies and pilots which culminated with the successful four-year run of *Wonder Woman*. He became partners with Aaron Spelling, working together from 1978-1989, and was executive producer on *Dynasty* and *The Colbys*. After their partnership dissolved, Cramer produced twenty Danielle Steel TV movies and mini-series, and Charles Bronson's last TV series, *a Family of Cops*. He retired from producing in 2000.

BATCOMPUTER OUTPUT END ...

HIRING THE BATMAN CAST: THEY MADE THE SHOW LAST

"**Somewhere along the line we came to the universal conclusion that the square-jawed naïveté and Frank Merriwell quality that Adam exuded was exactly right.**"
Harve Bennett, ABC Director of Network Program Development, interview in 1993 by Bob Garcia

Above left: Adam West: early publicity picture.

Above right: July 16, 1965 memo from Bill Dozier to Doug Cramer regarding Adam West, and Cramer's handwritten response.

Opposite page: Adam West publicity photo.

With years of experience in Hollywood, Dozier had an uncanny knack for matching any actor he met to the right role. Most actors would sign up instantly when he asked. He quickly cast veteran actor Neil Hamilton ("The only one I ever thought of for the role of Commissioner Gordon."), as well as Alan Napier, Madge Blake, and Stafford Repp. Dozier pursued Frank Gorshin for the Riddler and began a search for the Dynamic Duo.

Dozier firmly believed the actors portraying Batman and Robin should be relatively unknown. This would keep costs down, and he could cast a wide net to get just the right actors for these pivotal roles. The network, of course, demanded stars to draw an audience, so Dozier devised the plan to use only big stars for each week's "Special Guest Villain."

For the role of Batman, he initially had in mind Ty Hardin, but the actor was working in Europe and unavailable. Hardin's agent had another client he thought would be good, and he gave Dozier publicity photographs of Adam West. Dozier remembered he liked West from his Captain Q character on a Nestlé's Quik commercial, and set up a meeting.

"I had him come in and let him read the first script and we talked," Dozier said in a 1966 television interview with Fletcher Markle on the Canadian Broadcasting Company's magazine show *Telescope*. "He had an immediate and very intelligent insight into what we were trying to do. He grasped the duality of this thing immediately. That he would have to play it very straight and very square in order to have it come through as humor... So he turned out to be exactly right."

Even before the pilot was ordered, in a memo dated July 16, Dozier recommended Adam West as a potential Batman to Douglas Cramer at ABC who enthusiastically agreed with the choice. West's agent negotiated his contract terms on August 23, but it would take almost a month for the contract to be issued by Fox. On September 20, Adam West was signed for the role of Batman in the pilot with a series option.

West remembered that after the meeting, he spent weeks studying up on heroes with secret identities like The Scarlet Pimpernel and Scaramouche, and reading a number of comic books to get the feel of Batman in particular. He also read up on fictional detectives like Sherlock Holmes and Simon Templar. West wrote in his autobiography *Back to the Batcave* that he and Dozier discussed these matters during pilot preparations.

"Bill Dozier and I had some early discussions about how the character should be played," West wrote, "and the only real disagreement we had was over Batman's speech pattern. Lorenzo had sent a memo to Bill from Spain stating that Batman's delivery should be staccato, wooden, and straight ahead like Sgt. Joe Friday in *Dragnet*. I strongly disagreed. I felt that Batman would be wooden enough in his suit, virtually expressionless behind the mask. I told Bill that Batman should muse and connect his ideas and sentences fluidly, similar to the

way Basil Rathbone did as Sherlock Holmes, only a bit less tightly wound… Bill listened, thought for a moment, then gave me the okay to try it that way when we did the screen test…" And so the signature, deliberate, precise speech pattern of West's Batman was born. It didn't hurt that speaking slowly added to the star's screen time.

"Adam enjoyed it so much," recalled Lorenzo Semple Jr. "He was perfect. I actually believed he *was* Batman. He took it properly and seriously. On that type of show you have to do it absolutely straight. He was able to do it without any embarrassment. He was really good."

Looking for someone to play Robin was much more difficult. The talent search seemed to take forever, with supposedly hundreds of actors interviewed, although casting records indicate it was more like dozens. "We weren't having very much luck," said Charles FitzSimons. "We wanted to find somebody who had that very special Robin quality. I was in my office. It was six o'clock in the

Left: Adam West with his agent Jerry Herdan (right) and Lou Sherrell (left) from the Herdan-Sherrell Agency. Taken during the first day or two of filming for Ep#23.

evening, and a phone call came from the cop at the gate at 20th Century Fox. He said, 'There's a young man out here who heard you were looking for a Robin [Burt Ward has said he didn't know what role he was applying for], and he'd like to have a chance to see you.'

"I was so tired, I said, 'Look, tell him to have his agent contact me.' The cop came back and said, 'He doesn't have an agent.' So I said, 'Well, if he's about 5'6" or 7", if he's over eighteen but looks fifteen, has black curly hair, blue eyes and he's athletic, send him in.' Thinking the cop would say, 'Well, forget it.'

"The cop came back and said, 'He says he's twenty but he looks sixteen. He has black curly hair, blue eyes, and says he has a brown belt in karate.' So I told the guard to send him in.

"So Burton Gervis [Burt Ward] came into my office, and I nearly fell off my chair. Here was the personification of everything we were looking for visually. I called Bill

Dozier on the intercom and said, 'Robin has just walked into my office.' Bill said, 'Are you out of your mind?' I brought him into Bill's office, and Dozier nearly fell off of his stool. So we tested him, thinking it was a long shot... He was it. He didn't have to act. He *was* Robin."

It was Ward's inexperience that had sent him to the gate at Fox. Twenty-year-old Ward had been selling real estate and trying to make ends meet, while taking acting lessons and attending UCLA. Producer Saul David, to whom he had sold a house, recommended an agent. That agent told Ward that they were looking for someone his age down at 20th Century Fox. Ward went to the studio hoping to get a shot, and luckily found the right person at the right time.

When Dozier met Ward, he told him that he was a little big for the role, which prompted Ward to promise not to grow any more. Dozier laughed, and was sold on the young man. Now, he and FitzSimons had to sell West and Ward to ABC.

Below: Holding his copy of the False Face script, Burt Ward looks out from his apartment balcony in West Los Angeles.

USING IRWIN ALLEN'S PROPS, TO MAKE SCREEN TESTS TOPS

"[Our impromptu Batcave] was exciting to look at, because the true source of it all was a comic book. We wanted credibility, but we didn't want reality."
Art Director Jack Senter on the Screen Test set, interview in 1993 by Bob Garcia

Above: Executive Producer William Dozier with secretary Bonnie Paterson, the inspiration for Commissioner Gordon's secretary with the same name, as well as future wife of Unit Production Manager Sam Strangis. Dozier's beloved companion, poodle Mac is at right.

Screen tests were needed and Greenway had to film two sets for ABC to choose from. Dozier brought in Lyle Waggoner as Batman and Peter Deyell as Robin for the second test. Agreements were signed with West, Deyell and Ward on August 23, and Waggoner on August 24.

Charles FitzSimons enlisted the help of Jack Senter, the Fox supervisor of television production and Art Director on *Peyton Place*. After Senter and FitzSimons figured out what they needed to do, they approached Dozier. "The first time I went into his office, one of the bungalow offices on the lot that was really done up in style," Senter said, in a 1993 interview with Bob Garcia, "Bill Dozier was sitting behind his period desk with a French poodle on his lap. Bill looked at it this way. He said, 'Anything you guys want, go ahead and do it.' So we did and just had a blast."

Dozier gave them about four days to create the sets. "They wanted to get the visuals and the mood of *Batman*, but they didn't have a lot of money," Senter said. "And

I believe that money is not the solution to making these illusions, anyway... But we really and truly had no money, so a bit of 'thievery' went on. It was a real maverick situation."

Senter went scavenging through the many miles of Fox's back lot for what he needed. There were literally rows and rows of old sets available for the picking. "It just took a large crane and some manpower to get that stuff down there," Senter said.

"Down there" was a space on Stage 15 used by *Lost in Space* and other Fox productions. Senter took over a section of the sound stage about 200 feet long by eighty feet wide, with rock and sand. Part of "that stuff" was a huge U-shaped backdrop that draped around one eighty foot end of the stage. It was painted with stalagmites and stalactites. The top of the backdrop went to black. The stage lights were hung at seventy feet off the stage floor, so the full effect was that of a deep dark cave. They depended on rich purple and blue lighting and Director of Photography Dale Deverman to complete the illusion.

Top and bottom right: Batcave interiors

Two lights hung down from the "cave" ceiling to illuminate the Batcomputers below. The final set had a much darker look than the Batcave for the series.

"I used rock pieces for the foreground and filled in the spaces with 'computers,'" said Senter. "We had to boost their imagery because the computers were nothing but a bunch of tin boxes with reels going around. So we added a 'light show.' The special-effects crew put red and white panel lights on these gray boxes."

Irwin Allen was on the lot at the time with his extravagant productions, *Voyage to the Bottom of the Sea* and *Lost in Space*. Senter called him the "Master of the Light Show," and said laughing, "I don't think to his dying day, he knew how much stuff I stole from him for those four or five days."

Normally, television screen tests were done with actors facing the camera, and not in wardrobe, but these tests were different. Halfway through, the actors were seen in full Batman and Robin gear. "We also did it in full costumes," FitzSimons explained, "because Dozier and I

were worried that if we didn't do them that way that the network might run away from the project. So we spent the money." In recent years, the costumes have gained their own infamy on YouTube. The Batsuit was patterned after the 1940s *Batman* movie serials with a wide Bat-shaped emblem across Batman's chest, rather than the now familiar yellow ellipse behind the bat. Other notable differences were higher ears and lower eyebrows on the cowl, top-loading pouches on the Utility Belt, and cloth gloves with elbow-length cuffs.

Test scenes with Waggoner, Deyell, West and Ward were rehearsed on September 9 and shot September 10 using a four-page script written by Semple. Director Alex March, who the producers knew from *The Loner*, directed the test. In addition to scenes with both pairs of actors set in Wayne Manor and the Batcave, Ward performed three throws and two falls for the camera while wearing the Robin uniform (sans mask, cape and gloves), and gave an exhibition of karate by breaking a solid board with his hand.

LORENZO SEMPLE Jr.
SCREENWRITER & STORY CONSULTANT

Lorenzo Semple Jr. (1923-2014) had been writing television for ten years before working on *Batman*. Leveraging his screenplay for the 1966 *Batman* feature, he broke into film screenwriting with Raquel Welch's well-received *Fathom* (1967) directed by *Batman's* feature film director Leslie Martinson. In the 1970s, Semple teamed up with other screenwriters to script the box-office hits *Papillon* (1973), *The Parallax View* (1974), *The Drowning Pool* (1975) and *Three Days of the Condor* (1975). He went on to write the cult favorites *Flash Gordon* (1980) and *Never Say Never Again* (1983).

JACK SENTER

Jack Senter began at 20th Century Fox in 1959 and served as the Art Director on more than a dozen shows (i.e. *Peyton Place*, *Julia*, and *M*A*S*H*). He also taught set design, drafting and model making at the prestigious Chouinard Art Institute. In the 1970s, he became an independent Art Director working on a number of Disney movies (i.e. *Freaky Friday* and *Return to Witch Mountain*) and movies at other studios including *Oh God!* (1977), *Go Tell the Spartans* (1978), and *Far and Away* (1992).

BATCOMPUTER OUTPUT END . . .

ADAM WEST
AS
BATMAN
AND
BURTON GERVIS
AS
ROBIN

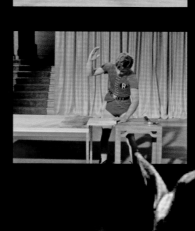

Dozier and FitzSimons also asked pilot director Robert Butler to interview Ward. They wanted to hear from the director that he could work with this "green kid." Butler thought Ward was perfect for the role. "We went off for an hour or so and we talked and read through the script," said Butler.

"I realized he was a just real primitive nice guy. Primitive as far as acting techniques. He was a good athlete and had a real ingenuous quality. I think we talked openly about [his inexperience]. As we talked about it and what he liked to do and what he felt comfortable doing – which was mainly the stunts, he loved physical action – I just realized [if] he could kind of play himself, he would be very, very good for

us. Which he *was.* I went back to Dozier and FitzSimons and said 'This guy's great. He's naturally kind of easy and innocent.'"

September 20, 1965 was an auspicious Monday in the show's history. William Dozier announced in a memo that Burton Gervis had become Burt Ward, changing his last name to his mother's maiden name. The stage name change was in fact stipulated in his contract. That day, Adam West signed for *Batman* with a Pilot Film and Series Agreement (Ward signed on Sept. 21) and Dozier authorized separate press releases stating West and Ward as being signed by Greenway, introducing them to the world as Batman and Robin.

Previous page: Images from the September 10, 1965 screen test for Adam West and Burt Ward, filmed on Stage 15 at Fox.

Right: Adam West (Bruce Wayne) and Burt Ward (Dick Grayson) answer a call from Commissioner Gordon.

FOX'S COMMITMENT, FITZSIMONS' FULFILLMENT

"We knew exactly what we were doing [on *Batman*]. It was completely created before we ever started to shoot a foot of film. *Batman* was one of the most rigorously planned things in television."

Charles FitzSimons, interview in 1993 by Bob Garcia

Above: Press photo released December 10, 1965.

From the end of July through all of October 1965, Greenway was one of the busiest places on 20th Century Fox's lot. Things sped up quickly after the screen tests, since the pilot had to begin shooting October 20, and to make matters worse ABC changed its schedule. In an August 23 press release, *Batman* was announced as a 1966-1967 season pickup but an October 19 ABC press release had Edgar Scherick announcing *Batman* would premiere January 12, 1966 as a twice-a-week series. The network decided to use *Batman* and three other series as mid-season replacements, which a Grey Advertising executive decided to promote as ABC's Second Season. "*Batman* was one of the first shows designed to be part of this Second Season," explained Scherick.

"The absolute fact was that after they got the script, they rushed it on the air," said Semple. "Whether because they thought it was wonderful, or whether they were desperate, I don't know, but it went on with incredible haste."

The studio had a remarkably deep and diversified talent pool. The same crews producing feature films also worked on television shows. Its stable of directors, cinematographers, special-effects men, makeup and wardrobe experts were all under a contract that included work on television shows whenever they were available. This crossover was a major strength of the studio in 1965. "In some ways what television did for Fox Studio," said William Self, "was to be able to keep those people on a year-round basis occupied when the movie business was reaching a point where it couldn't keep them busy."

The Fox production crew committed to the *Batman* pilot included Academy Award® nominee L. B. Abbott (*Voyage to the Bottom of the Sea*; *Tora! Tora! Tora!*) who was in charge of special effects; Ben Nye Sr. headed the makeup department; Margaret Donovan was the hair stylist; Jan Kemp and Pat Barto designed costumes and handled wardrobe; Edgar Graves was art director; James Blakeley was post-production supervisor, and studio construction chief Ivan Martin ran the set and prop construction crews.

The production unit also needed outside help. Lee Mishkin was brought in to animate the main title sequence. Car customizer George Barris was commissioned to supply, modify and maintain the Batmobile. Jazz musician/composer Neal Hefti was hired to create the theme and initially to score the pilot.

Dozier and FitzSimons transferred Assistant Director Sam Strangis from their western series *The Loner*. Strangis remembered being a bit confused when he got the script. He had been working on a super-serious revisionist western series written by Rod Serling, and they were taking him from that to *Batman*. He soon fell into the swing of things, becoming Unit Production Manager on the series and by the third season he was directing full episodes.

When costs were totaled for the pilot for a May 21, 1966 report, it was determined it cost $572,000. Twice what a normal pilot usually ran. It was expensive, but William Self's main goal was to protect the studio's investment. "I knew it was going to cost money," said Self in an interview with *Cinefantastique* in 1993. "It's normal to put money into a show over and above the network license fee to protect its syndication value. We did deficit financing on any show I ever did...The better it is, the more potential it has in syndication.. *Batman* was unusually high. I felt it was worth the gamble. We weren't being foolish in putting extra money into it. Of course, I think that has proven to be true. It's still running today [in 1993 *Batman* was still regularly syndicated on TV, and in fact to this day still runs on the US network MeTV]."

Only a few shows made at Fox during that era had

consistent, long-lasting syndication success. *M*A*S*H* and *Batman* were two of them. "I did not honestly anticipate that *Batman* would have the life it has had," Self continued. "It's become a cult show. Of all the many shows we were investing in at that time, I had no reason to believe that it would be the best investment. But *Batman* has done very, very well."

Charles FitzSimons credits *Batman*'s success to meticulous planning. "It took me several months [to get the pilot ready]," said FitzSimons. "From the time Dozier sat down with me at lunch and said we were going to do it, I started research on the comic books... [I needed] to plan the tests: from designing costumes and Batarangs to trying to find a certain kind of silk to make Batman's cloak, so that the hollows would be dark and the ridges would be highlights, and designing the mask he wore. There was an enormous amount of preparation involved... you don't come up with these things overnight."

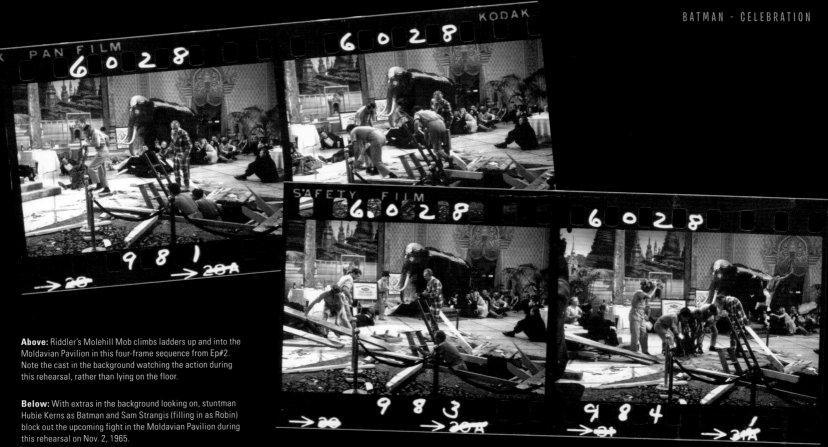

Above: Riddler's Molehill Mob climbs ladders up and into the Moldavian Pavilion in this four-frame sequence from Ep#2. Note the cast in the background watching the action during this rehearsal, rather than lying on the floor.

Below: With extras in the background looking on, stuntman Hubie Kerns as Batman and Sam Strangis (filling in as Robin) block out the upcoming fight in the Moldavian Pavilion during this rehearsal on Nov. 2, 1965.

BRINGING COMICS TO SCREEN: A VISUAL TREAT IN EVERY SCENE

"Jan [Kemp] and I pretty much saw eye to eye on the sharp but restrained Bruce Wayne duds. It was easy because my frame took 'off the rack' sizes. During the series I was elected one of the 'ten best-dressed men' in the world. Thanks, Jan."
Adam West, 2015 email interview with Bob Garcia

Costume designer and wardrobe manager Jan Kemp wrote in his bio regarding *Batman*: "When I received the assignment to work on the *Batman* series, I decided to get every copy of the *Batman* comic books that I could lay my hands on and shut myself away in a room with the phone off the hook and just absorb all the information I could about the characters and their behavior patterns. I soon realized this project would require a different approach in regard to costumes and I decided to give the actors a vivid combination of colors and styles that had not heretofore been used in films or television, and by so doing translate into real life the garish look of the comic-book pages. In spite of some opposition I did just that and the results are there to see; even today in reruns and syndication there is nothing quite like it."

In a 1994 interview, Kemp further explained: "I spent a lot of time in discussions with Charles FitzSimons. We decided we should try and get some kind of new color look on the show, which had never been attempted on television before...

Top and bottom left: From Ep#31: Adam West with Lee Harman, who transitioned from working with costumes in the first season, to makeup for second season.

Right: The Batsuit without trunks or Utility Belt. Director Oscar Rudolph (glasses) at right with Milton Stark (Dialog Coach, to right of Rudolph).

Opposite: The Penguin (Burgess Meredith), the Riddler (Frank Gorshin), Catwoman (Lee Meriwether) and the Joker (Cesar Romero) team up in the 1966 *Batman* movie.

The idea being that television [as a medium] was stereotyped and that it could only carry certain colors. I claimed and [was] later proved right that we could use all sorts of 'ultra-violent' colors and get away with it."

Kemp and Pat Barto (who worked on costumes for the actresses) brought together the shimmering leotards, black Lurex bodysuits (as worn by Catwoman), brightly colored tuxedos, and outrageously colored costumes that became the trademarks of the show. They worked with FitzSimons for months, buying special materials and dyes even before the screen tests were shot.

"It took a few months getting it all together before we got started and [was] quite a lot of work," Kemp pointed out. "Pat Barto was acting as coordinator with

me. The way they cast the shows and the way they were shooting them, we found we had to work together as a team. Every time Pat and I got something together and had decided on our colors and basic outfits, we would do a film test of it. Then [producers FitzSimons and Dozier] saw it and decided [whether] we should do a bit more with this color or make it more prominent and so forth." Film tests were tools used throughout preproduction on everything from costume color tests to hair color tests. For example, Adam West's October 5, 1965 close-up test for hair color can be seen on Kevin Burns' *Batman: Holy Batmania!* DVD.

"It was difficult to find materials that would look good with the colors we wanted," Kemp said. "Practically

Top: Above picture from Ep#7 shows how Utility Belt was tied in back. It also depicts a problem that surfaced during fights: Batman's cape would flip up and wrap around the neck, not only looking odd but getting in the way. Solution is shown below: two snaps on back of Batman's body suit where the cape would attach. Clips on shoulders (bottom right photo) also helped.

Opposite: Julie Newmar as Catwoman.

every piece of fabric had to be dyed to achieve the colors we were striving for, and initially I met with some opposition. However, as Mr. Dozier was fond of remarking: 'You have to overdo it in such a fashion that it becomes straight, and therefore funny!' Which was the premise that all the production departments used and gave the end result such a comedic camp quality that the audience seemed to enjoy."

Other department heads keyed into the color schemes that Kemp and Barto were creating. A yellow costume would result in the entire set having matching or complementary colors. Once the set was dressed in those colors, directors of photography would set up matching gels to properly light the set.

Adam West's Batsuit posed a number of challenges for Kemp. "I wanted to stay as near the comic-book look

as I could," the designer said. "Also I had the feeling that Batman himself should be an athletic-looking character. In that regard, I tried to use skin-tight material and things that would give an appearance of his athletic quality... We all knew from the story point that Bruce Wayne is a gentleman. He had to become a physical man to change over to Batman. I used Helenca [a synthetic fabric] for the tights which we dyed to reflect what we wanted in a color scheme."

Batman's cape presented its own set of difficulties. "We hunted around until we found a company which had a satin-silk fabric which we used as the cape," said Kemp. "[It] was intended to give an effect of a flowing look. This was a cape that worked and which kept to the original concept. We had to get that dyed to our color, because it wasn't quite the color we wanted...Sometimes we found

as we got into the show, that some of the colors would fade. It was a problem finding dyes that would stay dyed. For example, for the gloves and boots we used leather that had a stretch backing. That didn't carry the dye as well as the cape material did and was more subject to fading in the light and weather."

Mostly it was the cowl that caused Adam West problems, being very hot and cutting off much of his peripheral vision. "We tried figuring out how to make a cowl that would work for Adam," said Kemp, "[letting him

be] able to work, to hear, and to move without suffering from claustrophobia. Our effects department at Fox came up with a plastic combination that we formed. It crystallized to a hard substance that was the basis of the cowl, which we then covered with the fabric we were using for the costumes... We made modifications to the cowl as we got scripts and realized the type of action we were getting into. It necessitated modifications on his costume to enable him to work. It was like putting blinders on a horse; the poor guy inside was not seeing

too well. His peripheral vision was gone somewhat. So we had to try and eliminate as much of the problem as we could. Various modifications took place during the first two episodes, until we got an equitable arrangement that would work."

Adam West remembered: "The Batman costume had been carefully worked on for several weeks, then with me in the final fittings. It was necessary to manage look and comfort and measurability with the materials available at the time. I must say some were quite itchy and the cowl was quite hot after a few takes. Try to do action scenes under hot lights and not show sweat through the tunic. Super heroes don't sweat you know, especially someone as dapper as Bruce Wayne in maximum disguise. Jan had to use a hairdryer on my chest between takes. It looked a little silly but it quickly became ordinary."

The most famous of all Batman accessories was the well-stocked Utility Belt. "Batman always carried a lot of gadgets in his belt, and at various times he had all kinds of things he would use," Kemp said. "I designed that belt in collaboration with the prop department. They told us what they had to use in the way of weapons and we made our pouches to fit their gadgets. We would change them as the sequence required. It was a leather belt with a belt buckle produced for us by some metal shop that did it

in brass." That big yellow belt did have one drawback. As Adam West explained in *Back to the Batcave*: "The Utility Belt wasn't a problem unless I bent over suddenly, in which case I got a buckle in the gut or a Batarang in the side."

Robin's costume was pretty simple compared to the Caped Crusader's outfit. It was a basic green t-shirt with a red jerkin, green shorts, flesh-colored tights, yellow cape, green leather boots and gloves, plus the belt and black domino mask. Burt Ward complained about how hot and tight it was.

For the pilot, Kemp also designed Frank Gorshin's three Riddler costumes. Unfortunately, Gorshin was booked into Las Vegas and New York and couldn't make it to Hollywood for the initial fittings, which caused headaches for Kemp. "I had a lot of coordinating to do with phone calls to get measurements and to plan the costumes without his body to fit them to, initially," he said. "For his first outfit in the series, I had planned a set of leotards covered with question marks, then decided later on that we should have a change and put him in a suit. When he finally got time to come to the studio he kept the entire wardrobe department in stitches with laughter at his jokes and impressions." The third outfit was the crazy plaid suit The Riddler wore when he raided the Prime Minister's Climax Dinner.

Left: Burt Ward, playing Jill St. John's Molly in disguise as Robin, assists the Riddler's caper.

Opposite: Scenes from the Riddler's takeover of the Moldavian pavilion. See page 37 for rehearsal stills.

A QUICK WAY NEEDED FROM MANOR TO CAVE, THERE ARE ENDANGERED CITIZENS TO SAVE!

 It's a favorite scene in the classic *Batman* series. Bruce Wayne and Dick Grayson answer the "Batphone," get the lowdown on this week's villain from Commissioner Gordon, Bruce says "To the Batpoles!" and they run to and jump on their respective Batpoles (which are conveniently marked with each of their names). A quick "Batspin" later and the two are on their way down to the Batcave.

Lorenzo Semple Jr. delightfully described the final reveal in his script for the first episode: "[CAMERA] HOLDS on a pair of elevator-like doors [there were doors in his script!]. They WHIRR open suddenly and Dick and Bruce slide into view at bottom of the twin Batpoles. Only they are not plain, ordinary Bruce Wayne and Dick Grayson now, but fabulous BATMAN AND ROBIN... having wondrously acquired full Bat-regalia [sic] during their descent! Capes, tights, boots, gauntlets, bat-eared hoods and masks!"

The Batpoles were one of the first things Semple envisioned before the first episode was shot in October 1965. In a July 23 letter to Semple, Executive Producer William Dozier addressed the "Fire Station Poles" Semple envisioned in his initial outline. Dozier's comments included those of ABC executives about details, and discussions were exacting in this lead-up to the show: "[there] should be a large one for Bruce and a smaller one for Robin," adding that they should not be "literal about how they get their outfits on." Dozier suggested a "collection of various sound effects such as zippers zipping, hooks hooking, etc." But the production didn't go quite that far.

To show the genius of Semple, in his August 6 letter to Dozier, he remarked on the inevitable question raised by the existence of Batpoles: how do the Dynamic Duo get back up to Wayne Manor? "I leave the answer of that to you," he wrote. "I think it should just be forever a rich, piquant mystery. Just one of those bat-things [sic]." The question eventually was answered in "The Clock King Gets Crowned" with the "Compressed Steam Batpole Lift" but perhaps it should have been left a mystery.

The whole sequence was a bit of Hollywood magic, since the sets for Wayne Manor and the Batcave were never on the same sound stage. For the pilot, Bruce Wayne's study was on Stage 2 at the old Fox Studio on Western Avenue in Hollywood, miles away from where the Batcave set was built on Stage 16 of the 20th Century lot. For the series, the two sets were only a sound stage away from each other on the Desilu-Culver Studio lot.

Opposite: Burt Ward (Robin) and Adam West (Batman) prepare to race into the Batcave.

THE FANS MUST RAVE ABOUT THE NEW BATCAVE

"I walked onto the set, the first time, with total amazement. I thought, this really is a cave where Batman would solve crimes..."

Adam West, 2015 email interview with Bob Garcia

Jack Martin Smith, head of the Fox art department, assigned Edgar Graves as Art Director for *Batman*'s pilot. To finish the pilot's sets in the few weeks allotted, there were three or four groups of set builders, each one responsible for a different set. Ivan Martin, head of Fox's construction department (Mill, Paint and Plaster) oversaw the entire process. "[Martin ran] a top drawer operation," said Jack Senter. "It's one thing to visualize something, and it's another to get it all done. Ivan was able to do it for the money and in the proper style."

Stage 16 at 20th Century Fox was to house three sets: What a Way to Go-Go discothèque, the Peale Art Gallery office and the most famous set of all, the Batcave. "[It wasn't a normal set.] There were so many gadgets that were workable," said Ivan Martin. "It was an active set. All the parts worked, and everything worked fine." The Batcave was more than fifty feet tall, had twin poles that went from the floor to a high catwalk, a two-story Atomic Pile capable of supporting the weight of

several people, numerous Batcomputers and more.

In some cases, equipment in the pilot episode's Batcave was recycled from various Fox productions as was usual on the lot. The huge Atomic Pile, which was the Batmobile's nuclear power source, was part of a set from *Our Man Flint* turned upside down and redressed. One console was taken from *Fantastic Voyage*. They even grabbed a "force field generator" from *Lost in Space*, which was returned when the actual *Batman* series began shooting. Most equipment was jokingly labeled with its proper title such as "U.S. & Canada Crime Computer" and the "Chemo-Electric Secret Writing Detector."

Creation of the cave walls involved a whole new technology for the studio. They built a wire frame for the set and then sprayed it with polyurethane to get the "rock" walls. This was new and extremely dangerous work. The construction crew wore masks and used special equipment to build the rock formations. One advantage polyurethane had over other materials was that it dried quickly (usually in ten minutes) and when

dry you could carve the walls with knives to obtain the desired look. It was the same technique Martin used to build Ape City in *Planet of the Apes*.

Various colored dyes were added to the polyurethane for effect, and the walls were spray-painted by the art crew for highlights and shadows. Walls had to be bright so they would register when the show was televised. They looked fine in color, but most (about 90%) of America had black and white televisions, and the cave had to be brightly colored and sufficiently detailed to provide enough contrast to be seen by the viewing audience. The lightweight polyurethane was especially helpful in the creation of "wild walls"– tall walls that could be relocated when a camera needed to move to that spot on the set.

The entrance to the Batcave was a redressed natural cave located near a crossroads in Bronson Canyon, a section of Griffith Park, Los Angeles. The cave entrance was quite large and the crew made the entrance smaller with walls and doors that matched the cave's exterior. Later, foliage was added to better obscure the entrance. It was shot at an oblique angle because the cave was basically a long tunnel, and in any direct shot, light from the other side would be visible. A fold-down barricade at the road's edge was constructed for the Batmobile to speed across.

The stately Wayne Manor interior for the pilot was a revamped standing set from the TV show *Twelve O'Clock High*: the "Pinetree" set (the "old mansion"

Top left: A view around the first Batcave set, from far left of the Batpoles, across the left wall and up to the Atomic Pile.

Top right: A view looking into the Batcave from where the Batmobile would exit. Note crew member at far left along with partially exposed structure of Batcave walls.

Bottom: Jill St. John as Molly, masquerading as Robin.

Opposite top left: A full view of the Atomic Pile and foreground equipment in the first Batcave set.

Opposite top right: Stuntman Hubie Kerns and stuntwoman Pepper Curtis clamber about the Atomic Pile during filming of the pilot.

Opposite bottom: Right side of the Batcave, with Batmobile entrance.

headquarters for the Eighth Bomber Command) on Stage 2 at the Western Avenue Studio. In Bruce Wayne's study, the crew had to devise a simple way for the bookshelf to slide away, exposing the Batpoles, allowing Batman and Robin to slide "down" to the Batcave. Bill Dozier came up with the idea of a hidden switch inside a bust of William Shakespeare to activate the secret passageway. The stage crew wired that switch to a light behind the set, where a stagehand would be waiting. When the light went on, the stagehand would slide the bookshelf away, exposing the recess and the Batpoles. West and Ward would then leap onto the poles in true firefighter fashion and slide down, landing on cushions fifteen feet below. Sometime later in production, the Dynamic Duo's descent into the Batcave would be filmed miles away on Fox's Stage 16. The sequence was frequently reused as stock footage in future episodes. The exterior of Wayne Manor was a mansion on South San Rafael Avenue in Pasadena, California.

Commissioner Gordon's office was built on Stage 4 of the Fox lot. The interior of the TV studio, the Molehill Mob's Headquarters and the Underground Room under the Moldavian Pavilion were on Stage 2. The Moldavian Pavilion set was built on Stage 15, while underground passages used by the Riddler and his gang were filmed underneath that same stage. What A Way To Go-Go discothèque exteriors were on French Street at Fox.

In November 1965, after the pilot was finished, sets for the Batcave, the interior of Wayne Manor, and Commissioner Gordon's office all were either moved to or reproduced at the Desilu-Culver Studios where the remainder of the series was shot.

Above: Alan Napier (Alfred), Burt Ward (Robin) and Adam West (Batman).

Opposite: Burt Ward (Robin) examines a Batcave prop.

Following page, left: A view across the Batpoles and the left side of the second Batcave set.

Following page, top right: The second Batcave, viewing from right of the Atomic Pile to the secret entrance.

Following page, bottom right: Director George Waggner seated at far left, with Alan Napier (Alfred) and Burt Ward (Robin) in foreground, from Ep#91.

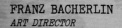

FRANZ BACHERLIN
ART DIRECTOR

Franz Bacherlin (1895-1980) worked on *Batman's* Batcave set. He also worked on *Journey to the Center of the Earth*, garnering an Academy Award nomination with his team (art directors Herman A. Blumenthal and Lyle R. Wheeler and set decorators Joseph Kish and Walter M. Scott). He worked on *Stalag 17*, *Twice Told Tales*, *The Magic Sword*, *Village of the Giants*, and other films.

BATCOMPUTER OUTPUT END...

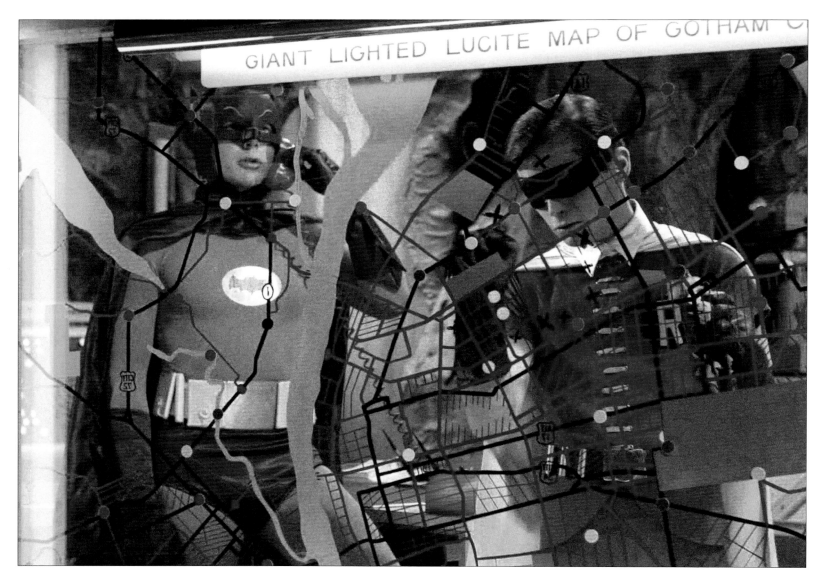

NEAL HEFTI WRITES THAT STRONG, GRAMMY-WINNING THEME SONG

"[Bill Dozier] tried to get [the theme song] credited as "*Word* and Music" by Neal Hefti. But they insisted on "*Words* and Music.""

Ann Rutherford-Dozier, interviewed in 1993 by Bob Garcia

Dozier suggested to FitzSimons that Neal Hefti write the show's theme song and score the series. Hefti had done albums with Sinatra and the Everly Brothers and Dozier was a fan. Greenway Productions signed the composer on September 14, 1965 to do the score. A press release stated that it would be Hefti's first score for TV. His famous theme included the repetition of Batman's name throughout. "So he not only got a composer's royalty," said FitzSimons, "but also a lyricist's royalty." Hefti received a 1967 Grammy for Best Instrumental Theme, as well as being nominated for Best Instrumental Performance and Best Instrumental Arrangement.

Neal Hefti had a tongue-in-cheek version of his hiring, which he included in the liner notes for his 1966 album *Batman Theme*: "When one is a composer-for-hire, he runs into many strange and unheard-of situations. For example, my phone rang one day recently. The voice at the other end was throaty and tense, but unmistakably

it was my friend William Dozier of Greenway Productions. He summoned me to a secret meeting at 20th Century Fox studios. Intrigued by his anxious tones and the sense of urgency about it all, I hung up the phone and raced to the movie lot without hesitation.

"When I arrived at his offices, instead of the usual greeting from a pretty receptionist, I was pinned to the wall by guards and frisked. Then mug shots were taken and I was fingerprinted. After pronouncing me clean, the guards whisked me into Mr. Dozier's office and quickly left the room. I stood in the hush of thick carpets before the great oak desk. Bill spoke.

"He swore me to secrecy and administered the loyalty oath, then came swiftly and precisely to the point. His eyes softened a little but he was no less stern as he said, 'Neal, I am going to commission you to compose the *Batman* theme.'

"My mouth went dry and my skin became chill as his words rang in my ears. I knew this would be hard, very hard, to keep to myself.

Previous spread: The Batcave was filled with gadgets to help the Dynamic Duo keep Gotham City safe from criminals. The Batcomputer was an integral part of the Batcave and essential for solving many of the crimes. Adam West (Batman) and Burt Ward (Robin) consulted it on many occasions.

Right: Nelson Riddle conducts his orchestra.

"Although I was unable to speak clearly, my friend knew that I was accepting this challenge by the humility in my eyes. He knew of my promise to keep confidence by the firmness in my handshake as he strode from behind his desk.

"I worked around the clock until my job was done. I planned carefully to take my 'batuscript' to the studio when it would not be noticed. The guards were there to meet me, and I was congratulated on keeping the great secret. *Batman Theme* was now a reality."

His son, Paul Hefti, now in charge of Neal Hefti Music Corporation, remembered his father talking about creating *Batman Theme*: "He told me he tore up more paper on *Batman* than on any other work he ever did. He had to find something that worked well with the visual of the two caped crusaders, and would appeal to kids as well as to their parents. What he came up with was a twelve-bar blues with a guitar hook and one word." Hefti delivered the theme around November 18 and recorded it for the show on November 22.

Hefti never did get a chance to score the pilot. He was getting too much work for feature film soundtracks. When it became apparent that Hefti could not do the show, William Self asked his friend, arranger and composer Nelson Riddle, to take over. The two had met when Riddle, was musical director of the short-lived *Frank Sinatra Show* (1957). Riddle would score the pilot in December and stay on to score the series.

BARRIS KUSTOM BUILDS A BATMOBILE WITH THAT PERFECT BOB KANE FEEL

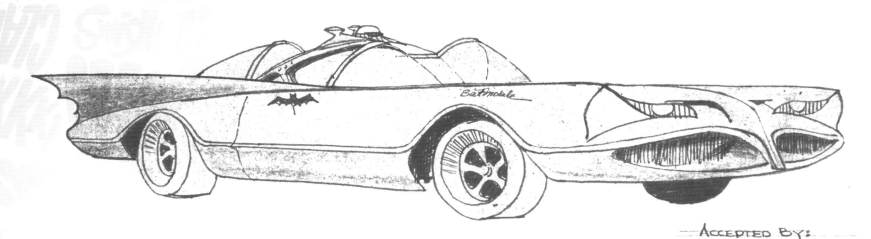

REVISED: 9-23-65

ACCEPTED BY:
Barris Custom City

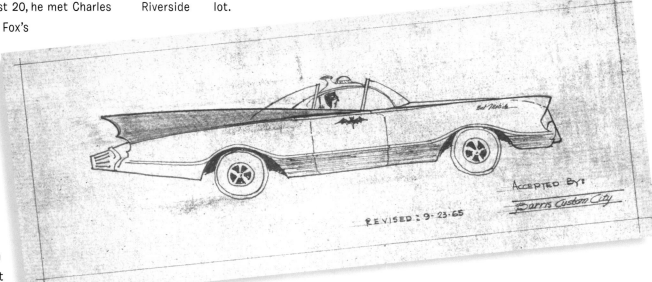

Semple couldn't help himself and had gone a little crazy on the Batmobile. As was usual with specialty cars, the producers turned to the booming California car-customizing industry to get it done.

George Barris, "King of the Kar Kustomizers," received a call from Greenway, and on August 20, he met Charles FitzSimons and Ike Danning from Fox's transportation department. They gave Barris a list of things the Batmobile needed and sketches done by art director Eddie Graves. Barris realized he had the perfect car on his lot and customizing it would save them time and money.

Barris had been part of Ford's 1955 Custom Car Caravan Tour, which featured a 1955 Lincoln Futura concept car built by hand at Ghia Body Works in Turin, Italy. When the tour was over, Ford Motor Company stashed it along with other cars at George Barris' shop in North Hollywood. In 1959, the car was repainted and tidied up for the Glenn Ford–Debbie Reynolds romantic comedy, *It Started With a Kiss*. It was then left to languish on Barris' Lankershim and Riverside lot.

Above and below: An early blueprint of the proposed Batmobile design.

Opposite page: Proofs of Batmobile pictures taken October 1965 on the Fox lot before final glossy finish and "fluorescent cerise trim" was applied to the vehicle.

REVISED: 9-23-65

ACCEPTED BY:
Barris Custom City

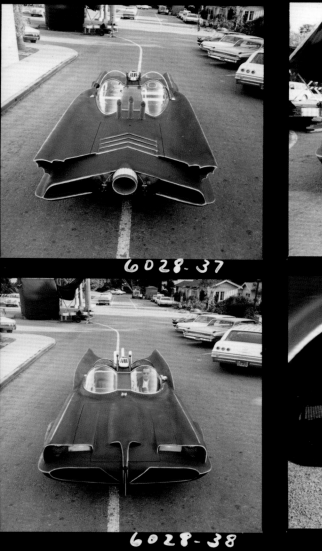

6028-41

6028-45

6028-37

6028-38

6028-42

6028-46

6028-39

6028-43

6028-47

6028-40

6028-44

6028-48

Barris took a look at Graves' sketches and saw how the Futura's front end could be modified into a bat's face, and the huge 1950s auto fins turned into bat wings. He set up an appointment to come back on August 25 with sketches of his own plus cost estimates.

Negotiations and sketch approvals dragged on for over a week until an agreement was reached on September 1. It took Barris a little over a month to deliver the car on October 7.

Above: Batmobile outfitted with "Batram" mounted on front (under bumper), as used in Ep#24. **Bottom middle:** Filming the Batmobile's Mobile Crime Computer for the pilot episodes. **Bottom right:** During Ep#51-52, Adam West visits with George Barris, builder of the Batmobile.

Left: The Lincoln Futura, from an original publicity still for the 1959 movie *It Started With A Kiss* which starred Glenn Ford and Debbie Reynolds.

THE BATMOBILE'S TRICKS, MADE EVERYONE FANATICS

BATMAN: To the Batmobile! Let's go!

ROBIN: Atomic batteries to power. Turbines to speed.

This page: Just a couple of the Batmobile's many well-labeled buttons.

Previous page: An "egg-ceptional" view from behind the camera during Ep#48, as Egghead "egg-spelled" the Dynamic Duo from Gotham City under threat of "eggs-ecution". Al Bettcher operates camera while Bill Bohny pulls focus.

Following page: From left: Boom Operator controls microphone, Sam Bishop (Key Grip, glasses, behind camera) and Al Bettcher (Camera Operator). Ward and West are inside Batmobile.

Along with Batman and Robin, the third star of the *Batman* television show was most assuredly the Batmobile. Black, sleek, powerful, with lots of labels on the inside, just to show you it belonged in this series. For audiences, the car just confirmed how cool Batman *really* was.

The Batmobile was true to its comic-book origins. Large, atomic powered, with a jet engine in the back, and no top; if it rained, the car would never have been practical, but, boy, it had cool stuff. Producer FitzSimons made a list for car customizer George Barris of items required to be built into the car. It read as follows:

✓ The switches and hand-throttle knob for the Turbo-electric Drive

✓ The Bing-Bong Warning Bell and Bat-Light Flasher

✓ The Mobile Phone between the seats with beeper and flashing light

✓ The Batscope, with TV-like viewing screen on the dash with control buttons and radar-like antenna with sizable parabolic reflector outside, with cockpit controls.

✓ Anti-theft System – flashing red lights – piercing whistle – little rockets built into tubes at the back of the cockpit that fire straight up with a fiery whoosh.

✓ Anti-Fire Control System – flood of foam from secret nozzle

✓ Turn-off switch for protection systems

✓ Radar-like screen that beeps and blips and points an arrow as it picks up Robin's directional signal

✓ Mechanics for Emergency Bat Turn – red lever so named on dash – reverse thrust rockets beneath headlights - Ejection Parachute Mechanism at rear.

✓ Bat-Ray projector mechanism - lever on dash so named – Hood Hydrolic [sic] Projector Device (Note: they talked about this ray possibly coming from the Bat-Eyes instead).

✓ Portable fire-extinguisher

✓ Receiver and sender computer to be installed in trunk of Batmobile

✓ Bat symbols on hubcaps

✓ *The color of the Batmobile and the Bat Symbols to be placed thereon shall be mutually agreed upon between owner and producer prior to the completion of the Batmobile.*

✓ *Special luminescent paint to define Bat outline at night, the placement of which shall be mutually agreed upon between owner and producer prior to the completion of the Batmobile.*

All of the gadgets were dictated by the script, and used to great effect by director Bob Butler. In an Audience Studies Incorporated (ASI) audience test, the Batmobile was an audience favorite. The report noted, "viewers responded most favorably to the sequences involving the Batcar [sic] especially the sequence where the Riddler tries to steal the car and fireworks shoot off." Over the years, writers added to the car's gadgetry with a battering ram, a smoke screen, a tire-repair device, a net in the trunk, and various dashboard gimmicks. Each new gimmick increased the Batmobile's status as the ultimate crime-fighting car.

Early in production of the series, the idea of a new Batmobile every season was briefly discussed, much like the new model year for automobiles, but renting the car was more economical. Difficulties did arise between exhibition demands and production needs, but the studio never did build their own Batmobile. George Barris eventually constructed three fiberglass replicas of the original Lincoln Futura.

#1 BATMOBILE SPECS
according to 1989 Press Kit

These specs had changed on the Batmobile as things wore out or were no longer available.

Designer/ Builder	George Barris, Barris Kustom City
Horsepower	500
Weight	5,500 Lbs.
Wheelbase	129 inches
Overall Length	206 inches
Height	48 inches
Transmission	B&M power racing automatic transmission
Tires & Wheels	Firestone traction grip oval tires. Wheels are [15] inch wide Base, [Rader steel rims].
Exterior Body Features	All steel painted Bat-Black with fluorescent Cerise trim. Batman symbol on doors and wheel hubs. Functional double-release parachutes. Twin top windshield bubbles of aircraft Plexiglass®. Concealed 12 volt headlights and tail lights for street driving. Dual large inner steel protective blades in rear 'Bat fins'. Push button operated center front steel chain slasher blade.
Interior Body Features	Twin body contoured durafoam bucket seats. TV screen with revolving closed circuit camera. Radar screen. Swivel Nozzle 5-way anti-fire system. Turbine exhaust and air-conditioning rear tube. Cable-controlled cutouts for sound transmission
Instruments and Dials	Half-diameter aircraft-type steering wheel. Right & left turning buttons on steering wheel. Dials and gauges in center of steering wheel.

BATMOBILE ON TOUR SHOWED THOUSANDS THE CAR'S ALLURE

 Within a week of the pilot episode airing, the publishers of *Motor Trend* magazine requested the car at their Pan Pacific Auto Show and their "The Wonderful World of Wheels" auto show in New York. The magazine promised "extensive coverage" in their magazines (*Motor Trend, Teen, Hot Rod,* etc.) which had a combined circulation of 2.5 million copies a month. George Barris requested appearances at the 13th Annual Custom Car and Speed Show and the 6th Annual International Custom Car Show. The requests never let up and George Barris spent most of 1966 pushing for permission to duplicate the original Futura.

These duplicates were built to be on tour, and there was also a very practical reason for the request. Transporting the Futura off-site led to logistical headaches in the production and it always ran a risk of damaging the one-of-a-kind car. The car once rolled out of its carrier and crashed into a parked car at a show. The 5500 lb car was unscathed, but the parked car was pretty banged up.

When Barris Kustom City (BKC) asked if they could fix the damaged vehicle, the owner laughingly declined. He had just had an accident with the Batmobile!

Still, it was no laughing matter to Barris, who insisted that more cars were needed. On October 11, 1966, an agreement was reached allowing BKC to manufacture two duplicate Batmobiles for exhibition. Somehow in November, *three* new automobiles were built: the #2, #3 and #4 cars.

They took fiberglass molds off of the Futura and mounted the new bodies onto three Ford Galaxie chassis lengthened by ten inches to match the longer wheel base and tread of the experimental car. These three weighed 3800 lbs each, 1700 lbs lighter than the original car. All had Edsel steering wheels and could easily be identified as the replicas by the black trim on their canopies. The original had chrome trim. The #2 and #4 never had working headlights. The headlight buckets were never cut out of the fiberglass. Both the #2 and #3 touring cars were simply beautiful, with new electronics and

Above: Note "Bat Car" on the sign. When exhibiting in the early days the term Bat Car had to be used by George Barris since "Batmobile" was restricted by legal agreements.

Opposite: Irvin Kuns, Lester E. Tompkins and George Barris, as the partnership Barris Kustom City, were responsible for building the Batmobile. The crew who customized the car included Tompkins, Michael "Gale"Black, Bill Cushenbery, Roy "Tubs" Johnson and Richard "Korky" Korkes.

bright bodies. Should you ever see one at an auto show or a convention you'll notice that they shine. The #2 and #3 Batmobiles had a 390ci V8 engine as did the Futura.

For local shows in California, Barris' wagon hauled the Batmobile in a trailer that had a huge painted sign on its side which read: "Batmobile, ABC Weekly Batman TV Series; Barris Kustom City 10811 Riverside Drive, North Hollywood, California, Ford Official Car." For state fairs around the US and Canada, a company called Promotions, Inc. exhibited the Batmobile in a bright yellow forty-foot trailer with "Direct from Gotham City" painted on the side. Towed by a semi, this trailer was equipped with a twenty-six-foot-long door that would fold down on one side and act as a viewing area. Stairs would be added so

people could walk up and look at the car.

The #4 Batmobile was built for drag racing. It had a large Holman & Moody 427ci V8 with a four barrel carburetor and a high-rise intake manifold. Beginning in early 1967, professional drag racer Bill Shrewsberry took the car on the racing circuit. He did two to three runs a day at the tracks. To make an impression, an actual flame thrower fired through the exhaust. The car had a larger beacon cage atop the center bar, and the rivets attaching the emblems to the doors are clearly visible.

In 2014, Mark Racop and his company Fiberglass Freaks were hired to restore the car. The company's online blog showing the step-by-step process is still available for viewing.

Top: Barris Kustom City made fiberglass molds from the original Batmobile in order to build three additional cars for use on tours and at automotive shows, with one as a drag racer on the professional US drag race circuit. After these molds were taken, the car needed to be repainted.

Bottom and opposite: Mark Racop's Fiberglass Freaks' restoration of the #4 Batmobile, the drag racer; various components of the car at different stage in the process, and a photo of the finished car itself.

ROBERT BUTLER SO TOTALLY "GOT IT" HE AND SEMPLE WERE A PERFECT FIT

"We were lucky to get someone with his reputation. He had already done a huge amount of work on TV. For both Butler and myself, *Batman* was a big deal."

Adam West, 2015 email interview with Bob Garcia

Robert Butler ... Would Batman really wear a robe like this?

After months of preparation, filming on the *Batman* pilot began on October 15, 1965. "Pilot" was a bit of a misnomer, since ABC committed to the series back in August. ABC even issued a press release October 19, the day before principal photography began, announcing their new series and a January 12, 1966 premiere. However most of Greenway and 20th Century Fox's paperwork for "Hi Diddle Riddle" and "Smack in the Middle" refers to the pair as the pilot.

Pilot director Robert Butler had ties to *Batman* early on. In a July 29, 1965 letter to executive producer William Dozier, writer Lorenzo Semple Jr. pointed out that he had "described this project briefly to my friend Bob Butler while I was in California and he dug it with tremendous enthusiasm and understanding."

Butler began working at CBS as an usher in the early 1950s and moved up the ladder becoming a production clerk, a stage manager and eventually, in 1957, an associate director on *Climax!* and later *Playhouse 90*. It

was on those shows that, after his daily unit work was done, he was able to sneak up into the sound effects booth to watch and study many of live television's legendary directors like John Frankenheimer, Franklin Schaffner and Arthur Penn. "Dozier knew me when he was a CBS boss, while I was a very efficient associate director," said Butler. "He knew me as a guy who knew production and would get the job done right."

In 1959, Butler was hired as a director on *Hennesey* and subsequently worked on such classic TV shows as *The Twilight Zone*, *The Defenders*, *The Untouchables*, *Dr. Kildare*, and *Ben Casey*. He directed the pilots for *Happy* (1960), *The Secret Life of James Thurber* (1961), and *The Greatest Show on Earth* (1963).

An August 26, 1965 telegram from Dozier informed Semple that Butler had agreed to direct *Batman*'s pilot. Semple was delighted since the two had been friends for some time. "We were very good friends and our wives knew each other as kids," explained Butler. "For a few years before Lorenzo went to Spain, we were young

Opposite top: Director Bob Butler contemplates upcoming scenes in the Batcave.

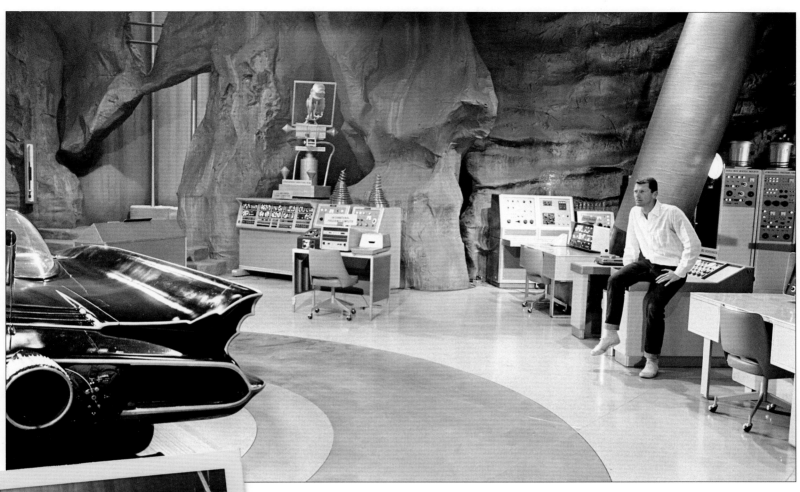

Batman caught red handed!

'newbies' together." The director signed on to *Batman* September 9 and officially reported for pre-production work on October 4.

Batman came at the end of a year-long run of directing all-new original material for Butler. It had started in November of 1964 with the pilot for *Star Trek*, "The Cage." He followed this with *Kilroy*, an original tele-movie shown in four-parts on *Walt Disney's Wonderful World of Disney*. Then he directed the *Hogan's Heroes* pilot and three additional episodes. Finally, he came to *Batman* where he would shoot the pilot plus four more episodes. This run had allowed him to develop the look and feel of several shows, but not get dragged down by the repetitive nature of working on a series.

Butler loved the energy of being in on the creation of

something. "On pilots everyone is hungry," he explained. "Everyone is paying attention. There is less goofing around. They want to sell it. They want to get it on the air. [Everyone has the attitude of] 'How can I help? What can I do?'"

He thrived on that new project excitement. It energized him. Sam Strangis, the pilot's Assistant Director, was impressed by Butler's "style and enthusiasm." "Bill knew his stuff, but it still takes a guy to put it on film. Bob Butler's techniques like the slanted camera on the villains, using hand-held, things that had never been done before. It was all Bob Butler. We wanted him back to do as many as he could, but he was too busy elsewhere."

ABC's Harve Bennett saw Butler as the director *Batman* needed: "Besides being a good director, he was like a kid. His enthusiasm was unbelievable. He had some

SAM STRANGIS
ASSISTANT DIRECTOR, UNIT PRODUCTION MANAGER, DIRECTOR

Sam Strangis (1929-) came to *Batman* as an assistant director. He became unit production manager and ended up directing nine episodes during the third season. He met and married Dozier's executive secretary Bonnie Paterson while working on *Batman*. Later he became Vice President in Charge of Production at Paramount doing *The Brady Bunch, Love, American Style*, and *Longstreet*. He started producing with *The Six Million Dollar Man* and went on to be producer or executive producer on a number of TV movies. In the late 1980s he was executive producer on the *War of the Worlds* TV series and in 2000 began his stint as co-executive producer of the hit show *CSI*, working there until 2003.

BATCOMPUTER OUTPUT END . . .

Sam Strangis - Assistant Director

Opposite: From this rehearsal outside the Gotham City Museum in Ep#24, Batman tries to reach Robin on the "Bat-Communicator."

Left: Burt Ward as Robin—although it is supposed to be Molly disguised as Robin—standing inside the Batmobile's cockpit for this Batcave scene from Ep#1.

great ideas. He had enormous panache. It was that final element that put the pilot over the top."

When Butler read Semple's script for the first time, he was delighted. "It was so economical and seemingly simple and clear," he said. As an example, he recited the script's description of the Riddler: "He contrives his crimes like artichokes. You have to strip off the spiny leaves to reach the heart of it. That isn't actually a joke, but it ain't naturalism for sure. That's smart [writing]. You have to be really smart to write dumb."

Knowing Semple helped him see the slyness of the script immediately. "I knew Lorenzo to be a crazy, wonderful maniac, so I knew what the script was about instantly, and just enjoyed it," Butler said. "That's not arrogance. It was

Below: Frank Gorshin (Riddler) ponders his next move.

just luck. I just got it instantly... Lorenzo was a very smart, sly, entertain[ing] guy. Always. So as I read this, I didn't really see Lorenzo as I read it, but I felt all that intelligence and specificity and economy. It was terrific."

Filming began with second unit work on Friday, October 15, 1965. After two days of rehearsal on October 18 and 19, principal photography followed from October 20 through November 10. Two additional days of second unit work were needed on November 11 and 12. Adding

it up, it took twenty-one days to shoot that one-hour pilot, something that would have been impossible at any other point in the series because of time restrictions. During the shoot, Butler consistently added a number of unscripted shots to scenes to better tell the story. "I think I was probably greedy about getting it right," admitted Butler. "It was scheduled for eighteen days [actually fourteen days] and it went to twenty-one in my eagerness to get it done really well."

Robert Butler busy directing...

ROBERT BUTLER
DIRECTOR

Robert Butler (1927–) went on to a very distinguished career after *Batman*, directing *Gunsmoke*, *Hawaii Five-O*, *Kung Fu*, *I Spy* and many others. He was awarded the Directors Guild of America Award for Outstanding Directorial Achievement in a Dramatic Series in 1973 for *The Waltons*. In 1974, he won the Emmy for Best Directing in Drama (A Single Program of a Series with Continuing Characters and/or Theme) as well as the Emmy for Director of the Year – Series, both for *The Blue Knight*. He picked up another DGA Award for Outstanding Directorial Achievement in a Dramatic Series in 1981 for the *Hill Street Blues* pilot "Hill Street Station," and won the Emmy for Outstanding Director in a Drama Series for that same episode. He co-created *Remington Steele* and followed it by directing several TV movies plus pilots/first episodes of *Moonlighting* (Emmy-nominated), *Sisters*, *Lois and Clark: The New Adventures of Superman* (Emmy-nominated), and *The Division*. On February 7, 2015, Butler was given the DGA's Lifetime Achievement Award in Television Direction, the organization's top honor.

BATCOMPUTER OUTPUT END . . .

SAVING TIME AND MONEY, WITH BIF, BANG, & ZOWIE!

> "It was so original to actually bring the comic script to the screen as pop art, with the actual POW lettering on the screen and the unusual camera angles."
>
> Bob Kane, creator of *Batman*, interviewed in 1993 by Bob Garcia

 Sound effects in title form for the pilot's fight scenes were indicated in Semple's script. But the screenwriter's revised draft script envisioned them and the entire scene much differently than the way they ultimately appeared:

VARIOUS CLOSEUP CUTS – THE DONNYBROOK
A series of VERY CLOSE, CRAZILY ANGLED, HAND-HELD SHOTS, succeeding each other with the utmost rapidity: monster swinging fists, uppercuts landing on jaws, a gasping mouth, a knee in someone's stomach, a kicking foot making contact with shin, etc., etc., etc. OVER these we hear violent SOUNDS OF PHYSICAL COMBAT and there are SUCCESSIVE EXPLODING TITLES:

POW!!! WHAMMM!!! BIFF!!!
GLIPP!! ZOWIE!!! URKKK!!!

At the end of this furious sequence, as FINAL TITLE EXPLODES AND FADES:
BACK TO SCENE – FULL SHOT

Batman and Robin, panting and disheveled, stand in midst of flattened, groaning, head holding Molehill Mobsters.

Director Butler chose to shoot wide, and with an emphasis on pageantry and speed. As the footage rolled in and time was running out, Charles FitzSimons saw the fight scenes needed extra coverage, but there was no way they could afford to reshoot anything. Out of pure necessity, he came up with a way of using "optical sound effects" over certain scenes in post-production. "The POWs, BIFFs, and BANGs covered the areas where you might have needed an additional shot," said FitzSimons.

Post-production coordinator Robert Mintz realized the editing department was having problems in delivering *Batman* episodes on time. The film editor would complete the editing of the show and then order the super-imposed optical sound effects afterwards. He would have to wait until they were optically laid into the scenes before the episode could be finished. "I started

Top: Fouteen Exploding titles from just one fight scene at the end of the second episode," Smack in the Middle," compared with just 4 simpler variants (along the bottom) from "The Clock King Gets Crowned" (Ep#46).

thinking about that, and I said, 'Wait a minute,'" recalled Mintz. "What if we gave the editor a big roll of ZAPs, a big roll of POWs, and he takes the scene, cuts it, lays in three frames, [and moves on]. It worked perfectly. It

saved the studio a fortune in optical effects. And the result was that it delivered on time, because the editor had full control." These slugs were introduced in the second season.

WILLIAM DOZIER AGREED TO NARRATE, DESMOND DOOMSDAY WAS GREAT

"Forgive me for flying in the face of unanimous acclaim, but a carping note: You must get rid of your voice-over announcer on BATMAN. Just awful! He's dragging you down (to a 50 share)."

A January 24, 1966 congratulatory note to Dozier from TV producer Grant Tinker

At several points in Lorenzo Semple's pilot script, he indicated using superimposed titles, akin to the text blocks used at the top of comic-book panels, for the reprise at the beginning of the second episode as well as the titles, plus an "announcer-type voice-over" for the cliffhanger at the end of the first episode. Eventually William Dozier chose something much faster and less expensive: a series narrator.

The necessity of a sizzle reel for network affiliates pushed Dozier into the role of that series narrator. "After we had been shooting about three weeks on the pilot, we had a lot of footage and the network wanted us to assemble it so they could show it to advertisers," said Dozier. "They were panicked to get a show on the air, and sold. So we immediately knew we had to have something to tie those scenes together so they'd make a little sense. The writers wrote some continuity stuff that would tie these various scenes together. Then I started auditioning professional off-screen announcers. I think

I auditioned about six or seven, and none of them had the right tone. I remembered what I wanted from radio shows like *The Shadow*; a lot of suspense and so on."

The announcers would come in, and Dozier kept telling them how the narration should be done. No one came up to his standards. Exasperated, FitzSimons finally said to Dozier, "Bill, there's only one person I know with that supercilious, superior quality in his voice, and that's you. Why don't you do it?"

Dozier, who hadn't done any voice work up to that time, agreed, and Desmond Doomsday (a Batman-esque pseudonym) was created. "We were up against the gun to get this film ready for the network to see, so I said, 'Well, okay. I'll do it for this and then let's get on with it.' I did it for the film we put together, and the network brass came out and ranted. They loved what they saw and asked, 'That voice, we have him tied up?' and I said, 'No, no. He's a big star.' I milked that for about five minutes and [said] I think if they played their cards right they could get him. [I] finally told them who it was."

Bottom: (From left) Burt Ward, Adam West, William Dozier.

Opposite: William Dozier's signature

"I did all of them from then on," Dozier continued. "I could do them exactly because I was familiar with all of the scripts. I knew the feeling of the particular episode... I would go to the dubbing room and knock off three or four of them in an hour. It was simple for me at least because I knew what they were all about."

"We never replaced him," said FitzSimons. "He did every one of them, and his voice was wonderful." It must have been a dream come true for Dozier, who was a great fan of radio and television announcers.

SHORT PAUSE! HOLD YOUR BREATH FOR THE DYNAMIC DUO

ABC'S MARKETING IS TOP NOTCH, MAKING BATMAN THE SHOW TO WATCH

"*Batman* would have attracted nobody but preschoolers were it not for ABC's ingenious promotion efforts."

Time magazine January 28, 1966 issue

ABC knew it needed to create an unusual mystique for *Batman*'s premiere, and Scherick started his famous ad campaign. "What we had to do was let the audience know that something was coming," he said. "I wrote a memo. I challenged everybody at ABC in the campaign we were undertaking, a mid-season campaign, to let America know [about *Batman*]. I wrote the slogan, very simple: 'Batman is coming, so is Robin.' If we do this right, it will open with a forty percent share of audience, but it has to be done everywhere. Everywhere people turn they have to see 'Batman is coming, so is Robin.' Even when Leonard Goldenson [ABC Chairman of the Board] goes to his private john there has to be a strip across his seat: 'Batman is coming, so is Robin.'"

The network ran a series of spots on their own airtime and their advertising agency, Grey Advertising, ran a series of print ads. In its January 28, 1966 issue, *Time* magazine wrote of the campaign: "*Batman* would have attracted nobody but preschoolers were it not for ABC's

ingenious promotion efforts. Skywriters emblazoned BATMAN IS COMING in the heavens above the Rose Bowl game. Every hour on the hour, television announcements bleated the imminent arrival of the Caped Crusader. Hordes of people who recalled Bob Kane's comic-book creation as well as the 1943 movie serial... pushed their toddlers out of the way to get a good look at the TV set."

The ad campaign was in addition to a huge ABC media blitz which had begun the previous month. In a four-page January 5, 1966 letter from Elliott Henry, ABC's Director of Network Press Information/Western Division, we can see the extent of the network's press push. For example: four national press mailings with photos had gone out since December 10, 1965, covering the first two weeks of broadcasts. On December 18, 1965, West and Ward had a color photo gallery shoot. Color and B&W sketches of Batman were circulated nationally. A 1,500-word publicity article was written for Newspaper Enterprise Association to run in their syndicate, ABC brought *New York Times* reporter Judy Stone to the set

Opposite: A full page newspaper ad appeared in the Jan. 12, 1966 *New York Herald Tribune*.

for cast interviews, and *Newsweek* ran a story in its December 20, 1965 issue. The letter goes on for another two pages, ending with "From this evidence I am sure that you, along with us, can more than assume that the nation will be quite BATMAN conscious come 7.30 p.m., Wednesday, January 12." Henry made the point that this letter didn't cover the network's on-the-air promotions or other advertising for the show.

ABC had arranged for a New York world premiere of the TV pilot at the York Theatre the night of January 12, 1966. William and Ann Dozier flew in from California. The invited guests were a who's who of New York City's most famous.

They included Jacqueline Kennedy, Mr. and Mrs. Peter Lawford, Mr. & Mrs. Leonard Bernstein, Senator and Mrs. Robert Kennedy, NY Mayor John Lindsay, Andy Warhol, and others. ABC also made arrangements for Adam West to appear on the January 10, 1966 episode of their daytime show, *The Dating Game*.

This was all the network planning, but Dozier wasn't going to leave such things in others' hands. On January 10, 1966 he had ABC send a telegram to forty-two journalists and critics throughout the southern United States that he met in Dallas and Atlanta the previous summer. The text was simple:

Dear–

I hope you will be able to watch the Batman premiere Wednesday evening and particularly that you will be able to see it in color. I think you will agree it is the Camp show of all time.

Warm Regards, Bill Dozier.

This was indicative of Dozier's hands-on approach to publicity. Before any major release, he either made a series of personal phone calls or sent a telegram to local news outlets.

HIRING PRODUCER HORWITZ
TO CREATE A SCRIPTING BLITZ

"Absolutely no thoughtful musing, and if I or any other writer accidentally put in such dialogue [or] stage directions, for 'batsake' knock them out with thick black ink…"

Lorenzo Semple Jr., in a November 1965 letter to William Dozier

Arguably, the hiring of Howie Horwitz as producer on October 21, 1965 was the beginning of the first season of *Batman*. Previously supervising producer on *77 Sunset Strip*, Horwitz began soliciting scripts while the pilot was still shooting. When it wrapped he had had thirteen story outlines in preparation. As those scripts arrived during November and December, they were sent to Semple for critique.

"I want to be mailed every draft that comes in," Semple wrote Dozier. "I'll phone or cable you my suggestions if they strike me as in any way inspirational. But I don't think you should count on me actively rewriting anybody else's scripts, partly because I'm lousy at it, partly because I don't think Executive Script Consultancy calls for it, but CHIEFLY (believe me, Wm.!) because it would stop my own writing dead in "bat-tracks" [and] I want this series to succeed at least as much as you do [and] I know that I can most help in this emergency situation by writing scripts."

True to his word, Semple delivered the first half of his script for "Fine Feathered Finks" on November 5, with the rest delivered on November 8. (Bob Butler needed to begin shooting "Finks" on November 22). And a few days later, he also turned in his outline for "Doom-Trap" which became "The Inescapable Doom-Trap" and was filmed as "Zelda the Great" and "A Death Worse than Fate." During the first season, Semple wrote the "Batnotes" (writers' guidelines), ten half-hour episodes and the feature film.

"I've learned in writing these, it's impossible to exaggerate [the] essential SIMPLICITY of proper 'Batscripts,'" Semple wrote to Dozier on November 9. "One simple villainous plot from start to end, by no means necessarily described in Part One, but strongly hinted at, and hinted at in terms of Batman's eventual involvement. That's to say, crook should (if possible) specifically declare that in some tricky way, Batman will be used in his scheme as more than merely a detective to be avoided. This is always a great What-The-Heck? element, and will help carry over the twenty-four-hour lacuna."

Above: Anne Baxter as Olga, Queen of the Bessarovian Cossacks, leans in for a kiss with Batman.

Opposite top: Adam West takes a break on the set of strange Albanian genius Eivol Ekdal's workshop.

Opposite bottom left: Another view of Eivol Ekdal's workshop, with Burt Ward and Adam West.

Opposite bottom middle: In Ep#9, Eivol Ekdal strafes his inescapable doom-trap with a machine gun to prove to Zelda that it is bullet-proof and unbreakable.

Bottom right: Batman and Robin cautiously enter the workshop of Zelda's criminal cohort.

That first season featured shows written by Robert Dozier, Fred De Gorter, Max Hodge, Rik Vollaerts, Stephen Kandel, Sheldon Stark, Dick Carr, and others.

For most writers, it was a one-time thing, and they moved on to other freelance work. One writer, Stanley Ralph Ross, wrote Catwoman's "The Purr-fect Crime" and "Better Luck Next Time" and stayed with the show until the end, writing a total of twenty-seven episodes. Ross had great fun writing for the show.

He sprinkled his scripts with dirty words in foreign languages (until they got letters), his old Coney Island addresses, the names of people he knew, anything and everything for fun.

Ross remembered that while Bill Dozier saw every script, his comments were usually minor. "He was a great noninterventionist," said Ross in a 1993 interview with Bob Garcia. "I once handed him a script and asked him if he wanted a second draft. 'Naw,' he said, 'I already did it

Top: Pre-production concept painting by Leslie Thomas, used as a guide during meetings and for set builders in developing the telescope scene on the roof of Wayne Manor at the beginning of Ep#9.

Above: "Good day, citizen! Are you certain you are eating all your vegetables?"

for you.' 'You did it for me?' I cried. 'Yes, there were only a few typos and I fixed them. I'll pay you for a second draft.' That's the type of guy Dozier was."

Horwitz looked over each script, and if a rewrite needed to be done it was handed to newly-hired story editor, Charles Hoffman, who had been producer on *Hawaiian Eye*. While assigning scripts and working with the authors was a top priority, Horwitz also line-produced the show.

Adam West remembered the producer fondly. "Horwitz seemed to be doing most of the on-the-line night-and-day producing work," he said. "He was small in stature but high on energy. Howie put on a marvelous front of being mean and pushy, but, underneath, he was a sweet man with a big sense of humor. And he seemed to love his job. It wasn't an easy one with the budget getting more constricted as the studio tried to cut back on an extremely expensive show."

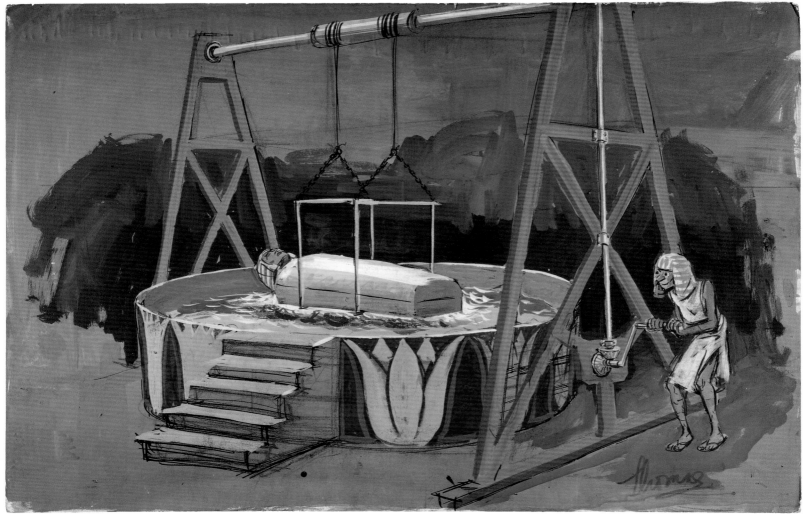

Above: Siren has hypnotized Bruce Wayne and ordered him to jump from the top of a tall building, as depicted in this pre-production concept painting for Ep#97 by Leslie Thomas. These visualizations of the script were used in meetings and aided set builders when constructing and decorating sets.

Opposite middle: King Tut's insidious drowning death trap for Batman, as depicted in this pre-production concept painting by Leslie Thomas.

Opposite bottom: A view across the Royal Oil Boiling Room for the Ep#88 fight. First picture, from left: Hubie Kerns (Batman stunt double), Dick Elmore (Royal Jester stunt double), Chuck Hicks (Tutling #1), Fritz Ford (Tutling #2) and Victor Paul (Robin stunt double). Second picture: Lee Meriwether (Lisa Carson) and Grace Lee Whitney (Neila) are held captive in background, then from left: Victor Buono (King Tut), Ford, Hicks, Paul and Kerns.

Third picture: Thanks to the Batcycle's Battering Ram, Batman was able to crash into King Tut's hideout and rescue Robin. Kerns socks Alfred Jones (Lord Chancellor stunt double) in this scene.

Right: Victor Paul (Robin stunt double) leaps into action to save Bruce Wayne (Adam West) from a fatal fall.

TV HISTORY WAS MADE, HORWITZ'S TEAM REALLY KNEW THEIR TRADE

"I didn't know it was going to work. Howie seemed to know and Dozier seemed to know, but I was more querulous. I didn't know until the second episode, and I just got into the swing of it. There was a rhythm to it. You have to remember we were breaking all the rules. But there was a [right] way of breaking all the rules."

Associate Producer William D'Angelo, interviewed in 1993 by Bob Garcia

 On November 15, 1965, Horwitz hired a colleague from Warner Bros., William D'Angelo, as his associate producer. "Howie Horwitz asked me to come join him. When I saw the pilot I was terrified, thinking that Howie had put us both out of the business," said D'Angelo in a 1993 interview with Bob Garcia. "I went home to my wife and said 'It's either going to be the greatest hit in the world or the greatest disaster.'"

Sam Strangis moved from assistant director on the pilot to *Batman*'s unit production manager. "We were the arms of Howie," said Strangis. "Bill was in casting and the look of the show, to make sure that nothing slipped by. I was in the money end of it, the production end, and the physical portion of it. Howie was the overseer, who would lay out what he wanted and we would extend it out, and it came out of us."

The production was behind schedule the day the pilot wrapped. When ABC moved the show (with such heavy post-production) to a mid-season replacement, it had effectively put a rush order on the entire first season. "It was something that had never been done in the history of television," said Strangis, "and it still hasn't been done since. The average half-hour show takes three days to prep. It takes three to four days to shoot it. And it takes ten days in post-production. That's the fastest you can do. That's seventeen days on each show.

"We began shooting in November," he continued. "We were on the air in January, twice a week. Now it is totally impossible for anyone to work during Christmas when the studio is down for two weeks. Then you have three weeks to put out two shows, [and afterward] two shows each week. We had three units going at one time. We were bicycling people back and forth. We were shooting until midnight to keep on the air. We were shooting shows and doing post-production as we shot film. We never missed a deadline. To this day, it's never been done [except by us]. That's what got [television production head] Bill Self mad, because he saw the cost. But it paid off. Fox made a fortune. They sold other shows because they had the

Previous spread, left page: Adam West sports a personalized example of a fashionable t-shirt which was quite popular at the time.

Previous spread, right page, top: This pre-production concept painting by Leslie Thomas visualized the secret hideout of Catwoman and the Joker as described in Stanley Ralph Ross's script. These paintings were used in meetings and helped set builders and designers when assembling props.

Previous spread, right page, bottom left: Eartha Kitt (Catwoman) and the Joker conspire to track down one million pounds of hidden gunpowder which they will use to break into the Federal Depository Building and loot the place.

Previous spread, right page, bottom right: Cesar Romero (Joker) was released early from prison but immediately linked up with Eartha Kitt (Catwoman) who had a hideout decorated and henchmen prepared.

Opposite: The second assistant cameraman hits the clapboard to synchronize the audio and video for the second take of this scene with Adam West from Ep#57.

number one show on the air."

Self clearly understood the problem. "It was a terribly rushed post-production problem," he said. "Because of the two episodes a week, and the late start, it meant a great deal of overtime, weekend work and everything else. Obviously, since I was the head of it, I was responsible for the production overages, the delivery schedule, the network relationship and all of that. I do remember we were under enormous pressure really in all those areas: in delivering the show on time, in keeping the cost down, and keeping the quality up. It was not an easy show."

Self was feeling a lot of heat from the 20th Century Fox board. "There was a lot of skepticism. The worst thing that could happen to me as the head of it was that the show would go off [the air] after one season or a half a season. That would mean all these extra bucks I was throwing in to keep the quality up would have gone down the drain."

"Every show came in fifty thousand dollars over, on the first pass, almost fifty percent of the total budget, and we had to pare it down," said Strangis. "It was a lot of money, because those guys would write big, and we never curtailed them. We said go out and write, and then it was

Bottom: Pre-production concept painting of the Kitty Car by Leslie Thomas. In this scene from Ep#110, Catwoman pulls up in her Kitty Car and "kidnaps" the Joker who has just been released early from prison due to good behavior. "Like sixty-four years ahead of time," remarked the Joker while in Warden Crichton's office, a line in the script that was cut from the final edit of this episode.

Opposite: Burt Ward, Adam West and Yvonne Craig: the Pied Pipers of Gotham City.

up to me to try and pare it down and still give them what they wanted. We had to find trick ways of doing it."

Getting everything ready was always a difficult and costly task. The schedule was such that at times they didn't get a shooting script until the Tuesday before the Monday they had to start shooting. "[Sometimes,] if while they were working on a script and there was something crazy, Lorenzo would call me and describe it,"

said Strangis. "I would go to the art director and tell him that it was coming up and to start putting something together. But that's about it. We never had enough time. I'd have three or four days to get gags ready and to get effects ready. It was a very impossible situation we worked through. Very few people knew really how tough it was. The creative people knew how impossible it was."

DESILU-CULVER MOVE REQUIRED, A NEW CREW TO BE HIRED

"All I want you to do is sprout your wings and fly. Go crazy."

Howie Horwitz to his newly hired art director Serge Krizman, from a 1993 interview with Bob Garcia

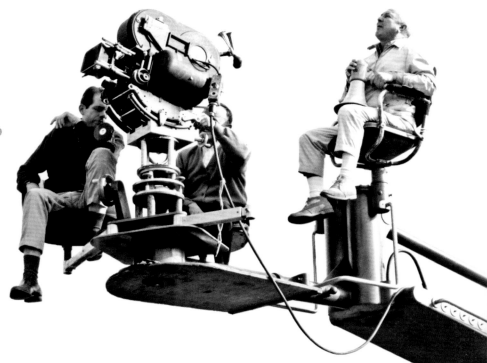

The first big expense took place before a foot of film had been shot. *Batman*'s production unit was moved from 20th Century Fox's lot down to the Desilu-Culver Studios because Fox had run out of room at their own studio. After the pilot, Ivan Martin's crew cut up the Batcave set, placed the pieces on sixty-foot low-bed trucks that were only two feet off the ground, and drove seven miles to the other lot. They reassembled it on Stage 16 for a total cost of $5,860. For an additional $32,260, a new Commissioner Gordon's office set was built on Stage 16 and a new Wayne Manor interior was constructed on Stage 15.

The new Batcave was much larger than the first. "[It] filled the whole sound stage," said Director of Photography Ralph Woolsey who shot the first ten episodes at Desilu-Culver. "And, of course, a director would call for action that needed more space than anyone thought would ever be called for. Once, we had to open the large sound stage doors, so we could get farther back and we had to tarp in the area to keep the daylight from getting in."

Villain's lairs and oversize interiors were shot on the lot's largest sound stage, Stages 3-4, which could be combined with Stage 2 to create an even more massive sound stage. Outside that building were Greenway's offices in what had been barracks during World War II. Howie Horwitz, William D'Angelo, Sam Strangis and eventually Charles Hoffman worked there. William Dozier also had a small office with enough room for a secretary. He hardly ever used it, doing most of his work up at 20th Century Fox.

The makeup chores for the series were given to Bruce Hutchinson. It was his first time as series lead. He and his assistants operated out of an L-shaped 12 x 12 room constructed in a corner of Stage 15, which was shared with hair stylist Kathryn Blondell. Since he needed to be on set every minute of those fifteen-sixteen hour shoots to do touch-ups, Hutchinson also had one dressing table with lights on each sound stage.

The makeup, hair and wardrobe departments shared a "honey wagon" which was used when the crew would go out on location. "We had a little room in what's

Above: Oscar Rudolph (Director, holding bullhorn) with Al Bettcher (camera operator) and Bill Bohny (assistant cameraman) filming Ep#70.

Opposite: Photo was taken Nov. 23, 1965, the second day of production for Ep#3–4. Burt Ward (Robin) and Adam West (Batman) rehearse exiting the Batmobile.

Opposite top: Alan Napier (Alfred assists from the Batcave while the Dynamic Duo are out on a mission.

called a honey wagon, which was a forty-foot semi-trailer of dressing rooms with a bathroom and couch," said Hutchinson in a 1993 interview with Bob Garcia. Only one of the makeup crew would work inside with the hairdresser and Hutchinson would work outside, where lights and a mirror were rigged on the side of the trailer. He set up a card table and worked on actors there. He liked it outside. "Daylight lighting is easier to work in than artificial lighting," he said. "You'd get a truer color.

You'd get a truer look."

"The scripts would hit our department first," said Hutchinson. "[Department head] Ben Nye would go to the production meetings and he knew up front what kind of character it was supposed to be... The production meetings were up at Twentieth Century Fox. If anything was unusual, he would get in touch with me, and tell me what would be going on. He would tell me, 'This is what's going on at our end. You come up here and we'll

Below: Adam West pauses between takes during the filming of *Presentation of Batgirl.*

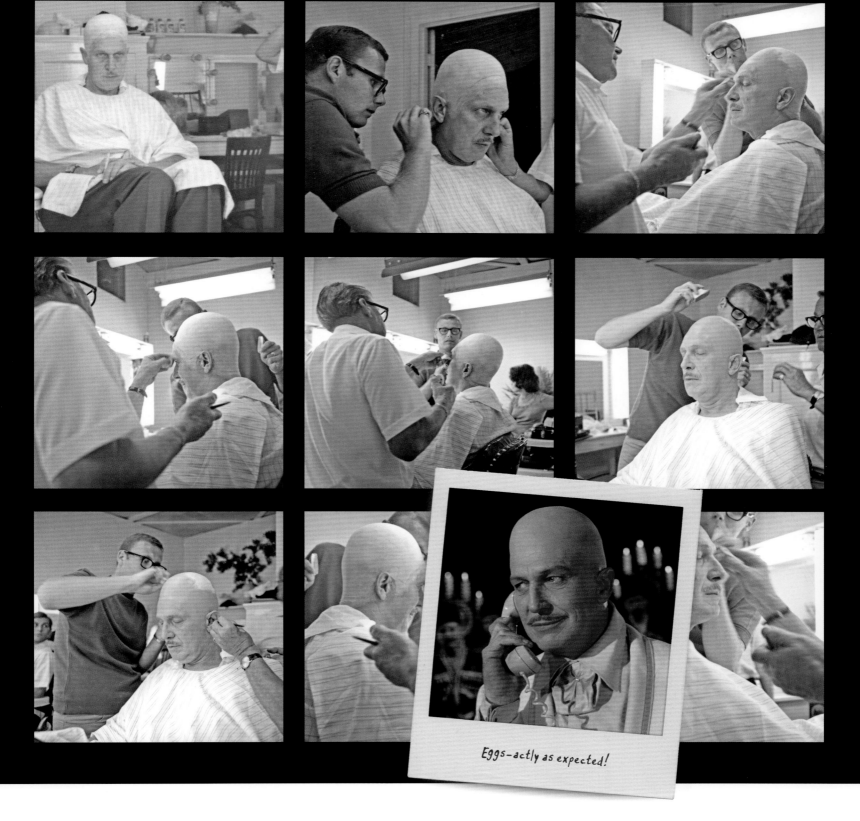

Eggs-actly as expected!

Above: Bruce Hutchinson (dark shirt) and an assistant makeup man build Egghead's dome, blending the oversize plastic bald cap to surrounding skin color.

get together and work it out.' Unless the character could be done without appliance work or anything, and then I would devise the character down at Culver."

Either way, the makeup department would then present the idea to the producers, and Dozier had final approval. "Most of the time we would hit it the first time," said Hutchinson. "Maybe we'd go back and redo minor things.

But we had a pretty good concept of what the character was supposed to be by the description in the scripts."

Hutchinson was at the studio at 5.30 a.m. Makeup and costume call for the actors was usually around 7.00 a.m., so he began each day applying Adam West's makeup in the star's personal dressing room. The mornings in West's dressing room became quite a ritual.

"Bruce was the makeup man with the most to do," West recalled. "He was a fine person and always good to be around. He became famous in his work and much of it owing to what he did with the colorful and bizarre *Batman* villains. Our dialogue coach, Milton Stark, also worked as my assistant. We became good friends. Milton was a sophisticated and kind man who saw the humor in most of the situations around us that grew tense. Milton, and the few who worked closest with me on a daily basis, would come into my dressing room first thing in the morning. They would put good jazz and music that swings on my player. Then they'd go to work and slap me together while Milton read the day's lines in my ear, lines that I'd fallen asleep memorizing the night before. It was quite a scene. Music, makeup, wardrobe and some impromptu solo dancing. But, it got us up to speed for the work ahead."

Art director Serge Krizman was brought over to *Batman* while he was working on *The Tammy Grimes Show* pilot. He was friends with Self, Dozier and FitzSimons and had over a dozen feature films and almost 250 TV episodes to his credit. "They showed me the pilot and Dozier showed me the original sketches by Bob Kane," Krizman said. "We had ample discussions on what the approach would be. Dozier had quite a bunch of comic books given to him by the publisher, to get the feel of it. It was, after all, Bob Kane's series. We had to evoke the memories of those who read it, once it got on the screen.

"I insisted on a uniform look for *Batman*, kind of like a corporate identity," he continued. Each villain was to have a singular color. "Color played an important part of the look of the show. We had conferences on costumes with designers Patricia Barto and Jan Kemp for a strong and definite coordination of colors. Even the effects and gadgets were color-coordinated. We were a tightly knit group from a visual standpoint."

Krizman's crew included an assistant, two to three draftsmen or set designers, and a sketch artist who would create art for the producer and director to get a handle on props. Illustrator Leslie Thomas did pre-production paintings of each set to show stage layout and color

Below: Pre-production concept painting by Leslie Thomas, used as a guide during meetings and for set builders when constructing the player piano roll perforating device in Ep#50.

design. Since props were constructed over at the 20th Century Fox lot, Krizman also had a coordinator, Tom Dries, who served in a supervisory capacity at the studio mill, paint shop and prop department.

A variety of directors were used in this first season not only because there was a need to shoot several episodes on top of each other, but also because there was a lack of available directors. Moving *Batman* up in the production schedule found many of 20th Century Fox's directors tied up with other ongoing series. So anyone available was called in to direct: Charles Rondeau, Norman Foster, Tom Gries, Larry Peerce, Richard Sarafian, Leslie H. Martinson, James Sheldon, William Graham, Murray Golden, James B. Clark and Don Weis.

Horwitz brought director of photography Ralph Woolsey from Warner Bros. to shoot the series. Woolsey found dutch-angling [a filming technique that produces a viewpoint akin to tilting one's head to the side] the camera was a problem for him and his camera crew. "It was more difficult then, because we were using double-headed BNCs, a standard sound studio camera, and it

was really very heavy," he said. "We obviously had a bigger job doing that than using [a] standard Arriflex camera [a common camera model name from the Arri Group]."

They also worried about keeping the lighting and sets bright enough, because *Batman* was going out to mostly black and white television sets. It was difficult to get more realistic colors and still have the black and white feed look light. The sets needed to be very bright. "We had much less sensitive film [than now]," Woolsey said. "We only had one film, an Eastman color negative. We occasionally had to push it or force-develop it [to] get more speed out of it. You had to counteract that then by [doing] other things."

"The Batcave caused the most problems at first, because it was dark," he continued. "The walls were essentially dark, and we had to put some life into them: some sparkle or glisten… Everything would merge into these horrible walls. Then, they had all this electronic gear with all these lights blinking on and off which we had to make brighter. If we didn't add in extra lighting or paint some walls with shiny black stuff and bang it with some pretty strong spots here and there, in black and

Right: Adam West stands next to Harry's pernicious perforator.

Below: Images from the series show details of the perforator.

white it would have been a gray blur."

During the ten episodes Woolsey shot, it was winter in Los Angeles and that meant rain. "We were rained out several times [when] we were supposed to go out, even when we were supposed to go out into the streets next to the stage," said Woolsey. "We didn't have too much lead time. They were working with their story changes. The optical effects were delayed now and then. And various types of props occasionally malfunctioned. So all of that left the policy makers pretty nervous. We would finish shooting at seven or eight at night and have to go over to another set, even another studio, and look over the set for the next day." After shooting ten episodes in seven weeks, Woolsey was replaced by Howard Schwartz and Jack Marta.

"Our camera personnel knew their stuff," said West. "Howard was one of the first to be filming an all-in-color TV series with its 'dutch angles' and other inventive and supportive camera tricks. He became well known in his field. Howard came in after another fine cinematographer, Ralph Woolsey [left]. He was a cheerful gentleman and wonderful with his work. I always enjoyed our collaboration in the difficult work on the sound stage. Ralph and Howard were our two most prominent cinematographers. Their contribution to classic TV was huge."

West and Ward received stunt training while shooting. "For the first year, they were being trained," said Strangis. "Whenever Hubie and Victor had time or weren't too tired, they would take the guys aside and teach them how to take shots or show them a few tricks." By the time the feature was shot, Kerns noted that West was able to do many of his own fight moves for the camera.

Opposite: Surrounded by cameramen, Adam West does close-ups for the cattle stampede scene in Ep#59. At right: Burt Ward with Cliff Robertson (Shame) behind him. Camera is covered to minimize potential noise picked up by microphone.

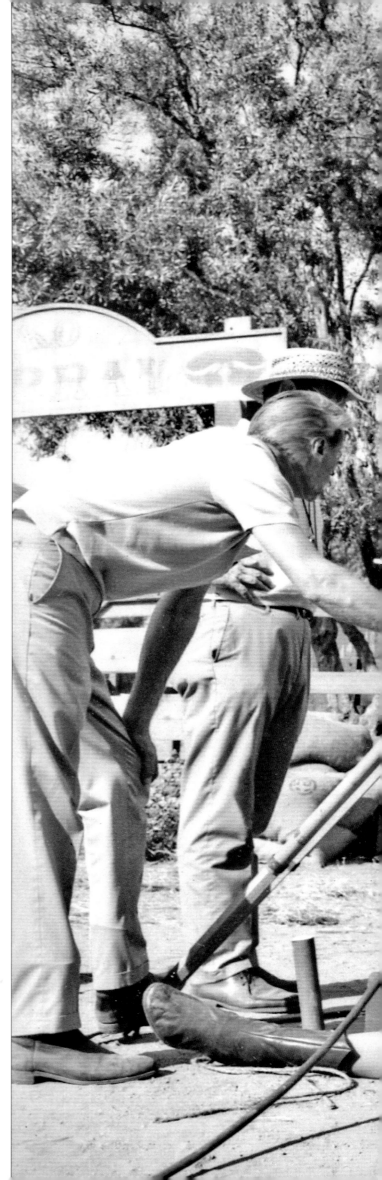

BATMAN'S HUGE DEBUT BRINGS MUCH HULLABALOO

"*Playhouse 90* was never like this."
William Dozier on getting famous movie stars for *Batman* villains in February 16, 1966 *Radio-Television Daily* interview

Below: Tallulah Bankhead as Black Widow.

Opposite: Vincent Price as Egghead.

"Movie stars do not do television," was the common axiom in 1966, but *Batman* proved to be the exception. "It was easy to get the special guest villains and special guest villainesses, which is what we called them," said Dozier. "Because they all recognized that it was a very different thing for them to do. It was a show that was very popular and they would have a big audience, and no actor can turn that down."

Batman's enormous popularity challenged the normal day-to-day work of producing the TV show. The network, Adam West's agent, even National Periodical Publications were trying to pry West and Ward away from shooting to do public appearances, radio and television interviews, and more. George Barris tried pulling the Batmobile off the lot for consumer shows. Studio executives and their friends, and friends of their friends, wanted to bring their kids to the set which eventually forced Greenway to limit these visits to Tuesdays and Thursdays.

Location shoots quickly became swamped with *Batman* fans. "I knew we were into something mystical

when we were at a location and Adam West was walking from his trailer to the set, and two old women were behind the yellow streamers line," said William D'Angelo. "One of them reached out and touched Adam's cape and then just stared at her hand. Then, she showed her hand to her friend. It was scary." The crowds appeared every time they went on location. Sam Strangis made deals with Warner Bros. Studio to use their lot to avoid crowds. But out of necessity the crew still occasionally had to go on location.

LITTLE FIRST SEASON SCENES FROM "FINKS" TO "FIENDS"

"We were fortunate in having a wonderful crew. I must tell you they were a great audience and that's a nice thing when you're playing for laughs."

Adam West, 2015 email interview with Bob Garcia

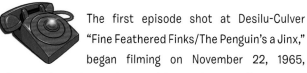 The first episode shot at Desilu-Culver "Fine Feathered Finks/The Penguin's a Jinx," began filming on November 22, 1965, long before the series would premiere on January 12, 1966. Krizman remembered that Fox's construction crew didn't believe how large an undertaking this series would prove to be. "One of the heads of construction happened to ask me what was my next crazy thing; well it happened to be the umbrella. So I said, 'We need a thirty-foot umbrella.' He said, 'Oh, yeah, sure.' I said, 'We do. Make it!' Eventually they just fell in and looked forward to the next crazy thing. It was more fun to do that than to make a breakaway door, which I did for years."

While Krizman was enjoying himself prepping the death traps and wild sets, Semple took a comment by Dozier to heart to "work in dames whenever possible," and changed the villain in his third script "The Inescapable Doom Trap" from comic-book villain Carnado to Zelda the Great. He told Dozier of the change in a letter Dozier

received November 15. Anne Baxter was announced in the role on November 26. Bruce Hutchinson remembered she was a garrulous special guest villainess that kept the crew in stitches.

On December 6, George Sanders signed on as Mr. Freeze for "Instant Freeze/Rats Like Cheese." Director of photography Woolsey had a great relationship with special-effects chief L. B. Abbott's work on these episodes. He was amazed at the ease and speed in which Abbott handled the assignment. "He would be on the set laying out these particular shots very carefully," he said. "One side of the screen would be on a diagonal and one side would be the freeze side. He would introduce a cold blue look on the freeze side, and double in the action on the proper side." Jan Kemp remembered the unique costume that was ditched in later versions of Mr. Freeze. The producers' haste to get the episode done and their desire to please Sanders caused a problem. "With George Sanders, everybody including George felt that he wanted to be inside a helmet," said Kemp, "And this would be

Opposite top left: Segments of giant umbrella handle are joined in preparation for filming Ep#3 in November 1965.

Opposite top middle: Construction crew assembles the Penguin's giant umbrella.

Opposite top right: Crewman checks lighting for scene with Burt Ward, Adam West and the Penguin's immense orange umbrella.

Opposite bottom: Several cranes were required to assemble and support the giant umbrella, shown here as it was prepared in the studio parking lot.

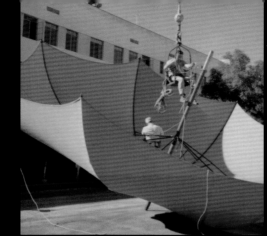

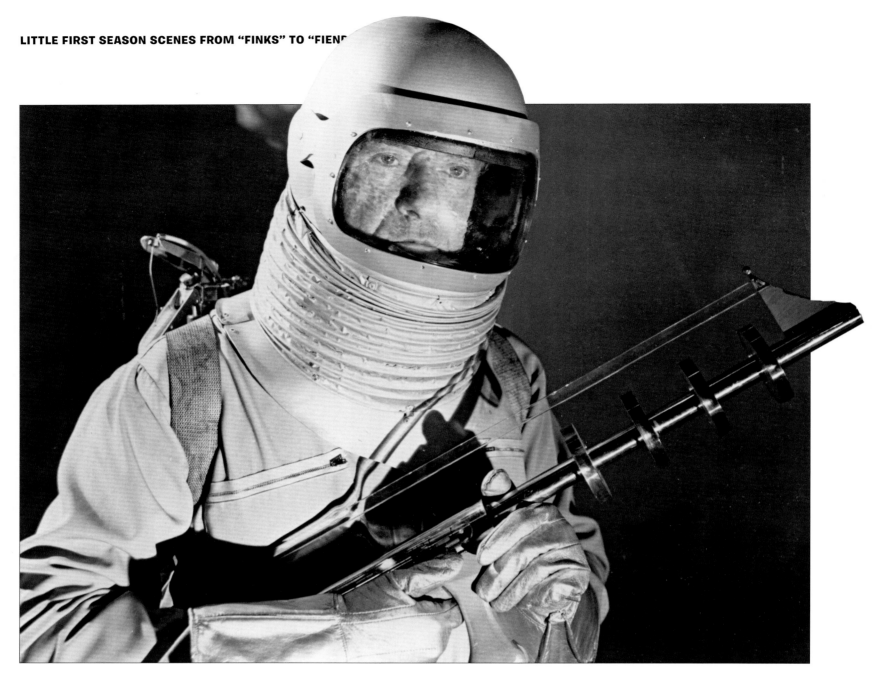

the way he kept himself in condition with the climate. The point I made to them at the time was that you were going to have difficulty with his speech. And as a matter of fact when we did the George Sanders episodes, we had to dub most of his dialogue at a later date... We did fit the helmet with miniature mics and stuff but the problem was that we'd still get a resonance on his voice which [didn't sound] quite [like] George Sanders... That was where the question of a lot of extra dubbing came in because of the voice quality. It was like putting a man inside a bucket; he's going to sound like he was speaking in an oil drum."

The next show in line to be filmed was "The Joker is Wild/Batman is Riled," written by William Dozier's son Robert Dozier who had been a TV writer since 1948, during the golden age of television.

On December 7, Nelson Riddle signed on as the series composer. Little did he know he'd be composing, arranging and conducting over the holidays. He was given "Finks" on December 23, 1965 and had to deliver it January 4, 1966.

The same day in January Adam West taped his appearance on *The Dating Game*. The next seven days, before the pilot aired on January 12, were taken up with re-editing and re-dubbing and testing the show.

On January 3, Frank Gorshin returned to film "A Riddle a Day Keeps the Riddler Away/When the Rat's Away the Mice Will Play." *Batman* aired January 12, and demands on Adam West's time increased exponentially.

The new director of photography, Howard Schwartz, was hired January 20 for Cesar Romero's return in 'The Joker Goes to School/He Meets his Match, The Grisly Ghoul.' Schwartz would be a stalwart of the production throughout his fifty-seven episodes. Makeup artist Hutchinson remembered Schwartz worked closely with him on this episode. Because of the film stock and intensity of the light required, the makeup used on Romero was not a standard white, but more gray (which photographed white). However, the lace of Romero's green wig was flesh-colored. Hutchinson tried to cover

Top: George Sanders as the first Mr. Freeze in Ep#7–8.

Top left: Malachi Throne (False Face) in the bank vault from Ep#18.

Bottom left: Myrna Fahey (Blaze) watches as Malachi Throne (False Face) adheres Adam West to subway tracks with quick-setting plastic cement…and the Express train is due inside of five minutes.

Right: Cesar Romero (the Joker) contemplates another pitch during the 3 o'clock prison yard softball game in Ep#5.

the lace with talcum powder and even makeup, but it didn't work. Eventually, Schwartz worked out a scrim solution that would diffuse the light so the lace would disappear. "He helped me a great deal," said Hutchinson. "He'd been around a number of years and he and his lighting man Bill Neff were very good to us."

On January 27 the Screen Actors Guild informed Dozier that he needed to get an SAG membership to continue being the announcer for *Batman*. The famous *LIFE* magazine cover shoot took place at Desilu-Culver on January 27. Adam West wrote that he hurt his back doing eighteen takes of jumping into mattresses to get that flying Batman look.

On January 31, Dozier wrote a cogent note to Horwitz, Semple, D'Angelo and FitzSimons about the cliffhanger in the Joker episode shot the week before. "The cliffhanger in last week's JOKER was noticeably weak… we must be certain always to have a recognizable *physical* jeopardy at the end of episode one, and almost always involving either Batman or Robin, or both. I think it is usually better if only one of them is in danger, because that leaves the other with the audience, scheming and fighting for his partner's release. If they are both in danger, it leaves no one, really, with whom the audience can identify as a fellow rescuer, struggling until 'tomorrow night' to effect a rescue of his (and the audience's) beloved partner."

This was also the day Dozier began his effort to make a *Batman* feature, having a talk with Edgar Scherick and two letters to Richard Zanuck. This undertaking took up most of his attention during the rest of the first season.

In a flash of synchronicity, this was also the day C. E. Parson, manager of public relations at Glastron Boat Company, followed up a conversation with Robert Lee at Fox, offering a Batboat to Greenway Productions. It was quite a nice turn of events, assuring the Batboat would be featured prominently in the feature film.

Charles Hoffman wrote "The Thirteenth Hat/Batman Stands Pat" a loose adaptation of "The New Crimes of the Mad Hatter" *Batman* #161 and which also incorporated

elements from a Hatter story in *Detective Comics* 230. David Wayne definitely got into the spirit of things as the Hatter, picking his bright red hair and mustache as well as the deep-black eyebrows, which gave him such a distinctive look. Stuntman Kerns remembered he and Victor Paul walked the set, trying to figure out how to stage the fight around the large death-dealing machine and the long jury box. It was basically a long corridor with lots of unbreakable obstacles. For the life of them,

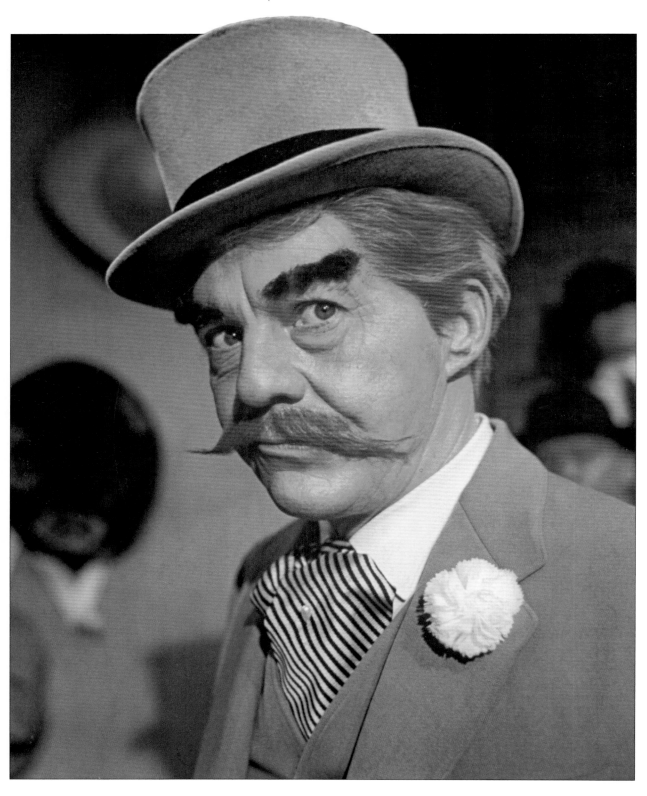

Left: David Wayne as Jervis Tetch, the Mad Hatter.

Not till I get your cowl, Batman!

they could not come up with a single good idea. Just before they were to meet director Norman Foster, Paul had a brainstorm. He started to rattle off exactly what he wanted to do, but was so excited and talked so quickly, Kerns couldn't follow him. When Foster walked in, Kerns turned to Paul with a big smile, and said, "Okay, Victor, explain to the man what we came up with."

Filming finished in early February for "The Purr-Fect Crime/Better Luck Next Time" which was one of Stanley Ralph Ross' first stints at scriptwriting. Teamed with veteran writer Lee Orgel, Ross was told to write a straight plot done deadly seriously. He did and the script

was so successful, that Ross eventually became the series' most frequently used writer. It was Julie Newmar's first appearance as Catwoman. In a 1993 interview with Bob Garcia she remembered there wasn't much prep time. "Put on your wings," she said. "Zip up your costume. Try the best to do your makeup, and you're right on stage. We did have the script [to study] for one day [before shooting], but most of that [day] was consumed in costume fittings and stuff." The shooting schedule matched the prep time. "Because of the cost, because of the schedule, because of the implicit needs and pleadings of the producer, we would

even shoot the rehearsals," Newmar said. "And I am famous for being able to shoot rehearsals. Because it saves [the producers] money, and you want to please the producers." Producer Horwitz and his wife Harriett became great friends with Newmar. Her visits delighted their three daughters, who adored the star.

In "The Penguin Goes Straight/Not Yet, He Ain't" the Penguin and his goons stole the Batmobile. Batman and Robin followed in the Batcycle (the one and only appearance of the Harley-Davidson Batcycle), and remotely launched the henchmen into the air via the Batmobile's ejection seat.

Above: Howard Schwartz (Director of Photography) lines up a shot with Burt Ward and Adam West. Bill Bohny (Assistant Cameraman) is at left of camera for this setup from Ep#19.

Opposite, top left: Kathy Blondell (Hair Stylist), Julie Newmar (Catwoman), Pat Barto (Costume Designer) and Howard Schwartz (Director of Photography).

Top middle: Burt Ward and Adam West on platform; Bill Bohny (Assistant Cameraman, left of camera), Al Bettcher (Camera Operator) and Howard Schwartz (Director of Photography, on floor, looking left).

Top right: Burt Ward, James Sheldon (Director), Adam West and, two special effects men.

Stuntman Hubie Kerns remembered the ejection sequence test firing as quite harrowing. When the launch button was hit, the dummies were apparently blown over 100 feet in the air. The blast was so large, anyone in the Batmobile would have been killed. The car survived intact. So the next day, when they shot the scene, Paul, Kerns and Strangis sat off camera with fingers crossed that the actual ejection wouldn't hurt

Meredith's stunt double Albert Cavens. Fortunately, it didn't. Finished in late March, though scheduled to be finished much earlier in the season, "The Bookworm Turns/While Gotham City Burns" was delayed because of a schedule conflict for Roddy McDowall. This production-heavy episode included the first Batclimb to feature a guest star, Jerry Lewis. Krizman loved the huge book death trap

Make her Purrrrfect!

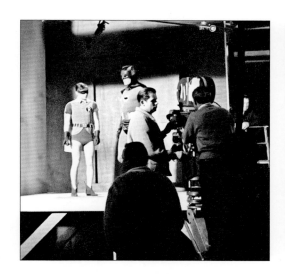

he designed for these episodes. "That was shot at Warner Bros. at New York Square," he said. "I had to build this thirty-foot-high, twelve-foot-wide and three-feet-thick book and it had to open in half, like a real book. [Batman and Robin] had to walk inside, and it would be a trap. The book closed on them. The special-effects department did excellent work on that. When you have two parts of a thirty-foot book open and close and not see guide wires on it, it was engineered quite well." The script also called for Robin to be hung upside down on a bell clapper in a belfry, not a favorite scene of stuntman Victor Paul. The scriptwriter probably thought they would find an existing set from Fox's storage. Unfortunately that wasn't the case. "The belfry well was forty feet high and had to be built from scratch. I couldn't find a bronze bell that was eight feet high," said Krizman. "So it had to be made all out of plastics."

On March 28 Semple's final draft of the *Batman* feature arrived at Greenway. Krizman began designing the sets and equipment needed for the feature film. He turned over the TV series to art director Jack Collis who covered six of the season's final eight episodes. Collis had been A.D. on Greenway's western series, *The Loner*.

Bruce Hutchinson remembered a problem during Victor

Below: Bookworm and his female accomplice, Lydia Limpet, survey the scene of his big book caper.

Above: Pre-production concept painting by Leslie Thomas, used as a guide during meetings and for set builders in devising Bookworm's headquarters.
Bottom left and right: Roddy McDowall as the leather-bound Bookworm.

Above: From left: Bruce Hutchinson (makeup), Jan Kemp (wardrobe) and Victor Buono (King Tut).

Opposite page top: Pre-production concept painting by Leslie Thomas, depicting Robin's deathtrap at the Wayne Memorial Clock Tower.

Opposite page bottom: Having readied the boy Wonder to have his bell rung, Bookworm and his criminal crew prepare to depart the clock tower.

Buono's makeup test for "The Curse of Tut/The Pharaoh's in a Rut": "The first time we made him up they wanted this exotic Egyptian-looking makeup on him," said Hutchinson.

"Well, we did the makeup. Everyone looked in the mirror and fell on the floor. He looked like some old opera diva. [Buono] said laughing, 'I [can't] go out of this trailer looking like this.' So we just washed his face and put this little chin piece on and the costuming, and he sold it."

William D'Angelo noted that during the final episodes of the first season, location shooting was almost impossible.

"I remember we went to Rancho Park to shoot," said D'Angelo, "and we just couldn't work. The crowds were just too big. Three to four thousand people showed up. We couldn't find a way to shoot. We were surrounded and they were in every shot. We begged, cajoled, and the studio police and the regular police ordered them away but they wouldn't listen. Everyone had to see Batman and Robin."

The four Riddler episodes late in this season, "The Ring of Wax/Give 'Em The Axe" and "Death in Slow Motion/The

Riddler's False Notion," brought Gorshin back to the fold. "The Joker Trumps an Ace/Batman Sets the Pace" did the same for Romero.

Very little information surrounds these episodes, as Greenway continued to gear up for the feature. Semple delivered the final draft of the script for the feature April 5, signed a contract to write eight half-hour episodes for the second season on April 7, and completed his work on

the feature script April 15. As production wound down on the season, and it was apparent that Lorenzo Semple Jr. wouldn't be coming back as executive script consultant, Charles Hoffman was hired on April 11 as full-time script editor and head writer for the second season.

The season wrapped photography for "Fine Finny Fiends/Batman Makes the Scenes" on April 15. William Dozier made his first cameo in the series. This time,

Left and right: William Dozier (left) and Howie Horwitz (right) were pictured among other criminals when Batman used the "Memory Batbank" on Alfred, who had been brainwashed by Penguin.

Below: (from left) Alfred (Alan Napier), Robin (Burt Ward) and Batman (Adam West), look at the Penguin on the "Memory Batbank."

Right: The Fox lot at mid-morning on October 20, 1965, the first day of principal photography. Scenes 165 and 166 were the first to be filmed. Crewmen at left are helping to operate the Mobile Crime Computer in the vehicle's trunk. Sam Levitt (Director of Photography; with hat) is at the camera, Neil Hamilton (Commissioner Gordon) next to camera, Adam West (Batman), and at far right, Sam Strangis (Assistant Director).

he and producer Horwitz were two of the criminals in the photos Batman showed Alfred.

A true family atmosphere pervaded Bill Dozier's production. Sam Strangis, unit production manager, remembered that when his wife died of leukemia in the first season of the show, his friends on *Batman*'s cast and crew helped keep his life together. "She was only thirty-five years old and I was thirty-six," said Strangis. "Under normal conditions, I don't think a normal human being would have continued on the way I did with three kids at home. But the show itself grew on you. It was part of your life. I think that if I didn't have the show, I probably would have flipped out. It was fun. It was hard work. It was family... We were all very, very close. The whole group of us. The crew, the cast, the guest stars. Everybody was close."

BURT WARD AS ROBIN WAS IDEAL, HE PLAYED THE ROLE WITH ZEAL

"He was just perfect. He was a very eager kid, worked hard. It was a delight to see him sort of come alive."

Executive Producer William Dozier, interview conducted by Kevin Burns

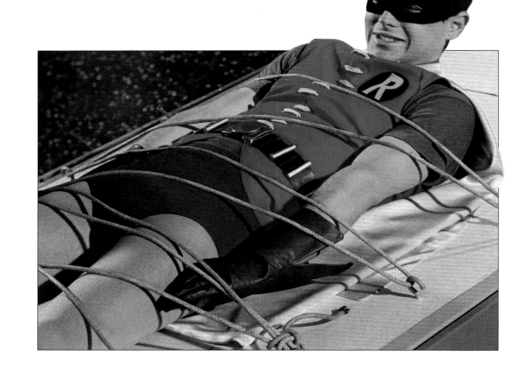

Burt Ward began his stint as Robin as an untrained actor, with no experience at all on the set of a television show. He didn't know the "right" way to perform for television, and just let his instincts take him through each episode. For example in "Hi Diddle Riddle," the Batmobile pulls up to the back of the Peale Art Gallery. Adam West exited through the car door, but Ward stood up and walked across the top of the car. Director Robert Butler remembered that the casual stroll was all Ward's doing. "He got up in the seat and jumped up over the back of the car," Butler said. "I didn't [tell him to] do that. It was him. It doesn't make any sense. Why go the long way? Because he was just so into his character."

Ward enjoyed the physicality of being a Super Hero. He pushed to do as many stunts as he could (though stuman Victor Paul did anything truly dangerous). Ward had experience in throws and falls since he had a brown belt in karate. He was full of energy and it showed as he seemingly leapt into every scene he had. Butler remembered the

first time West and Ward had to jump onto the Batpoles in Bruce Wayne's study. "They were so behind it," Butler chuckled.

Ward learned the discipline to train when he was ice-skating professionally as a boy. That discipline served Ward well during one of his scenes in "Hi Diddle Riddle." The Riddler was attempting to steal the Batmobile and knocked out Robin with a drugged dart. Placing the unconscious Boy Wonder in the passenger seat, the Riddler attempted to drive away, but the Batmobile's anti-theft device kicked in. The special effects crew shot fireworks out of the three rocket tubes in back of the vehicle, a few feet behind Ward. Stray sparks came drifting down and burnt holes in his costume and also landed on the actor himself. But under strict instructions from Butler, Ward didn't cry out or move until he heard "Cut!"

At conventions, Ward has often recounted occasions when he was injured on set, remarking that at times he wasn't sure he would survive the series. One of his injuries can be seen in the Mr. Freeze episode "Deep Freeze." During a scene in Mr. Freeze's hideout, where the Dynamic Duo blast open a jail cell door to escape, Ward was injured when residue from the explosion launched from the cell door and straight at him. He was burned around the right elbow and forearm as well as on the side of his face. He was sent to First Aid and then to the hospital. Being the disciplined trooper he was, he never missed a day of that shoot, even filming subsequent scenes with a bandaged right arm.

According to Yvonne Craig, this was typical of the actor during her association with him in the third season. "I was very impressed with Burt," she remembered. "I've said this often: Burt Ward always knew his lines, was always on time on the set and never got into anything with anybody. And [more importantly] this was his first job! He was doing a very difficult job because you're looking at somebody who is obviously not fifteen, playing a fifteen-year-old. And from experience [I know how tough it was], I played sixteen-year-olds until I was well into my thirties. It was a difficult job he had to do and I thought he did it very well. I was amazed at his professionalism."

Ward learned a lot during his years working on the show. He became the perfect Robin: overly enthusiastic, physically capable, willing and able to deliver the most outlandish lines with great sincerity and conviction. Holy perfect casting!

Far right, top left: In Ep#106, Adam West rescues Burt Ward from certain doom in the Winch-Room.

Far right, top right: Burt meets *Batman* fan and fellow actor Bill Mumy - *Lost in Space*'s Will Robinson.

Far right, bottom left: Burt in his dressing room.

Far right, bottom right: Glenn Wilder (Henchman #2) rehearses fight details with Burt.

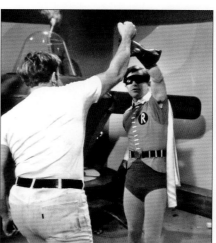

HOLY IS ROBIN'S GO-TO PHRASE, HE SAYS IT IN SO MANY WAYS

"Holy Contributing
to the Delinquency
of Minors."
Robin (Ep#105)

The September 2, 1965 Shooting Script Review by ABC's Department Of Standards & Practices commented on sixteen different aspects of the Pilot's First Draft. Among them: on page 7 and throughout, "the repetitive use of 'holy' becomes offensive." It was not specifically stated to delete them or even how to address the matter although one would infer that there were too many if they were considered repetitive. Fortunately, the phrases were not eliminated at this point and they would become one of the more fascinating aspects of the series.

More than 400 "Holy...!" exclamations were delivered throughout the 120 episodes, 1966 movie and *Presentation of Batgirl* film. Nearly all were explosively delivered by Robin, although a few came from Dick Grayson. Several other characters uttered the phrase including a police officer and even Alfred, while Batman came up with two himself. Some came from narrator Desmond Doomsday during episode introductions or cliffhangers. There were occasional repeats and therefore some phrases have multiple episode references.

Holy Agility! (Ep#95)

Holy Almost! (movie)

Holy Alphabet! (Ep#15)

Holy Alps! (Ep#38)

Holy Alter Ego! (Ep#67)

Holy Anagrams! (Ep#103)

Holy Apparition! (*Presentation of Batgirl*)

Holy Armadillos! (Ep#78)

Holy Armor Plate! (Ep#17)

Holy Ashtray! (Ep#1)

Holy Asp! (Ep#27)

Holy Astringent Plum-like Fruit! (Ep#120)

Holy Astronomy! (Ep#71)

Holy Audubon! (Ep#66)

Holy Backfire! (Ep#10)

Holy Backfire's Right! (Ep#10 by narrator)

Holy Ball and Chain! (Ep#15)

Holy Bank Balance! (Ep#51)

Holy Bankruptcy! (Ep#82)

Holy Banks! (Ep#48)

Holy Bargain Basements, Batman! (Ep#113)

Holy Barracuda! (Ep#1 by Dick Grayson)

Holy "Bat-Graves"! (Ep#51 by narrator)

Holy "Bat-Logic"! (Ep#60)

Holy "Bat-Trap"! (Ep#21, Ep74 by narrator)

Holy Benedict Arnold! (Ep#16)

Holy Bijou! (Ep#83)

Holy Bikini! (movie)

Holy Bill Of Rights! (Ep#47)

Holy Birthday Cake! (Ep#10)

Holy Blackbeard! (Ep#36)

Holy Blackout! (Ep#96)

Holy Blank Cartridge! (Ep#61)

Holy Blizzard! (Ep#7)

Holy Bluebeard! (Ep#50)

Holy Bombshell! (Ep#22 by narrator)

Holy Bouncing Boiler Plate! (Ep#17)

Holy Bowler! (Ep#14)

Holy Bullseye! (Ep#29)

Holy Bullseye, Batman! (Ep#77)

Holy Bunions! (Ep#37)

Holy Caboose! (Screen Test)

Holy Caffeine! (Ep#83)

Holy Camouflage! (Ep#26, 43)

Holy Captain Nemo! (movie)

Holy Carats! (Ep#115)

Holy Caruso! (Ep#50)

Holy Catastrophe! (Ep#119)

Holy Catastrophes, Batman! (Ep#77)

Holy Cats! A Cat! (Ep#19)

Holy Chicken Coop! (Ep#54)

Holy Chilblains! (Ep#94)

Holy Chocolate Eclair! (Ep#62)

Holy Chutzpah! (Ep#81)

Holy Cinderella! (Ep#29)

Holy Cinemascope! (Ep#76)

Holy Cliche! (Ep#37)

Holy Cliffhanger! (Ep#27 by narrator)

Holy Cliffhangers, Batman! (Ep#77)

Holy Clockwork! (Ep#33)

Holy Clockworks! (Ep#81)

Holy Coffin Nails! (Ep#52)

Holy Cold Creeps! (Ep#109)

Holy Complications! (Ep#95)

Holy Complications indeed, Robin! (Ep#95 by Batman)

Holy Conflagration! (Ep#12)

Holy Contributing to the Delinquency of Minors! (Ep#105)

Holy Corpuscles! (Ep#41)

Holy Cosmos! (Ep#40)

Holy Costume Party! (movie)

Holy Cow! (Ep#15 by First Girl Cheerleader)

Holy Cow Juice! (Ep#16 by narrator)

Holy Crack Up! (Ep#66)

Holy Crossfire! (Ep#10)

Holy Crucial Moment! (Ep#108)

Holy Crying Towels! (Ep#102)

Holy Cryptology! (Ep#79)

Holy Crystal Ball! (Ep#83)

Holy d'Artagnan! (Ep#37)

Holy Davy Jones! (Ep#62)

Holy Dead End! (Ep#81)

Holy Demolition! (movie)

Holy Deposit Slip! (Ep#65)

Holy Detonation! (Ep#104)

Holy Detonator! (Ep#29)

Holy Deviltry! (Ep#36)

Holy Dilemma! (Ep#108)

Holy Disappearing Act! (Ep#119)

Holy Disaster Area! (Ep#51)

Holy Distortion! (Ep#54)

Holy Diversionary Tactics! (Ep#75, 99)

Holy Edison! (Ep#44)

Holy Egg Shells! (Ep#102)

Holy Encore! (Ep#26 by Dick Grayson)

Holy Entanglement! (Ep#12 and Ep#18 by narrator)

Holy Epigrams! (Ep#54)

Holy Escape Hatch! (Ep#94)

Holy Explosion! (Ep#29)

Holy False Front! (Ep#28)

Holy Fate Worse Than Death! (Ep#57)

Holy Felony! (Ep#20)

Holy Finishing Touches! (Ep#112)

Holy Fireworks! (Ep#40, 69)

Holy Firing Squad! (Ep#61)

Holy Fishbowl! (Ep#10)

Holy Flight Plan! (Ep#65)

Holy Flip-flop! (Ep#62)

Holy Floodgate! (Ep#56)

Holy Floor Covering! (Ep#93)

Holy Flypaper! (Ep#4)

Holy Flypaper, Batman! (Ep#85)

Holy Fly Trap! (Ep#39)

Holy Fog! (Ep#33)

Holy Forecast! (Ep#43)

Holy Fork in the Road! (Ep#79)

Holy Fourth Amendment! (Ep#97)

Holy Fourth of July! (Ep#6)

Holy Frankenstein! (Ep#41, 82)

Holy Fratricide! (Ep#49)

Holy Frogman! (Ep#14)

Holy Fruit Salad! (Ep#15)

Holy Fugitive! (Ep#50)

Holy Funny Bone! (Ep#81)

Holy Gall! (Ep#115)

Holy Gambles! (Ep#73)

Holy Gemini! (Ep#100)

Holy Geography! (Ep#20)

Holy Geography indeed, Robin! (Ep#20 by Batman)

Holy Ghost Writer! (Ep#66)

Holy Giveaways! (Ep#51, 119)

Holy Glue Pot! (movie)

Holy Golden Gate! (Ep#26)

Holy Graf Zeppelin! (Ep#65)

Holy Grammar! (Ep#6)

Holy Graveyard, Batman! (Ep#10)

Holy Greed! (Ep#50)

Holy Greetings Cards! (Ep#43)

Holy Guacamole! (Ep#60)

Holy Guadalcanal! (Ep#62)

Holy Gullibility! (Ep#106)

Holy Gunpowder! (Ep#43)

Holy Haberdashery! (Ep#3)

Holy Hailstorm! (Ep#16)

Holy Hairdo! (Ep#43)

Holy Hallelujah! (Ep#10)

Holy Halloween! (movie)

Holy Hallucination! (movie)

Holy Hamburger! (Ep#91)

Holy Hamlet! (Ep#65)

Holy Hamstrings! (Ep#113)

Holy Handiwork! (Ep#69)

Holy Happenstance! (Ep#13)

Holy Hardest Metal in the World! (Ep#117)

Holy Harem, Batman! (Ep#57)

Holy Haziness! (Ep#105)

Holy Headache! (Ep#29, 31)

Holy Headlines! (Ep#6)

Holy Heartbreak! (movie, Ep#50)

Holy Heart Failure! (movie, Ep#100)

Holy Heidelberg! (Ep#63)

Holy Helmets! (Ep#13)

Holy Helplessness! (Ep#119)

Holy Here We Go Again, Batman! (Ep#109)

Holy Hieroglyphics! (Ep#27, 41, 96)

Holy Hi-Fi! (Ep#28)

Holy High-wire! (Ep#42)

Holy Hijack! (Ep#53)

Holy Hijackers! (Ep#46 as Dick Grayson)

Holy History! (Ep#77)

Holy Hoaxes! (Ep#91)

Holy Hole in a Donut! (Ep#9)

Holy Hollywood! (Ep#83)

Holy Holocaust! (Ep#73)

Holy Homecoming! (Ep#108)

Holy Homework! (Ep#107)

Holy Homicide! (Ep#29)

Holy Hoodwink! (Ep#70)

Holy Hoofbeats! (Ep#101, 115)

Holy Hors d'Oeuvre, Chief O'Hara! (Ep#58)

Holy Horseshoes! (movie, Ep#46)

Holy Hostage! (Ep#35, 91)

Holy Hot Foot! (Ep#22)

Holy Hot Spot, Batman! (Ep#39)

Holy Houdini! (Ep#17, 35, 57, 80)

Holy Human Collectors' Item! (Ep#85)

Holy Human Flies! (Ep#29 by Jerry Lewis)

Holy Human Pearls! (Ep#73)

Holy Human Pressure Cookers! (Ep#120)

Holy Human Surfboards! (Ep#104)

Holy Hunting Horn! (Ep#81)

Holy Hurricane! (Ep#27)

Holy Hydraulics! (Ep#56)

Holy Hypnotism! (Ep#57)

Holy Hypodermics! (Ep#114)

Holy Hypotheses! (Ep#84)

Holy Hypothesis! (Ep#48 by narrator)

Holy Iceberg! (Ep#7)

Holy Ice Picks! (Ep#19)

Holy Ice Skates! (Ep#93)

Holy Impossibility! (Ep#49)

Holy Impregnability! (Ep#26)

Holy Incantation! (Ep#107)

Holy Inquisition! (Ep#35)

Holy Interplanetary Yardstick! (Ep#118)

Holy Interruptions! (Ep#8)

Holy Iodine! (Ep#23)

Holy I T and T! (Ep#47)

Holy Jack In The Box! (Ep#5, 25)

Holy Jackpots! (Ep#21)

Holy Jailbreak! (Ep#44)

Holy Jawbreaker! (Ep#41)

Holy Jelly Molds! (Ep#73)

Holy Jet Set! (Ep#87)

Holy Jigsaw Puzzles! (Ep#59)

Holy Jitterbugs! (Ep#34)

Holy Journey to the Center of the Earth! (Ep#117)

Holy Jumble! (movie)

Holy Keyhole! (Ep#55)

Holy Key Ring! (Ep#55)

Holy Kilowatts! (Ep#40)

Holy Kindergarten! (Ep#31)

Holy Knit One, Purl Two! (Ep#113)

Holy Knockout Drops! (Ep#21)

Holy Known-Unknown Flying Objects! (twice in Ep#118)

Holy Koufax! (Ep#5 by Dick Grayson)

Holy Las Vegas! (Ep#15)

Holy Leopard! (Ep#21)

Holy Levitation! (Ep#62, 107)

Holy Liftoff! (Ep#46)

Holy Living End! (Ep#86)

Holy Lodestone! (Ep#4)

Holy Long John Silver! (movie)

Holy Looking Glass! (Ep#25)

Holy Lovebirds! (Ep#37)

Holy Luther Burbank! (Ep#101)

Holy Madness, Batman! (Ep#82)

Holy Magician! (Ep#15 by Dick Grayson)

Holy Magic Lantern! (Ep#29)

Holy Mainsprings! (Ep#45)

Holy Marathon! (movie)

Holy Mashed Potatoes! (Ep#72)

Holy Masquerade! (Ep#27, 45)

Holy Matador! (Ep#60)

Holy Mechanical Armies! (Ep#113)

Holy Memory Bank! (E#p70)

Holy Merlin the Magician! (movie)

Holy Mermaid! (Ep#70)

Holy Merry-Go-Round! (Ep#46)

Holy Mesmerism! (Ep#89)

Holy Metronome! (Ep#50)

Holy Midnight! (Ep#29 by narrator)

Holy Miracles, Batman! (Ep#66)

Holy Miscast! (Ep#76)

Holy Missing Relatives! (Ep#96)

Holy Molars! (Ep#32)

Holy Mole Hill! (Ep#26)

Holy Movie Moguls! (Ep#76)

Holy Mucilage! (Ep#23, 98)

Holy Multitudes! (Ep#70)

Holy Murder! (Ep#16)

Holy Mush! (Ep#22, 64)

Holy Naiveté! (Ep#70)

Holy Nerve Center! (Ep#89)

Holy New Year's Eve! (Ep#16)

Holy Nick of Time! (Ep#21)

Holy Nick of Time, Batman! (Ep#74)

Holy Nightmare! (Ep#22, movie)

Holy Non Sequiturs! (Ep#98)

Holy Oleo! (Ep#37)

Holy Olfactory! (Ep#89)

Holy One Track Batcomputer Mind! (Ep#97)

Holy Oversight! (Ep#85)

Holy Oxygen! (Ep#34)

Holy Paderewski! (Ep#50)

Holy Paraffin, Batman! (Ep#24)

Holy Perfect Pitch! (Ep#50)

Holy Piano Roll! (Ep#49)

Holy Pincushions! (Ep#104)

Holy Polar Front! (Ep#53)

Holy Polar Ice Sheet! (Ep#94)

Holy Polaris! (movie)

Holy Popcorn! (Ep#4)

Holy Potluck! (Ep#52)

Holy Precision! (Ep#81)

Holy Pressure Cooker! (Ep#30)

Holy Priceless Collection of Etruscan Snoods! (Ep#108)

Holy Pseudonym! (Ep#55)

Holy Purple Cannibals! (Ep#101)

Holy Puzzlers, Batman! (Ep#33)

Holy Rainbow! (Ep#9, 39)

Holy Rats in a Trap! (Ep#18)

Holy Rat Trap! (Ep#68)

Holy Ravioli! (Ep#5)

Holy Razor's Edge! (Ep#117)

Holy Recompense! (Ep#48)

Holy Red Herring! (Ep#5)

Holy Red Snapper! (Ep#2 by narrator)

Holy Red Snapper, Batman! (Ep#72)

Holy Reincarnation! (Ep#29)

Holy Relief! (Ep#49)

Holy Remote Control Robot! (Ep#82)

Holy Reshevsky! (Ep#19 by Dick Grayson)

Holy Resourcefulness! (Ep#64)

Holy Return From Oblivion! (Ep#111)

Holy Reverse Polarity! (Ep#90)

Holy Rheostat! (Ep#44)

Holy Ricochet! (Ep#13)

Holy Rip Van Winkle! (Ep#63, 114)

Holy Rising Hemlines! (Ep#106)

Holy Roadblocks! (Ep#105)

Holy Robert Louis Stevenson! (Ep#108)

Holy Rock Garden! (Ep#118)

Holy Rocking Chair! (Ep#43)

Holy Romeo and Juliet! (Ep#22)

Holy Rudder! (Ep#34)

Holy Safari! (Ep#6)

Holy Sahara! (Ep#46 by narrator)

Holy Sarcophagus! (Ep#41)

Holy Sardine! (movie)

Holy Schizophrenia! (Ep#7)

Holy Sedatives! (Ep#68)

Holy Self-service! (Ep#69)

Holy Semantics! (Ep#47)

Holy Serpentine! (Ep#6)

Holy Sewer Pipe! (Ep#11)

Holy Shamrocks! (Ep#53)

Holy Sherlock Holmes! (Ep#8)

Holy Showcase! (Ep#2)

Holy Show-Ups! (Ep#105)

Holy Shrinkage! (Ep#25)

Holy Shucks! (Ep#75)

Holy Skull Tap! (Ep#120)

Holy Sky Rocket! (Ep#28)

Holy Slipped Disc! (Ep#113)

Holy Smoke! (Ep#2, 24, 28, 32)

Holy Smoke! (Ep#16 by police officer)

Holy Smokes! (Ep#16)

Holy Smokestack! (Ep#25)

Holy Snowball! (Ep#7)

Holy Soapsuds! (Ep#52 by narrator)

Holy Sombrero! (Ep#14 by narrator)

Holy Sonic Booms, Batman! (Ep#72)

Holy Special Delivery! (Ep#110)

Holy Spider Webs! (Ep#25)

Holy Split Seconds! (Ep#85)

Holy Squirrel Cage! (Ep#46)

Holy Stalactites, Batman! (Ep#58)

Holy Stampede! (Ep#59)

Holy Standstills! (Ep#97)

Holy Steam Valve! (Ep#88 by Alfred)

Holy Stereo! (Ep#79)

Holy Stew Pot! (Ep#30, 82)

Holy Stomachache! (Ep#82)

Holy Straightjacket! (Ep#61)

Holy Stratosphere! (Ep#66)

Holy Stuffing! (Ep#5)

Holy Subliminal! (Ep#33)

Holy Suborbit! (Ep#77)

Holy Sudden Incapacitation! (Ep#96)

Holy Sundials! (Ep#45)

Holy Surprise Parties! (Ep#105)

Holy Switch-A-Roo! (Ep#13)

Holy Taj Mahal! (Ep#25)

Holy Tartars! (Ep#109) Batman responds "Unholy Tartars, Robin."

Holy Taxation! (Ep#38)

Holy Taxidermy! (Ep#28)

Holy Tee Shot! (Ep#25)

Holy Ten Toes! (Ep#104)

Holy Terminology! (Ep#71)

Holy Time Bomb! (Ep#98)

Holy Tintinnabulation! (Ep#106)

Holy Tip-offs! (Ep#91)

Holy Titanic! (Ep#80)

Holy Tome! (Ep#30)

Holy Toreador! (Ep#60)

Holy Trampoline! (Ep#79)

Holy Transformation! (*Presentation of Batgirl* by narrator)

Holy Transistors! (Ep#18)

Holy Transistorsville! (Ep#39)

Holy Travel Agent, Batman! (Ep#28)

Holy Trickery! (Ep#19)

Holy Triple Feature! (Ep#31)

Holy Trolls and Goblins! (Ep#58)

Holy Turnabouts! (Ep#52 by narrator)

Holy Tuxedo! (Ep#53)

Holy Uncanny Photographic Mental Processes! (Ep#86)

Holy Understatements! (Ep#103)

Holy Underwritten Metropolis! (Ep#113)

Holy Unlikelihood! (Ep#86)

Holy Unrefillable Prescriptions! (Ep#119)

Holy Vacuum! (Ep#15)

Holy Vanity Case! (*Presentation of Batgirl*)

Holy Venezuela! (Ep#9 by Dick Grayson)

Holy Vertebra! (Ep#55)

Holy Voltage! (Ep#68)

Holy Waste of Energy! (Ep#117)

Holy Wayne Manor! (Ep#33)

Holy Weaponry! (Ep#37)

Holy Wedding Cake! (Ep#82)

Holy Wernher von Braun! (Ep#43

Holy Whiskers! (Ep#27)

Holy Wigs! (Ep#18)

Holy Zorro! (Ep#84)

Examples omitted from scripts:

Ep#2: Holy Windshield Wiper!

Ep#81: Holy Brass! (pg. 7)

Ep#73: Holy Jello Molds, Batman! (pg. 86; changed to Jelly Molds)

Ep#83: Holy Syntax! (pg. 29)

Ep#85: Holy Cancellation! (pg. 39)

Ep#86: Holy Tête-Bêche! (pg. 42)

CATWOMAN IS A WOW, JULIE NEWMAR TAKE A BOW

CAT THRONE

Adam West on Newmar's Catwoman:
"With several varieties of beautiful flowers named for her (a rose, a daylily, and an orchid), one gets a vision of what others see in Julie Newmar. She truly is as attractive as one of her roses. Inside and out it's true.

"As Catwoman in our classic series she said 'come hither' to men of all ages. And she was funny. It was important that she was able to give Catwoman an impish, putting-you-on quality. I remember her humor well. One evening in my dark cottage on the Desilu-Culver lot, I stumbled on a large object as I stepped inside after an insanely full day of running around in cape and cowl. It was a large, lightly humming vibrating relaxation board wrapped in a gold ribbon. A birthday present from Ms. Newmar. The note, in her precise hand, read 'I know I make things difficult for you, please relax with this comfy exercise board, love Julie.'

Her personality and character were warm expressions of humor and caring for others. She was graceful and quite professional. I had a high regard for her."

Julie Newmar won the Tony Award for Best Supporting Actress in the Broadway play *The Marriage-Go-Round* (1959), and has been nominated for two TV Golden Globes Awards. Her career began as a staff choreographer at Universal Studios. She moved from there to stage to film to television. Statuesque and beguiling, she was the perfect choice to play Catwoman, though she, like Cesar Romero, had no idea what-the-heck Batman was to begin with.

"I was bi-coastal at the time," said Newmar. "I happened to be living in New York in my lovely penthouse in Beekman Place. My brother came down from Harvard and was visiting with five or six friends. We were going out to dinner. The call came in and I picked up the phone. It was someone from the casting office. They're desperate. They're *always* desperate. Suzanne Pleshette had probably hung up on them. She's the only other one I know who was considered. They were asking me about something called *Batman*. As soon as my brother heard

Above: Pre-production concept painting by Leslie Thomas, used as a guide when constructing Catwoman's Cat Throne.

Above bottom left: Julie Newmar brushes up on her lines while Kathy Blondell brushes up Newmar's hair and Pat Barto realigns necklace.

Following page: Catwoman peers down on her prey—the Dynamic Duo—from behind bulletproof glass inEp#37.

Following page bottom left: Catwoman, sans gloves, from her first appearance in Ep#19-20.

Following page bottom middle: Newmar (Catwoman) with stuntman Paul Picerni.

Following page bottom right: Julie Newmar runs through dialog with a script assistant on the set of Catwoman's maze.

the word 'Batman,' he leapt off the couch and came over to me and pushed me out the door to get on that plane and get out there. He told me that everyone at Harvard broke from their studies, watched this show. Hello! When you get a recommendation like that, you fly out to California."

Though unfamiliar with the character at first, she came to love being Catwoman. "It was a great role," she said. "The type of female that Catwoman was, so spontaneous and creative and maddening and sexy and insouciant. She had so many qualities that weren't all rather ladylike. She could do bad stuff and get away with it. On top of that, it's comedy, and comedy elicits the unused intelligence in the back of my brain, which I fancy a lot. Straight drama is fairly simple, but [with comedy] now we're creating something magical. To have fun with something is a very special focus, a very special energy."

For her character's great success she credits her friend Stanley Ralph Ross who wrote every Catwoman episode but one. "Never did I change a word of Stanley Ralph Ross, the Great Bear, the genius who wrote the encyclopedia of show business [*The Motion Picture Guide* with Jay Robert Nash]," said Newmar. "He worshipped me as Catwoman. He was a genius, and you don't tell a genius what to do. He already knows. Every time he wrote the Catwoman character or that version of Batman, he added a love interest to it. Maybe that's true in life, that enemies almost have a diabolical flirtation with each other."

This flirtation with Batman fueled Catwoman's popularity. In a leotard Newmar described as fitting "like melted licorice" and with not a bit of skin showing, Batman and Catwoman brought very steamy scenes to network TV in a perfectly acceptable family way.

Above: Julie Newmar as Catwoman rests on the Moldavian Mammoth, during the filming of Ep#37. **Bottom left:** Newmar and James Griffith (Trusty, light blue shirt) are surrounded by other convicts (from Ep#44). **Bottom middle:** Valerie Kairys (Kitty), Pat Becker (Cattie) and Julie Newmar (Catwoman) in Catwoman's lair. Kathryn Blondell (Hair Stylist) is at right. **Bottom right:** Batman asks for Catwoman's help in stopping Sandman.

FRANK GORSHIN IS THE ONE TO MAKE THE RIDDLER LOADS OF FUN

Adam West on Gorshin's Riddler: *"When I was with [Frank] we saw the funny and bizarre moments we wanted to create, so we had plenty of laughs and Frank relaxed with me. With Batman and Riddler moments we sometimes had a tough job not totally losing it. We became great friends and I couldn't resist playing his butler in one of his movies,* Angels with Angles.

"It was comfortable for me to have an actor like Frank around. He certainly helped me keep a light, fun and creative atmosphere on the stage. At the same time, Frank was as serious about the results as I was. Frank was always interesting and he was always a friend."

Frank Gorshin (1933-2005) was nominated for an Emmy for his performance of the Riddler in "Hi Diddle Riddle," one of three Emmy nominations the show garnered for 1966. He split his career between live performances doing impressions, eventually becoming a headliner in Las Vegas, and his television/film career, where he would boast of more than forty TV appearances and seventy film roles. Gorshin reprised his role as the Riddler in the TV movie *Legends of the Superheroes* (1979). He returned to the DC Universe in 2005, when he voiced the animated character of Dr. Hugo Strange for three episodes of *Batman: The Animated Series*.

"Riddle me this, Batman," was a jest and a joust. Gorshin's Riddler was mocking our hero and challenging him at the same time. It became a part of popular vernacular almost overnight. A subtle line delivered by a brilliant performer who transformed a comic-book villain into a force to be reckoned with. Gorshin's Riddler delighted in outwitting Batman. He clearly couldn't restrain his laughter and glee, and brought the audience in on the joke.

Above: Frank Gorshin (the Riddler) with Susan Silo (Mousey) from Ep#11 and 12.

Somehow Bill Dozier knew the actor and impressionist would be the perfect Riddler and pursued Gorshin for the part. "I was flattered that he did think of me," said Gorshin. "I was excited too, because as a kid I loved the *Batman* comic. I relished [playing the role]. I wanted to do it. So I didn't have to audition or anything. They asked for me, and I agreed."

"Oddly enough, I was a fan of the Riddler," he said. "I knew exactly who he was and how I would bring him to life. Riddler was a true maniacal character, one that could turn on a dime. Sweet one second, bat crazy the next. He was an honest character."

Semple's script delighted the comic in Gorshin. "It was definitely going to be a comedy," Gorshin said. "When I found out they were gonna have balloons on screen saying POW and ZAM, how could it be anything else? Then I read the dialogue and it was pretty apparent that it was going to be tongue-in-cheek. It was going to be for laughs and at the same time it was going to have an appeal for kids, because there was going to be a lot of action involved with it... I thought it was really clever. Lorenzo Semple was a brilliant writer, and I thought, this is going to have legs. It was a pioneer. It was a whole new thing. It was also exciting being on the first show, and setting the pace so to speak. I was the forerunner, and I love that responsibility, because I thought it was going to last a long time."

Gorshin's success as the Riddler loomed large over his entire career. "I became a headliner [in Vegas] because of the strength of that role," said Gorshin. "[Because of] the numbers of people who had seen it, I became box office... And I think of the dichotomy of what I've experienced from it. It has been the very thing that elevated me, as I say, to a headliner performer, and has been... the very thing that kept me from doing other things. Because the identification was so strong for me as the Riddler... I loved the role. I loved the idea of playing that role and enjoyed the idea of doing it."

Top: Mole Hill Mob members Joe Nappi (left) and Frank Arno along with Frank Gorshin (the Riddler) and Jill St. John (Molly) react in surprise as the Batmobile's rocket-launching tubes continue to fire.

Middle: Allen Jaffe (Harry), Jill St. John (Molly) and Frank Gorshin (the Riddler) with Burt Ward (Robin).

Bottom: (From left) Joe Nappi (Mole Hill Mob member), Frank Gorshin (the Riddler), Frank Arno (Mob), Allen Jaffe (Harry), Joe Gray (Mob), Jill St. John (Molly), Michael Morelli (Mob) standing over Burt Ward (Robin).

Above: Batman and the Riddler's boxing ring duel in Ep#96, as visualized in this pre-production concept painting by Leslie Thomas. **Bottom left:** The Riddler describes how the evening's boxing match is going to be thrown. From left: Gil Perkins (Cauliflower), Nicholas Georgiade (Kayo), James Brolin (Kid Gulliver) and Frank Gorshin. **Bottom right:** (From left) Frank Gorshin, Peggy Ann Garner (Betsy Boldface) and Gil Perkins (Cauliflower).

CESAR ROMERO IS A WIN, THE JOKER ALWAYS MAKES US GRIN

Above: Adam West and Cesar Romero filming on the beach.

Adam West on Romero's Joker: *"Cesar Romero amazed me with his energy. His Joker was always at a full court press. Cesar was not a young man when he joined our classic series. However, he never slowed or lost the manic laugh and energy in scenes that sometimes demanded the athletic abilities of a decathlon champ.*

"I decided to study him a bit. I wanted to see what he did to maintain. I would use it myself after nine or ten hours of the daily filming grind. He took no foreign substances that I could see. There would be no Congressional hearings or investigations with our Joker. He didn't pose around with some exotic Tai Chi movements. He didn't even have a yoga pad. I found he merely sat in his canvas chair and went instantly to sleep. And some minutes later when called to the set, he would be instantly awake and super intense. To me it seemed an amazing ability. I don't sleep that well even at night."

Cesar Romero (1907–1994) began his movie career in *The Shadow Laughs* (1933) featuring the pulp hero The Shadow. He subsequently played everything from leading man to the debonair villain, and worked in television from its early days in 1948 up until 1992.

"I never thought very much of *Batman* because I never saw the comic strip," said Romero. "When I was called about this I didn't know what Bill Dozier was talking about. He explained that they had done the first episode with Frank Gorshin playing the Riddler and one with Burgess Meredith playing the Penguin, and now they were going to do the third with the Joker as the villain. And it meant absolutely nothing to me. Why he wanted me for the Joker I will never know. His wife Ann Rutherford said he saw me in something that made him want to cast me… I went to the studio and it was just great. I thought 'My God. This is really fun.' When I read the script I said, 'Why sure I'll do this. I'd love to do it.'"

Jan Kemp, *Batman*'s costume designer/wardrobe

Above: Diana Ivarson's character (Baby Jane Towser) was a nod to blonde Baby Jane Holzer who had appeared in several of Andy Warhol's movies.

head, remembered it was Romero's reaction to his costume that defined the character for the actor. "Cesar Romero, always the epitome of the well-dressed gentleman, was cast as the Joker," said Kemp. "At our first meeting, I said to him that I would like to preserve that image in his costume and planned to give him a smartly tailored dress tail suit. He nodded his approval. I explained further; 'Of course, it will be a burgundy color with black stripes on the pants. You should have a green shirt and a floppy black silk tie with white face makeup and green hair, not forgetting green socks!' He started to giggle with this insane cackle. The producers were there, and he had us all in stitches with this stupid laughter about this costume... he decided to keep the laugh in the show as his trademark."

Of course, laughter was the trademark of this villain from his comic-book beginnings, but that costume sold it to Romero. "It was a very easy character to go into," he explained. "Once you get into that costume

and get the wig and makeup on, you change completely. When I get in an outfit like that, I'm not going to sit there and go: 'ha, ha, ha'. I'm going to go 'HA, HA, HA, HA!' Just whoop it up, laugh and scream. It was a ball to do. I thoroughly enjoyed playing the Joker."

One thing fans enjoy is that Romero never shaved his mustache even though it was covered in white clown makeup. "I grew my mustache when I was twenty-three years old, because I was very much in love with a lady ten years older than I," explained Romero. "She wanted me to look older and I grew the mustache. I've had it ever since. When I was going to do the Joker, which was just one week's work at the time, I wasn't going to shave it off and told them that. I told them to just pile makeup on it. That was perfectly all right with them, so it didn't really make any difference at all."

Left: Cesar Romero (the Joker) sports his latest invention—a Joker Utility Belt—allowing the Clown Prince of Crime to more successfully engage and enrage Batman. "With bright green hair and alabaster face, he'll look hugely bizarre," wrote Executive Producer William Dozier in a Dec. 17, 1965 note to Lorenzo Semple Jr. **Above:** Pre-production concept painting of the Joker's lair by Leslie Thomas.

BURGESS MEREDITH MAKES US CHORTLE, HIS PENGUIN IS IMMORTAL

All the better to smell the fish...

Adam West on Meredith's Penguin: *"Fans often ask who my favorite Batman villain was. That pusillanimous poltroon with the feathers always comes to mind. The fine actor who portrayed the Penguin always comes to mind, as well. Burgess Meredith had already become legendary because of his many notable film and stage roles. He was always interesting and full of stories. When Burgess and I had scenes together it was always a learning experience for me.*

"When we premiered our Batman movie at the Paramount Theatre in Austin, Texas, we all arrived together on a swanky plane. But what should appear in the sky about to land at a nearby runway? It was Burgess dressed as the Penguin and privately flown by his charming wife. Well, his late and colorful arrival certainly topped ours. We had a great time and I was even asked to dance with the first lady. However, after a few seconds of rhythmic moves and small talk, the Penguin cut in. Upstaged again. Burgess and I became friends and occasionally amused each other at dinner."

Burgess Meredith (1907–1997) was called "One of the most gifted and versatile performers of the American stage and screen" by Ephraim Katz in *The Film Encyclopedia*.

He received an Emmy for Outstanding Performance by a Supporting Actor in a Comedy or Drama Special for *Tailgunner Joe* (1977) and a National Board of Review Award for Best Supporting Actor for *Advise and Consent* (1962). He was also nominated for two Academy Awards®, for *Rocky* (1976) and *The Day of the Locust* (1977), a Golden Globe®, another Emmy and the BAFTA Award. His most famous role is probably George Milton in Director Lewis Milestone's *Of Mice and Men* (1939).

Meredith's enthusiasm for the part of the Penguin was remarkable. His contempt for the Dynamic Duo came through in his dialogue delivery, often dripping with unparalleled venom. Mumbling into his cigarette holder, his quick ad-libs would often be funnier than the script. Charles FitzSimons often said: "Why he never won an Emmy for that performance, I'll never know."

Top left: Rehearsal scene with Burgess Meredith as the Penguin in a rare picture without his hat.

Top right: Bruce Hutchinson (Makeup) works on attaching prosthetic nose to Burgess Meredith (the Penguin).

Opposite: Burgess Meredith fires up another tricky umbrella.

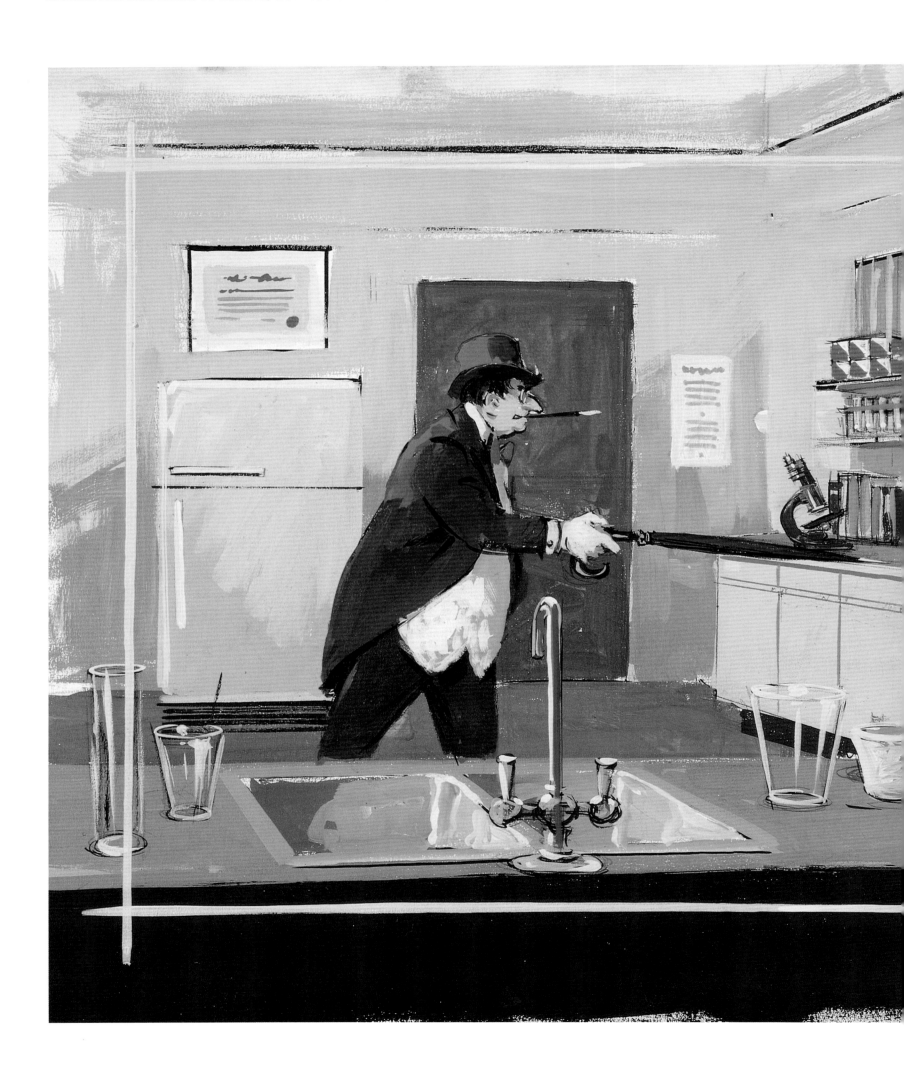

"Burgess Meredith was absolutely brilliant," said associate producer William D'Angelo. "Lorenzo created the character, but Burgess brought so much on top of what was on the paper; it was incredible to see. He absolutely loved doing that part. He called us every week to ask when the Penguin was coming back. He would have done every episode if we had [more] of them for him."

Even the hours in makeup didn't hinder Meredith's enthusiasm. "The minute he got that makeup on," said makeup artist Bruce Hutchinson, "he became that Penguin, and he was that character all day long, until all that came off. He was a laugh riot. He loved this character. He would kind of waggle around as the Penguin did on the show, with the umbrella, hat and monocle."

He had a razor-sharp sense of humor, and we had more fun with him," continued Hutchinson. "I think it was the first [character with which] he could just kick back and have a wonderful time, because he had always been a pretty serious actor. And that was the difference on that show that really made it."

Bob Butler, the director who first worked with Meredith as the Penguin, admired how well the actor developed what he was doing in the role. "[The Penguin] was a man who enjoyed dressing up in clothing à la a penguin, who liked wearing a tuxedo all the time and walking like a little bird," said Butler. "That was the reality in the TV show, and Meredith got behind that instantly. He didn't worry about the psychology of a man who would be that way... He was exquisite. He was a formally trained actor and he knew that this whole thing wasn't too far from *commedia dell'arte*. You just get behind it; you just play this bizarre reality for all it's worth."

Left: Pre-production concept painting by Leslie Thomas. In this scene, the Penguin has invaded Gotham General Hospital, intent on destroying the existing supply of B-6 Vaccine which combats Lygerian Sleeping Sickness.

THE SECOND SEASON STARTS, INCLUDES EPISODES IN THREE PARTS

> "I thought the *Batman* series was wonderful, so inventive and clever. There was such a sense of humor on the whole set. The producers really loved it. They had a huge hit on their hands. They paid great attention to it. It was produced as a real movie. They didn't skimp at all."
>
> Vincent Price, Egghead, interviewed in 1993 by Bob Garcia

On March 9, 1966, five weeks before the first season finished production, ABC sent a wire to 20th Century-Fox Television exercising their option "for fifty-two new color programs in the *Batman* series," officially authorizing the 1966–67 season. Eight more episodes would be added to the order, bringing the total to 60 half-hours, the most of the three seasons and half of the show's entire 120-episode output.

Since the second season had the largest number of episodes, it racked up a number of interesting statistics. The sixty episodes were done by ten directors, compared to the first season's thirty-four episodes handled by twelve directors. Season two brought in twenty-two writers to cover nineteen different villains. The season featured a new Riddler and two new portrayals of Mr. Freeze. It had the first three-parter, a two-parter with the fewest "Holy" exclamations by Robin (just three in "That Darn Catwoman/Scat! Darn Catwoman") and Madge Blake's (Aunt Harriet) favorite episodes (with Liberace). It introduced the Compressed Steam Batpole Lifts and

Negate Bruce's Change option to the series. It not only unveiled the reverse Batclimb, but featured the first solo Batclimb by Batman and the first – and only – Batclimb by Alfred. It introduced the Alfcycle, Pengymobile, Jokermobile and, thanks to the movie, a Batboat, Batcopter and an updated Batcycle.

The three-part episodes were quite a departure from the first season. There were thoughts of turning at least one three-parter into a theatrical release, "The Zodiac Crimes/The Joker's Hard Times/The Penguin Declines." In early December, Post-Production Coordinator Bob Mintz instructed film editors "to cover themselves with dupe negative on any scenes being cut down for the TV version that might possibly run longer in a theatrical version." This would preserve the original negative of a lengthier sequence for use in a movie, while a dupe was used to assemble the final version of the TV show. No such theatrical versions of the shows have been found.

Below: From Ep#62: compressed steam is how they ascended to Wayne Manor.

HORWITZ BUILDS A RELIABLE STAFF WHO WROTE SCRIPTS FOR A GOOD LAUGH

"There were only a few people who really understood the way I was doing Batman. It was my sense to make him stoic and yet vulnerable and tongue-in-cheek; a crazy guy running around in tights doing funny things for the adult audience, and just being sort of Robin Hood for the kids."

Adam West, 2015 email interview with Bob Garcia

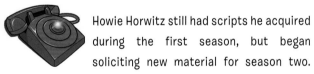 Howie Horwitz still had scripts he acquired during the first season, but began soliciting new material for season two. With an eye toward this season, in an April 15, 1966 memo, William Dozier recommended that Horwitz commission "two King Tut and one Mad Hatter, plus two Catwoman, two Riddlers, two Jokers and two Penguins, and two Mr. Freeze... all the rest new"

From Tony Award-nominee Jay Thompson came "The Impractical Joker/The Joker's Provokers." It was a heavily rewritten version of Thompson's "Hickory Dickory Doc," an early story submitted October 28, 1965. Its first draft was dated November 15, with a revised draft on March 7, 1966 and it had a great unused cliffhanger. Batman and Robin had climbed into the Joker's apartment. The Joker used his black box to freeze Batman and Robin in their tracks, reversed them so they were climbing backwards down the building and then slashed through the Batropes. Quoting Thompson's script: "We hear the evil laughter of the Joker as we see Batman and Robin falling, falling, falling to the concrete below." This unused cliffhanger is resolved as the Joker changes his mind, causing the Duo to fall upward, at least saving their lives for the moment. This was Thompson's only foray into episodic television. His book for the stage musical *Once Upon a Mattress* received a Tony nomination and he had directed *Born Yesterday*, *Pocketful of Wry*, *Annie*, *Sweet Charity* and many other classics on Broadway.

A story outline that arrived in May, during filming of the feature, was Lorenzo Semple Jr.'s "The Penguin's Nest/The Bird's Last Jest." It was the first to go before the camera for season two, although it was not the first episode broadcast. Les Martinson was scheduled to direct, but ultimately decided he would not have the time or energy to properly prepare since it was so close to when the *Batman* movie was wrapping up.

Charles Hoffman was signed to be script editor and head writer beginning with season two. He would become the second most prolific scripter with his name on twenty-two episodes, and as script editor, he would work

Tutlings! Sic 'em!

Above: Camera operator shoots hand-held work with an Arriflex for Victor Buono's (King Tut) ride down the mining shaft in Ep#117. Ted Cook (Property Master, wearing glasses) holds onto cart. Cave and shaft sequences were filmed on Stages 2 and 3 at Desilu-Culver.

on every script during seasons two and three. Hoffman had written the Mad Hatter script for season one, "The Thirteenth Hat/Batman Stands Pat," which was thought of by Greenway as "one of the best we did this year" and catching "the exact flavor and spirit of the series."

"He could do a rewrite overnight," associate producer D'Angelo observed about Hoffman. "Charlie would come [to work] in the morning and just sit in front of the typewriter. He didn't do anything else. He was an old-fashioned writer. He was terrific... To meet Charlie, he was a fooler. He was a shy fellow and very educated, and articulate. In appearance, very square; you wouldn't believe that kind of stuff would come out of his typewriter. He had a great sense of humor."

Hoffman, along with Stanley Ralph Ross and Stanford Sherman, virtually took control of writing the series around the middle of this season. They were responsible for forty-seven of the final fifty-six episodes. Only Semple would prove more influential.

Stanley Ralph Ross worked on twenty-seven episodes. "It was the greatest show business experience of my life," recalled Ross. "We were such a close-knit family that some of us still stay in touch. I see people I knew from *Batman* all the time. They loved to put me on... I did a cameo in

Batman as Ballpoint Baxter, the world's greatest forger, with thick glasses. A near-sighted forger. I kept hawking Howie [Horwitz]. I wanted a part. He said, 'Stanley, you're a writer, leave me alone.' I persisted, 'C'mon, please, gimme a part. Please.' He said, 'Alright.' He gave me a part where I had nothing to say. Not one line. He said, 'If you are really funny, you can get laughs without any lines.'"

Ross came up with a perfect comedic hook for Egghead. "When I started to write Egghead, I looked up every word in the dictionary that started with 'ex' or 'ecc': Egg-centric, Egg-splosive..."

Another important writer was Stanford Sherman. He was a very young man who had once studied to be a rabbi.

Bottom left: Vincent Price (Egghead) and Adam West (Batman).

Bottom Middle: Egghead approaches the Electro-Thought Transferrer during an Ep#47 rehearsal, with Burt Ward in the background.

Bottom right: Vincent Price (Egghead), Gail Hire (Executive Secretary Miss Bacon) and Adam West (Batman).

Below: As Commissioner Gordon, Bruce Wayne and Dick Grayson watch, Chief O'Hara brings Ballpoint Baxter into Gordon's office at the end of Ep#62. The non-speaking role of Baxter was portrayed by series writer Stanley Ralph Ross.

Above: Vincent Price shows off his egg-cellent finger dexterity.

Following spread, top right: As a big-time movie producer, the Penguin required his own personal transportation.

Following spread, middle right: Bill Neff (Gaffer) positions light on scene with Carolyn Jones (Marsha) and Adam West from Ep#76.

Following spread, bottom right: Burt Ward and Adam West in Catwoman's deathtrap. No Utility Belts because the Feline Fury burned them!

Following spread, full page: Catwoman's two-ton echo chamber deathtrap for the Dynamic Duo in Ep#63 magnified the sound of a dripping faucet ten million times.

While working on *Batman*, he would usually write late into the night, and just come into the office to hand in his assignments. He contributed eighteen episodes, of which two were three-parters.

Modifications to scripts happened on a regular basis. Some were minor, but occasionally they were very significant or even involved major rewriting.

A few examples:

- "The Penguin's Nest/The Bird's Last Jest"

originally had Commissioner Gordon imprisoned in the trunk, but this was changed to use Chief O'Hara instead since Gordon was involved in the cliffhanger of another episode.

- Alternate episode titles considered for "Penguin Sets a Trend/Penguin's Disastrous End:"
"General Penguin Sets A Trend"
"Penguin And Marsha's Disastrous End"
"Penguin And Marsha Reach A Dead End"

"Penguin And Marsha Fail To Blend"

- In early versions of the script for "The Cat's Meow/The Bat's Kow Tow," the character Allan Stevens had been named Connie Jarson.

The show's original casting director, Larry Stewart, left in May 1966 during the feature film, and Michael McLean took his place, getting actors for the new roles. Associate Producer Bill D'Angelo and McLean agreed it was a blast to go to work each morning. "It was a funny group of guys," McLean said. "Whatever silly nightmare Bill and I dreamed up the night before we could get away with." The two became fast friends on the show. They often went out after a day's work, or stayed late into the evening hunting up extras or sometimes principal villains for the next day's shoot.

Horwitz had a clever way of keeping that family spirit growing. Each crew member eventually acquired a "Bat" nickname. Dozier's secretary on the production was called "Bon-Bon". Jan Kemp was "Head-Rag-Picker." Michael McLean received memos addressed to "Batcaster." Stanley Ralph Ross was "Ballpoint," after his cameo. Horwitz affectionately became "Batleader," while Dozier was called "Super Bat-Chief." The nicknames added to the magic.

The feature film finished shooting June 2. Editing was finished the following Friday with a screening set for Director Les Martinson, Editor Harry Gerstad, Charles FitzSimons and William Dozier. Another screening was set for Monday morning on June 13 with another later that afternoon with sound and music running. June 13 also marked the first day of production for the second season, and once again, the principal cast and most of the crew did not have much time off.

NEW DIRECTORS GOT READY, KEEPING PRODUCTION STEADY

"Our directors were the best with working our kind of television. They came and they went. Several were distinctive with their own style and grasp of the material. The show was so hot we had no trouble in finding outstanding people who wanted to be a part of it."

Adam West, 2015 email interview with Bob Garcia

Below: Director Oscar Rudolph works with Alan Napier and Yvonne Craig in Ep#106.

While Robert Sparr, Jeff Hayden, Sherman Marks, Murray Golden, Larry Peerce, Don Weis and James Neilson directed episodes this season, the series increasingly became the showcase of three other directors: George Waggner (who insisted his screen credit appear as george waGGner), James B. Clark and Oscar Rudolph. They were the men whom Horwitz would depend on to make the weekly schedule.

Waggner was the director of Universal's *The Wolfman* (1941) and *Man-Made Monster* (1941) and he produced *The Ghost of Frankenstein* (1942) and *Frankenstein Meets the Wolf Man* (1943). He was undeniably a top professional who directed ten episodes during the second and third seasons, and who always wore a suit no matter what the weather. "When Otto Preminger the director was hired to play Mr. Freeze, George Waggner was onboard to direct," said Adam West."

James Clark, who directed fifteen episodes, considered *Batman* ancient history, only remarking later in life that, "It was fun. It was a great show. I made a

James B. Clark directing...

Above left: (From left) Otto Preminger (Mr. Freeze), George Waggner and Milton Stark (dialogue coach).

Above right: Among the cast and crew: James Clark (under the light), Bill Bohny (assistant cameraman, right of camera), Thomas Del Ruth (second assistant cameraman, dark jacket), Bill Derwin (assistant director, dark glasses).

lot of them. I loved it. I was at the end of my career. I've been retired for twenty years and never looked back. I loved everybody. Howie Horwitz was a wonderful man. The people making it were all fine talents at 20th Century Fox where I was born and grew up. It was wonderful."

Oscar Rudolph joined the series this season. Charles FitzSimons recalled, "Oscar Rudolph had directed the entire Ann Sothern series, *Private Secretary*. He was very proficient, very responsible and was a very good friend of mine. He had directed a pilot for me and for Dozier at Screen Gems, so I brought him over to *Batman*, and he did more *Batman* episodes than any other director." Of the nineteen directors on the series, Rudolph ultimately helmed thirty-six episodes of *Batman*, directing thirty of the final fifty-two episodes. Prior to *Batman*, Rudolph was noted as one of Hollywood's most reliable directors, working on *December Bride* and *My Favorite Martian* in addition to second unit work on *Whatever Happened To Baby Jane?* (1962) and other feature films.

"Oscar got the work done quickly with a lot of threatening tongue-in cheek bluster," recalled West. "He saw the humor in this crazy show with its absurdities abounding. He was truly funny and a fascinating little gent who looked like a junior Olympic wrestler.

"Oscar Rudolph and Larry Peerce couldn't have been more different," West continued. "Larry Peerce was

a demanding director with a creative bent I greatly admired. On stage or location he could be heard with as big and resonant a voice as his opera star father, Jan Peerce. Larry was urbane and funny and I enjoyed his time with us. He also did a great impersonation of me and he had a good grasp of what we were all about and why the show was such a phenomenon." Peerce continued on to an illustrious career, during which he directed the Robert Dozier-scripted *The Incident* and the hit *Goodbye, Columbus*.

"Four *Batman* episodes were directed by Tom Gries," added West. "Tom's credits were long and ran the spectrum of TV and theatrical. Will Penny, the western with Charlton Heston, had been a success for him, and he had won a number of Emmys for his small screen work. The only serious disagreement we ever had with *Batman* was with something so seemingly petty it became hilarious. A restaurant booth with Batman and a few others sitting in it was supposed to revolve and disappear with us into the wall. Within the context of the scene we disagreed on whether it should disappear clockwise or counterclockwise. Which would be funnier. On cue and with dialogue, we tried it one-way and then the other and then the other and so on. I got dizzy, the crew broke up and Tom won his point." Result: the booth spun clockwise.

THE CAST & CREW LOVED ALL THE MANY FANS, EVEN WITH THEIR WACKY PLANS

"[Adam West] was an incredible celebrity, mobbed everywhere. He was extremely decent about it always. He loved his fans, giving autographs, and being Batman."

Lorenzo Semple Jr., 1993 interview with Bob Garcia

 One of the wonderful things about the show was how the directors, cast and crew treated the children who were visitors to the set. "Usually they don't let children on a movie set, because they will yell or cry out or say 'Oh' or something or spoil takes," said Dozier. "We had kids on the set all the time, and they never had a take spoiled. Never. [The children] were so enthralled by what they were watching, so wrapped up in those characters, [they] never spoiled a take… [I think it was because] what they saw on the set was what they saw on the screen."

Adam West proved to be a true hero with these children. "Adam was wonderful with the kids," said Dozier. "He would visit them between setups and let them come and sit on his knee and so on and so forth. We had billions of kids all summer long each year it was on. We let them come on the set with their parents and the kids had a ball."

Fans of the series wrote in to request autographs and photographs, with some perhaps even hoping to receive a note from one of their heroes. "We were not prepared for the enormity of the impact made by *Batman* on the viewers of America," wrote William Dozier in his May 3, 1966 response to a mother from East Palo Alto, CA. She had contacted the executive producer after her daughter wrote to Burt Ward two months earlier and then kept asking, "Why doesn't Robin write?" Dozier continued, "We have received over sixty thousand such letters since *Batman* went on the air a little over three months ago. I personally have answered three or four hundred letters, and we have a department which does nothing else but answer fan mail. [Setting up the equipment and people to do the work] was not adequate at the outset and took a while to develop," Dozier went on to reassure the concerned mom that her daughter and her friends would soon hear from their favorite heroes.

By late summer, 20th Century Fox and ABC had been heavily promoting the *Batman* feature and the start of *Batman*'s second season. On August 23, a Tuesday, Adam West and Burt Ward had a temporary break in filming. Both departed for a "Batman Tour" of New York City to promote the feature film's release. This included scheduled interviews on both local and network radio and TV, plus appearances on *The Merv Griffin Show*

Top: From Ep#101: The Dynamic Duo applied a flower decal on the Batmobile when they were scheduled to be guests of honor at a Flower-In that afternoon.

Left: Adam West greets some fans outside of Stage 2 at Desilu-Culver during filming of Ep#41-42.

(which aired September 1) and *The Mike Douglas Show*. They visited movie theatres in Flushing, Jamaica, Queens Village, Brooklyn, Manhattan, the Bronx and New Jersey with a grueling thirty-seven theatre visits scheduled. Estimates were that 1.25 million people saw the pair. Undaunted, West and Ward were back at the studio Monday morning with a 7.30 a.m. makeup call.

MAKEUP & WARDROBE TALES FROM PENGUINS TO DUSTY TRAILS

"They were all so eager to do the show, we could put *anything* on them and they loved it."

Bruce Hutchinson, 1993 interview with Bob Garcia

"I had been an apprentice," recalled makeup man Bruce Hutchinson. "*Batman* was my first show that was my own, and I was heavily into it. [I had my] own artistic input because I was away from 20th Century Fox down in Culver City. There were a lot of times when I had to just come up with something right away. I couldn't call the [Fox makeup] department and say, 'Well, this is what they want; how do you feel about it?' I just had to think on my feet."

Fox's makeup was developed and manufactured on the 20th Century Fox studio lot. Whenever Hutchinson needed to refresh supplies, he went to the department's laboratory to personally choose his makeup.

"I learned an awful lot those two years," said Hutchinson. "In fact, I had the best time I ever had in the business working on that show. Some of the most incredible people came through then. I met more people in two years than I have in the thirty years since. It was just a great experience."

Most of the actors would put themselves in Hutchinson's care, but a few wanted to do their own, for example: "Cliff [Robertson] had his own ideas about his makeup," said Hutchinson. "He wanted to be very dark and very leathery looking. So I just kind of let him go. I'd put on the basic stuff and he did the rest himself. A lot of makeup men get upset if the actor wants to do his own makeup. But if it works for the character, I don't object."

"Talking of cowboys," said Jan Kemp, "we did two episodes with Cliff Robertson playing the part of Shame, a take-off of cowboy badmen. For his outfits, I used a combination of fringed leather garments and modern print shirts using a spotted silk tie, tied with a Windsor knot, and a white hat instead of the usual black hat worn by the bad cowboys. My favorite character in those two shows was a Mexican henchman in shabby clothes wearing a huge sombrero and speaking with an impeccable English accent. This is the kind of camp humor that the

Batman series became known for. I developed an aptitude for making things a little larger than life."

Tallulah Bankhead, one of stage and screen's Grand Dames, appeared in "Black Widow Strikes Again/Caught in the Spider's Den" as the Black Widow. "Tallulah had emphysema," remembered Bruce Hutchinson. "But the minute they said 'Action,' she was eighteen years old. She was delightful and sweet."

FILM SETS, FIRST AID, & SHOWERS CAUSE SHOOTING TO TAKE EXTRA HOURS

"There never was an accident of any consequence. [The scripts] weren't designed that way. The show was supposed to be fun and enjoyable and if somebody was going to be bleeding on the set, that's not very funny. So we avoided physical action that was too physical and it worked."

William Dozier, interview conducted by Kevin Burns

All sorts of problems can arise on a set and cause delays. Sometimes actors arrive late, causing the entire production to come to a standstill right at the beginning of the day. Or they might return late from lunch.

Delays occurred weekly, but one was particularly notable. On August 4, 1966, Burt Ward reported to makeup at 10 a.m. as scheduled. He had a set call at 10.30 a.m. but was dismissed at 11 a.m. and rushed out of the studio and to the hospital. His wife, Bonney, had given birth to their daughter Lisa Ann Ward.

Later that same day, a delay for a much more common reason occurred: stuntman Remo Pisani hurt his leg in a fight and was sent to First Aid. Small accidents cropped up throughout production. With Ward gone, the company ran out of work at 4.30 p.m., although Hubie Kerns and Victor Paul remained on the set until 6.45 p.m..

The Ma Parker episodes seemed to have encountered more problems than usual. On August 11, during the first day of filming, a power failure occurred late in the afternoon, resulting in a thirty-five-minute delay. The next day, crewman Don Bishop stepped on a nail on the set and had to go to First Aid. Day three found the company a half day behind in shooting due to previous delays. On day four, Sandy Kevin (in the role of a Truck Guard) was hit in the face by a machine gun clip; he was given first aid on the set. On day six, Adam West hurt his head on a stage door and was sent to First Aid, resulting in a two-hour delay. August 19 was day seven of what was supposed to have been a six-day shoot.

At about 10.30 a.m., the Company moved from Stage 8 to 15. Interestingly, they were going to shoot the last few scenes in the Prison Death Chamber. At about 10.50 a.m., Shelley Winters slipped in a pool of water on the Stage 15 floor and was given first aid, all resulting in a half-hour delay. Winters did return to the set to film her remaining three shots. Even an eighth day of filming was required on August 23 with the six principal cast members. These Ma Parker episodes were the first directed by Oscar Rudolph, and after this experience, he

Previous spread, left page, left image: Adam West pulls down cowl in preparation for filming, assisted by costumer at right.

Previous spread, left page, right image: From left during Ep#59–60: Bill Derwin (assistant director), Adam West (Batman), set costumer, second set costumer.

Previous spread, right page: Taken during the first day of principal photography for the pilot, Charles FitzSimons (assistant to the producer) observes at right, while costumers prepare Adam West's cowl.

Opposite: Shelley Winters (Ma Parker) and Adam West pose between takes during Ep#43–44.

must have wondered if the place needed an exorcism.

Other productions occasionally got in the way of *Batman*. Monday, August 29 was the second day of filming "An Egg Grows in Gotham/The Yegg Foes in Gotham." The day was planned for work at Fox Hills on Stage 9 with the Chicken Shack interiors and then filming on New York Street for the jewelry store, rear steps of City Hall and two Gotham City streets. However, filming for the movie *Caprice* pre-empted the *Batman* unit from using New York Street and they had to return Thursday to film those scenes. Bottom line: five hours lost in the two moves, additional transportation expenses and incidentals and a half day of production that had to be made up.

Sunny southern California usually made weather a non-issue for filming, but that was not always the case. Filming for "Penguin Is a Girl's Best Friend" began Monday,

December 5 with all exterior shots planned, and of course it rained. Director Clark still got in a good amount of work, although everyone was dismissed around 4.30 p.m. and the day ended two hours behind schedule. The next day began with exterior scenes planned at Warner Bros. New York Street, but the company moved to Stage 3 at Desilu-Culver at 9.45 a.m. due to rain. The crew bus arrived at 10.25 a.m. They would film Hilda's Cave but not until 2.20 p.m. because the set was not ready! The company finished at 5.45 p.m., and was now three-quarters of day behind. Wednesday had interiors on Stage 3 planned for the entire day... and the weather was clear. On December 15, the same company was hit with a fifteen-minute power failure while on Stage 15. The next day, a thirty-minute power failure on Stage 2 affected work on "That Darn Catwoman/Scat! Darn Catwoman."

Left: Chief O'Hara's police car was pancaked by the Penguin's solid gold tank. Several policemen helped remove the flattened vehicle. In back: Burt Ward, Stafford Repp (Chief O'Hara), Adam West, and Neil Hamilton (Commissioner Gordon).

There were the silly incidents to just make folks laugh: "We're doing a fight on this Learjet, and the owner is standing there watching us," said Victor Paul regarding "The Duo is Slumming". "They're trying to shove me into the engine. Of course it's not going, but the heavies are pushing me inside the jet engine. I'm supposed to be hollering 'Batman, Batman!' One guy got on the wing and the plane tilted down. It actually leaned way over, and touched the ground. Finally, the owner runs out and says, 'What are you doing? This is a two and a half million dollar plane and you guys are going to ruin it!' "

"I had on that skin outfit and the big white hat," said Charles Picerni about the "Batfight" in "Come Back, Shame" and his doubling for Robertson, "and my hair was a bit longer than Cliff's. I had to do that fight behind the bar when Victor was swinging [an] axe handle. Oscar

Rudolph said to me, 'Don't lose that hat no matter what you do.' Sure enough, I get that hat and pulled it down, and Victor hit me, and the hat fell off as I was going over. I fell right into that hat. Put it back on and went right into the fight."

While the Batmobile encountered its share of scratches, dings, dents and mechanical trouble during filming, it fortunately never suffered enough damage to prevent it from being used. Lighting and camera angles occasionally make it appear that a substitute may have been filmed, most notably in episode 69 during scenes in the Batcave. However daily production reports indicate otherwise, and while Barris eventually did build three more, it was Batmobile #1 which appeared in every episode.

RIGHT: Adam West waits for the crew to set up a shot of the Gotham City Convention Hall in Ep#52.

A STRANGE PROP EACH DAY KEPT KRIZMAN AT PLAY

"I used to laugh when I came on set. They used to have weird-looking balls of string hanging and these ugly-looking chairs with cat skin. It looked much more marvelous on the screen. Those colors just gave it that zing."

Julie Newmar, 1993 interview with Bob Garcia

Very bad for your diet...

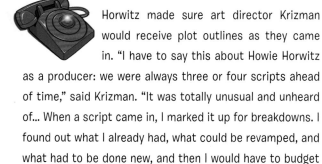

Horwitz made sure art director Krizman would receive plot outlines as they came in. "I have to say this about Howie Horwitz as a producer: we were always three or four scripts ahead of time," said Krizman. "It was totally unusual and unheard of... When a script came in, I marked it up for breakdowns. I found out what I already had, what could be revamped, and what had to be done new, and then I would have to budget for the whole thing."

"When there were changes, it was only in the dialogue," said a grateful Krizman. "What was in the scripts originally, that was what stayed. It was heaven for me, because if you can plot things three or four shows ahead of time you can plot your revamps. You think about one set, and say that three shows from now that thing can become whatever, with this or that change. Then you design it and build it that way. So when the revamp came in, it was already able to go. That was entirely to Horwitz's credit."

Krizman wasn't on set to see most of his work being filmed. He was too busy. He explained: "During the actual shooting, unless there was a new thing that had to be made, or I was making the sets for the first time, I was usually so busy making the next show [that] I wasn't at the shooting site too much."

An outsize prop cake was built for John Astin's Riddler episodes, "Batman's Anniversary/A Riddling Controversy." "The giant cake was fun," said Krizman. "It had three tiers, and was thirty-five feet high. We built most of it with plywood except the top which we put foam rubber in so the Dynamic Duo would sink. We had a small elevator installed so they would have something to stand on as they were lowered into the foam rubber. The candles on the bottom were fully lit with electric lights. It was one of the most elaborate death traps the show had." Batman and Robin escaped using their "Experimental Heel-and-Toe Bat-Rockets." As the rockets "ignited," the stunt doubles were pulled up and away.

Krizman gave Alfred a bicycle that the faithful butler christened "my Alfcycle" for "The Joker's Provokers." It had two-way Alfradio between the handlebars, and he adjusted the Batmobile's radio so they could communicate.

Opposite, main: Victor Paul (Robin stunt double) and Adam West on steps leading to top of cake. Sequence was filmed January 10, 1967 on Stage 16, same sound stage used for the Batcave, as evidenced by rock formations visible at right.

Opposite, bottom left: Rehearsing the sequence where Experimental Heel-and-Toe Bat-Rockets launch the Caked Crusaders skyward. Hubie Kerns and Victor Paul (Batman and Robin stunt doubles) are suspended over Riddler's trap.

Opposite, bottom middle: Nick Carey (Special Effects) hands script pages to Adam West and Burt Ward.

Opposite, bottom right: As an elevator slowly lowers Adam West and Burt Ward into the giant cake, they appear to be sinking into quicksand.

It appeared again in "Come Back, Shame," while in "The Catwoman Goeth," Alfred was seen cleaning the cycle in the Batcave. In that same episode, he also used it to give Batman a ride when the Caped Crusader's Batmobile was stolen. In "The Joker's Epitaph," Alfred can be seen holding the Alfcycle for a split second as the Batmobile pulls away at the end of Scene 159. Alan Napier was to ride away on the cycle, but it collapsed under him. The Alfcycle never appeared again.

WITH CAMEOS & INVITED GUESTS BATMAN PICKED FROM HOLLYWOOD'S BEST

"[Dozier] seemed to know everyone who was anyone in a tough town full of talent. And he knew how to creatively mix that talent in order to get the best results. Eli Wallach as Mr. Freeze, Shelley Winters as Ma Parker, or for example, Roddy McDowall as Bookworm."

Adam West, 2015 email interview with Bob Garcia

 Casting director Michael McLean remembered that they tried to accommodate all the actors who wanted to appear on the show. "It was the 'in' thing at the time," said McLean, "and everyone wanted to be a part of it. There was no way we could use them all, which is why we invented the Batclimbs." The Batclimb came straight from comic books and appeared in the first TV episode. Batman himself referred to Batclimbing in episode forty-eight "The Yegg Foes in Gotham." A total of thirty-three climbs were accomplished in some manner during the series, including variations such as a Robinclimb ("Give 'Em the Axe"), Alfred's Batclimb ("The Joker's Epitaph") and a solo by Batman ("King Tut's Coup"), but most were by Batman and Robin together. There were more Batclimbs made without encountering anyone, but it was those fourteen surprise guests who flung open the window that viewers remember the best.

After the first window cameo by Jerry Lewis during a Batclimb in "The Bookworm Turns," the bit became a

staple during the second season. Only two Batclimbs were used during the third season, neither with guests at the window.

There was an air of secrecy about the whole thing. Hair stylist Kathryn Blondell remembered that they were never told beforehand who they would be working on. Wigs or costumes would come down from the 20th Century lot to Desilu-Culver, and the crew would just have to prep whoever showed up.

Not all cameos were done with a Batclimb. In episode "The Cat's Meow/The Bat's Kow Tow," the operator of Mr. Oceanbring's Salon For Men was portrayed by Jay Sebring. "He was a famous hairdresser," recalled Charles FitzSimons. "He had his own salon and was very expensive. And he was a friend of Bruce Lee's." Among the stylist's star clients: Bill Dozier, Stanley Ralph Ross, Milton Berle, Bobby Darin and Frank Sinatra. At the time, a Sebring original ran $50 with subsequent trims at $26.

Cyril Lord, The Carpet King, earned a cameo in "The Duo Defy," supposedly because he had sold Bill Dozier

Above: Faithful butler Alfred made his own Batclimb (or rather, "Alfclimb") in Ep#82.

some Persian rugs. These sequences usually were written on a short deadline. "I would have to come up with stuff that ran twenty-two seconds or so," recalled Stanley Ralph Ross. "They would call me up and say, 'Stanley, we've got so-and-so coming in tomorrow.' Sometimes I wrote it on the set. More often than not, I had a day. That was all decided by Bill Dozier and Howie Horwitz and it was all personal friends and stuff. People were waiting in line to do it. Everyone wanted to be on the show."

Batclimbs certainly took care of those actors who wanted to appear on *Batman* but didn't have time to do more than that.

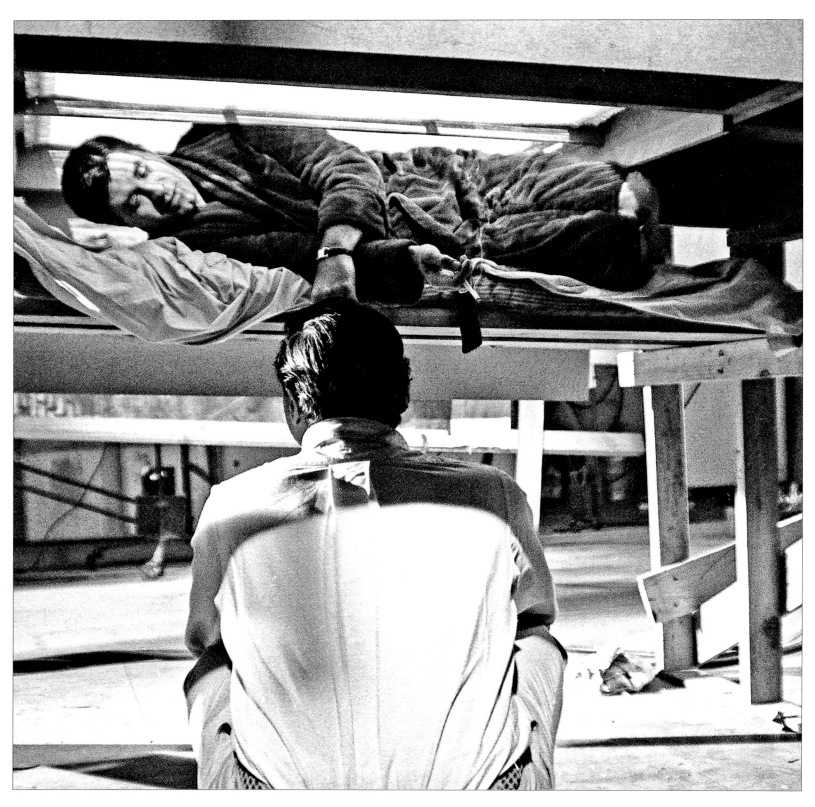

Above: The first Batclimb with a guest cameo, from Ep#29, used a different cityscape background than those seen in future Batclimbs. In this episode, the Dynamic Duo used a bazooka and grappling hook because the building walls were too high for a Batarang toss.

Right: Burt Ward and Adam West practice dialogue and Batclimbing in this rehearsal from Ep#39.

Left Page: During this Batclimb rehearsal for Ep#29, Jerry Lewis reclines on a platform, waiting for cue to open the window and greet Gotham City's wall-climbers.

Sammy Davis Jr. visits Gotham City

Below: Andy Devine (Santa Claus), with Burt Ward and Adam West working on the Batclimb for Ep#66. When first broadcast, his episode aired three days before Christmas on December 22, 1966.

GUEST STARS RECALL THEIR BEST MOMENTS OVERALL

Left: Julie Newmar in disguise as well-known wealthy recluse, octogenarian Miss Minerva Matthews in Ep#38.

Below: Julie Newmar's Catwoman, disguised here in Ep#63 as Edna Klutz from the Duncan Dance Studios, gives Dick Grayson the free dance lesson he won.

"The fun things were the show's extraordinary requirements of me," recalled Julie Newmar about her role in "The Cat and the Fiddle" as an octogenarian. "Being glamorous is easy. I can get up and put the makeup on. It takes time to do it, but I'm facile at it. But [acting at] being eighty-years old, when you're thirty-something, that's a different challenge. That took work. It took observation. It took time. When you are [acting] eighty years old, I noticed at the time, I could do things I couldn't do as a pretty woman. You could be more aggressive. So it's wonderful to play something you're not. Every actor likes to indulge in this manner. It's a form of patting themselves on the back.

"I played the dance teacher that comes into Wayne Manor," said Newmar recalling "The Cat's Meow." "That was fun, because I got to go to wardrobe and ask for a dress that makes me look like a school teacher from 1910. Then, since my feet are size 8, I asked for shoes that were size 11, something so big that it makes me look clumsy when I walk. Then my hair was tied back in

a knot. And thick, thick, thick glasses, so he wouldn't see my eyes. And finally being very bossy dealing with Burt Ward. It was great fun. I was taking giant steps, and stepping all over him. Trying to manhandle that little boy as a school teacher. The challenges are the things that made it fun."

Dozier decided to call in Vincent Price for "An Egg Grows in Gotham/The Yegg Foes in Gotham" as the illustrious villain Egghead. "They were shows that were very much on the tip of everyone's tongue," said Price. "Everybody was talking about *Batman*. Everybody wanted to be in them. I was delighted when they called and asked me to do it... [The villains] were nasty, but funny... I was just sort of starting my villainous career at that point. It was a good idea to make fun of it. I think my villains have sort of remained [popular], because I spent the rest of my time making fun of them."

Price was delighted when he heard Edward Everett Horton would be co-starring as Chief Screaming Chicken. "One of the people I always wanted to work with all my life,

Batman and Chief Screaming Chicken

Above: Edward Everett Horton (Chief Screaming Chicken) and Adam West (Batman) exchange a "traditional Mochican greeting" in Ep#47
Right: Vincent Price (Egghead) schemes with Chief Screaming Chicken.

was Edward Everett Horton," recalled Price. "I loved him. He was such a great actor. He was very old at that point in time, and very quiet, but very sweet with that wonderful funny face... I just loved working with him."

Writer Stanley Ralph Ross's script described Egghead's hide-out as "a fantastic place" including "a half-egg-shell-shaped chaise lounge," egg-shaped desks, egg-shaped mobiles hanging from the ceiling and "a painting of an egg on the wall." Art director Serge Krizman attacked his mission with gusto, designing a lair where Egghead could hatch his schemes. "I had a marvelous time with Egghead's headquarters, with its seven-foot-long half-egg couch. It was almost contemporary art," said Krizman.

"He was brilliant," Price observed regarding Krizman.

"His sets were marvelous and he too had a sense of humor... In my apartment, all the furniture was hard-boiled eggs cut in half. The painting on the wall was bacon and eggs. For all the world, it looked like the most modern picture you ever saw in your life. It was so inventive."

Because Egghead was original to the show, there was no comic-book reference to work from, and everything had to be created by the production staff. "The most marvelous thing was, there was nothing to go on," said Krizman. "Not much background at all, so I did what I did."

Jan Kemp had to develop Egghead almost from scratch, although Ross's script did describe a man with an egg-shaped bald head, white tropical suit and a yellow vest. "First of all, they said they were going to use Vincent Price," said Kemp. "I had to figure out how I would do an 'Egg-head.' So with [the] effects department, we came up with idea of the skull. Then I started to think about what I should do with that. It finally came to my mind that I would use this white-colored costume with yolk trim in silk, and make it much like a tuxedo. So we would preserve the kind of feeling of an egg as a body. We discussed this with Vincent and he was very pleased with the idea. So I went ahead and started making up the designs, getting the pattern together, and getting the materials together to have the suit done. Three suits actually. It was a very high collar on the shirt. I had the shirtmaker make the shirt with a special collar. I used a satin for the cravat, which was fluffed up with some chiffon under it. The vest was much the same as the silk.

We had enough contrast in the suit [to show against the set]. I was lucky I found a fabric that had the right color so there was no question of dyes fading."

The Egghead design included an oversize bald cap for Price to wear. "He had a full bald head and a piece underneath the cap to make his head look more elongated, more egg-shaped," said makeup supervisor Bruce Hutchinson. "The first time we did the Egghead on Vincent Price, he came in after we finished for the day, and we said, 'Okay let's take this thing off.' So we spent twenty minutes to a half hour gently removing this bald cap, which was glued down. And the next day, he came in and said, 'This is really boring. I hate this.' He reached back and ripped the thing off his head. From that day forward that was the only way he would take it off. He said it was like taking a band-aid off a little bit at a time. You just have to rip it off. We would put a new cap on him every day. I would loosen the back by his nape, and he would just take hold of it and pull forward with both hands and it would come right off. His hair was all matted down. [The appliance] was just a piece of plastic; it was like wearing Saran Wrap on your head all day."

"They had to put a vent on the back of the makeup so I wouldn't sweat," remembered Price. "I had to wear that all day long, and in a television show, you work ALL day. I'd get there at 7 a.m.. It took a long time to get on."

"Actually, we left a little bit of it not glued down and the perspiration would drain out of the back of his neck," said Hutchinson. "He wore a very high collar which was designed by wardrobe which kept the nape of the neck

Left: (From left) Vincent Price (Egghead), Gail Hire (Executive Secretary Miss Bacon) and Edward Everett Horton (Chief Screaming Chicken) tally up some ill-gotten gains.

Above: Liberace portrayed two roles in Ep#49–50: Chandell (aka Fingers) and his twin brother, Harry.

Right: From Ep#50: Liberace (Chandell) and James Millhollin (Alfred Slye) are tied up and on their way to being perforated into human player piano music rolls, while Sivi Aberg (Mimi) watches.

area pretty well concealed, so you couldn't really see much of that."

Kemp came up with the idea to drain the sweat away from Price. "I shouldn't be telling you this," said Kemp. "I don't want to spoil the illusion. Vincent and I always wanted to preserve the idea that he was a cool, very hard-headed Egghead, [but] we had a tube running down from the vent into a little bag/pocket in the costume. There wasn't much room in that costume. He was wearing a dress suit which was quite form-fitting."

Even with the prosthetic, Price enjoyed making that Egghead episode with director George Waggner. "He was very good... There was lots of action, and it's always difficult to do action quickly. The camera can't get it or [someone] wants to improve it."

Price became close to Jan Kemp during the show's run. "During the time we were working on this, his wife and my wife were both expecting," said Kemp. "We became and remained very close friends. Sometime later, he was in New York doing a Broadway play... He sent me a clipping and attached was a note saying he felt he had been remarkably well taken care of, but never more so than by the costume department, particularly

Jan Kemp who he said was 'My personal Pierre Cardin.' I thought that was a very nice compliment."

"Liberace's manager called us and we wrote a show for him where he played two parts," recalled associate producer Bill D'Angelo. "The day he arrived, he had laryngitis. We told him to mouth the dialogue. But he was on every page of the script, because he had two parts. We just shot it and looped it later."

Liberace's role in *Batman* turned out to be a wonderful event for costume designer/wardrobe head Jan Kemp. "I went to his home in Hollywood," said Kemp. "His manservant took me on a tour of the Liberace wardrobe, a series of ante rooms off a circular staircase where, stored in glass-fronted cases, hung all his fabulous jeweled stage costumes. After I had selected the costumes he would wear in the show as the pianist, because part of the play was that he was this fabulous concert pianist like himself, Liberace joined me for tea in his living room which was filled with crystal glass pieces, many of his trademark candelabra, in one corner his glass grand piano, in another a Wurlitzer organ. We made plans for him to come to the studio the following morning for a fitting as the role of his twin brother Harry... Having just

Bruce Hutchinson applies more makeup

seen all his superbly jeweled garments hanging in such profusion, I felt awkward about this fitting. He came down and I got him a selection of yuck, cheap, gangster-type mohair suits. He put them on, and he was ecstatic. There he was preening and turning in front of the mirrors, and he said an emphatic remark I'll always remember: 'I do so like dressing up!' I thought to myself, 'This is more like dressing down.'"

"Liberace was so kind," said dialogue coach Milton Stark. "During lunch periods he would sit at the piano and say, 'What do you want me to play?' They'd ask anything. He'd play it for them. He was very congenial, very, very nice and a real professional."

"Otto Preminger called me one day from New York," William Dozier remembered. "In the middle of the night," added Dozier's wife, Ann Rutherford. Dozier continued, "He said, 'Bill! I must do *Batman*. I can't go home. My kids won't let me come home if I don't.' So I said, 'Otto, you come on out and we'll do one.' So he did [and I] paid him the same as everybody else." Preminger became the second man to portray Mr. Freeze after George Sanders.

The first Mr. Freeze costume, worn by George Sanders, had a helmet with microphones in it to capture his voice. But echoes in the helmet forced them to go back and loop dialogue, increasing post-production costs. Jan Kemp eliminated the problem by redesigning the costume. "When we came up with Preminger," said Kemp, "what we did was take away the helmet and give him a collar

Top left: Otto Preminger (Mr. Freeze) poses with his Freeze Gun.

Bottom right: Dee Hartford (Miss Iceland) and Otto Preminger (Mr. Freeze) in between scenes.

that has little jets to blow the ice-cold air around him. In fact, I think we made a point in the script about this, that he was wearing this device that kept him cool. We could see his face and see his character and everything and wouldn't have the problem with dialogue."

For "The Puzzles Are Coming/The Duo is Slumming," Fred De Gorter's script actually began as a Riddler vehicle entitled "A Penny for your Riddles/They're Worth a Lot More!" His first draft, dated April 22, 1966, was probably intended as an early second season episode. Frank Gorshin

did not return to reprise his role, so De Gorter rewrote the script for a new villain, Mr. Conundrum. A revised final draft of "The Conundrums are Coming/The Duo is Slumming" was dated September 27, 1966. Later, the script was modified for another new character, the Puzzler (also the name of a Superman villain in the comic books), hence the final title. In the comic-book texts, Riddler had also been referred to as the Conundrum Champion, the King of Conundrums and the Prince of Puzzlers.

Below: Maurice Evans (the Puzzler), wearing his "perfect garb for flying the Retsoor" jet, offers a puzzle to Batman while on the phone with the Caped Crusader.

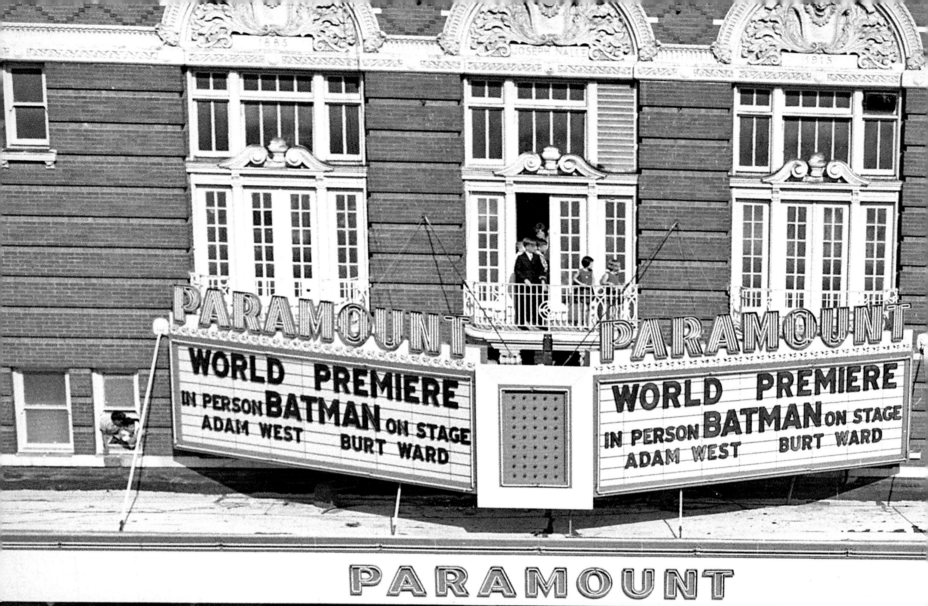

STUNTMEN KERNS & PAUL DARE TO MAKE STUNTS THAT REALLY SCARE

"Batman was a tough show to do. You were restricted because you had a lot of kids in the audience. You couldn't do anything that was too dangerous. It had to be cute."

Victor Paul (Robin stunt double, stunt choreographer), 1993 interview with Bob Garcia

Hubie Kerns and Victor Paul were the two veteran Hollywood stuntmen doubling for Adam West and Burt Ward. Luckily, neither had any qualms about wearing tights. Paul worked for years in swashbucklers where tights were *de rigueur*. Kerns had sweated through sword and sandal epics like *Samson and Delilah* and *Spartacus* wearing a lot less. In this case, it was just a Batsuit. *Batman*'s unit production manager Sam Strangis, who knew the pair from his own days as a stuntman, brought them in to meet director Bob Butler on the pilot. After that, Strangis kept them on for the series.

In addition to doubling for the Dynamic Duo, they were responsible for choreographing the show's fights. "Sam knew we understood how to save time," said Paul. "When you're shooting a half-hour show you have to move. He gave us a free hand, and the directors never gave us any static. They didn't have time to tell us how to shoot it. They were happy to see what we had."

Kerns and Paul also hired the stunt crew. They had been around the business since 1948, and knew most everyone. "We went through almost every stuntman in Hollywood," said Paul. "We had certain guys we loved calling back because it was like bread and butter. We'd have some regulars, because they knew our style. Other guys who didn't get our style, we wouldn't ask back because it took so long to catch on with what we were doing."

Charlie Picerni was one of the stunt regulars who worked on *Batman* beginning with the pilot. He had met Paul on *The Untouchables*. "I was good friends with Victor and when he started *Batman*, he would call me on practically every show," he said. "Hubie and Victor were acting as [what would now be called] stunt coordinators. Previous to those years, there really weren't stunt coordinators. There were assistant directors who would lay everything out. But on *Batman*, there were so many fights, they used Hubie and Victor."

On the days when fights were scheduled, Kerns and

Paul usually came in at 6.00 a.m. to look over the new set to determine how the fight was going to be done. After they blocked out the action, they would meet with the episode's director and discuss how to shoot the fight. Then they would talk to art director Serge Krizman and give him a list of things to make as breakaways, walls to reinforce, or whatever they needed to make the fight dynamic and destructive. Krizman would inform them of what special props had been built for the week's episode.

"We went through so much balsa wood," said Paul, "they must have cut a couple of trees down just for us alone. We used the same tabletops for every fight though. Instead of building brand-new tables for each fight, we built tops out of real wood, and then we'd have balsa wood legs. So after we'd crash into the top of the table, we'd just put another set of legs on it. We did the same for the chairs. For the next fight we'd just paint the table and chairs a different color. It saved a lot of money and time that way."

Picerni remembered the daily routine well: "There were so many stunt guys in the fights, we would come in the morning," he said, "and we would rehearse first. The director would come in during rehearsal and make any changes, but they weren't that involved. Then we did the fight. There would be a master shot with two or three cameras, and then we shot coverage." The master shot and shooting coverage took about an hour. They included the principals in as many close-ups as they could to save time. The fights were shot around 9.00 a.m. or first thing in the afternoon. Kerns remembered they tried to work with the stuntmen as early as they could to save the production on overtime costs.

"While I was preparing for the day," Adam West said, "my stunt double, Hubie Kerns Sr., would be rehearsing his *cour de ballet* for the next big fight scene. Later I would join him to synchronize our moves so that when we shot the required battle I wouldn't be too badly injured. Hubie and his crew knew all the tricks of their dangerous work."

Previous: Stuntmen Victor Paul (Robin stunt double) and Hubie Kerns (Batman stunt double) speed down a Gotham street—actually a highway in southern California—in the Batcycle.

Left: Hubie Kerns and Victor Paul walk into the Archer's net trap in Ep#35. Four grips held ropes out of camera range, and at the precise moment, the entire net was quickly pulled upwards, trapping the Dynamic Duo in the middle.

Top left: From an Ep#47 fight rehearsal with stuntmen Victor Paul (Robin), Pete Kellett (Benedict) and Hubie Kerns (Batman).

Top right: Left to right from Ep#80: Chuck Couch (the Riddler stunt double), Hubie Kerns (Batman stunt double), Chuck Bail (Down stunt double), Victor Paul (Robin stunt double), Vince Deadrick (Across stunt double, back to camera).

Kerns remembered one particular day when things didn't go as smoothly as usual. "We came in one morning to plan the fight in the afternoon, and they're painting the floor," he said in a 1993 interview with Bob Garcia. "There's nothing on the set. They're just putting up the walls, and Sam Strangis says to us: 'The fight is the first thing we're going to do.' Victor and I looked at each other and we were mad. We took great pride in our work, and we needed plenty of time to work things out. So we asked Sam why, and he told us they don't have the cast yet. They can't do what they were going to do, so they had to film the fight. While we waited for them to finish painting the floor, we tried to figure out what we were going to do. The moment we were dressed, we had to go in there and shoot it. I hate to say it, but that fight with all that pressure was one of our best fights.

"Now after that," Kerns continued, "they sent us down to Stage 3 and told us to look over the set and figure out the fight for tomorrow. So we were sitting around, and we had all the other stunt guys with us. We're joking and taking ideas of what each stuntman wanted to do, and generally having a good time, when all of a sudden, in come the grips pushing the camera. I yelled, 'What are you guys doing here?' They told me that they were going to do the fight next. I said, 'You can't,' and they said 'Well, we're going to.' Those two fights, that we didn't get to prepare for, were two of our ten best fights."

Paul went to the dailies of the fight sequences to see what looked good on screen and if any stuntmen needed to be called back for extra coverage. The extra work on his part was particularly helpful during the first season. The production was hard pressed to meet deadlines, finding it difficult to jump into a twice-weekly show schedule immediately after shooting the pilot. "First season, we had a six-day schedule but we went eight, nine, or ten days," said Kerns. "Very seldom did we ever finish in six. We had lots and lots of golden hours. The long hours would end up with us shooting at night. So while we ran into night, we hardly ever planned night shoots." One crewman even named the boat he bought after the first season, "Golden Hours."

"Hubie and I got along like brothers," said Adam West. "We had to. I wanted to stay alive and not be ingested by a giant man-eating clam or tiger." The tiger was particularly dangerous for Kerns in the Catwoman episode "Better Luck Next Time."

In a 1993 interview with Bob Garcia Victor Paul remembered it as a frightening stunt. "The tiger was supposed to come out of the room and attack Batman," Paul said. "But the tiger was around all day. We started at seven in the morning, and we didn't get around to this shot until eight at night. So they opened up the door to the tiger's room, and they couldn't get this tiger to come out. It was tired or scared or whatever it was. Someone got the brainstorm to hang some meat next to Hubie's leg, so when it smelled the meat, it'd attack Hubie.

"Hubie took out his 'Bat Claws' from his Utility Belt and climbed the wall," Paul continued. "He was on a cable. So when he began to climb, I turned to the special-effects guys and told them: 'This is one time, you suckers better pull him out fast. When this tiger comes out, they better start pulling, because Hubie can't see

in his mask.' I looked down, and saw that tiger coming and it leapt at the meat and missed Hubie's leg by mere inches. It banged into the wall and dropped back. Hubie asked me [afterward]: 'What did it look like?' I told him, 'It looked like that if it hit you, it would've killed you.'"

Kerns had to wear an alternate version of the infamous Batman cowl, which afforded both West and Kerns little ability to see, particularly up and down. Costume designer/wardrobe manager Jan Kemp discussed the difference between the two cowls. "We did have to

Below: The Ep#20 sequence with Catwoman's ferocious Batman-eating tiger was assembled from a carefully edited series of shots with Adam West in close-ups, stuntman Hubie Kerns, and an animal trainer, whose white mustache can briefly be glimpsed several times.

make more modifications on his than Adam's," he said, "because for the stuff the stuntman had to do, he needed more vision. The modifications were only minor in regard to eye slit openings and a better opening for the nostrils." Which was to say that Kerns still had huge blind spots in his field of vision.

Paul remembered the only drawback to his costume was that it was so skintight there was no way he could hide any elbow or kneepads. "I had more burnt elbows and knees than anybody you'd ever seen," he said. "I'd

drop down from a chandelier or whatever and skin my knees and elbows."

While Kerns was principal stunt driver of the Batmobile, Batcycles, and Batboat (at low speed; he was not an expert in the water), he occasionally turned the costume over to other stunt specialists. For Batcopter scenes and the Batboat's high-speed scenes, professional pilots were hired. Each of whom were dressed as Batman. In "The Puzzles are Coming/The Duo is Slumming," the Puzzler lashed Batman and Robin inside the basket of

Left: Battle of the stuntmen: as Pete Kellett (Benedict) and Al Wyatt (Egghead) subdue Victor Paul (Robin), Hubie Kerns (Batman) swings across on an egg mobile to rescue the Boy Wonder.

Top right: Stuntman Al Wyatt (Egghead) is about to heave a piece of egg-shaped furniture onto Hubie Kerns (Batman stunt double), who has just smacked Dick Crockett (Foo Yung stunt double) in Ep#47.

VICTOR PAUL: ACTING STUNT COORDINATOR
STUNT DOUBLE FOR ROBIN

Victor Paul (1927-2011) had a long and illustrious career in motion pictures. He was a champion swordsman and was in a number of great swashbucklers: *The Buccaneer* (1958, uncredited); *Blackbeard the Pirate* (1952, uncredited); *Swashbuckler* (1976); and *The Prisoner of Zenda* (1979, uncredited). Whenever Maureen O'Hara was in a swordfight, she requested Victor Paul as her opponent, because she knew how conscientious he would be to take care of her. He was also Tony Curtis' preferred opponent. Beginning in 1959, Paul added television shows to his credits including *Tales from the Crypt* (1990), *When Things Were Rotten* (1975), *Monster Squad* (1976) and *Star Trek* (1988). He continued working as a stuntman on feature films including *Dirty Harry* (1971, uncredited), *Diamonds are Forever* (1971, uncredited), *Conquest of the Planet of the Apes* (1972, uncredited), *Battle for the Planet of the Apes* (1973, uncredited), *The Blues Brothers* (1980) and *The Rocketeer*. He served as stunt coordinator on *Zorro, The Gay Blade* (1981), *Mobsters* (1991) (co-coordinating sixty-five stuntmen) and *Don Juan de Marco* (1994). Paul was a Lifetime member of the Stuntmen's Association of Motion Pictures and an inductee into the Hollywood Stuntmen's Hall of Fame.

BATCOMPUTER OUTPUT END . . .

Opposite: Stunt doubles Victor Paul (Robin) and Hubert Kerns (Batman) in a very early costume test shot, possibly taken prior to Ep#3–4.

Below: Charles Picerni (left, stuntman) with Paul Picerni (right, Brown). Although Charlie did not appear in Ep#83–84, he did visit his brother on the set long enough to clown around for several photographs.

a hot-air balloon, set to automatically release when the altimeter reached 20,000 feet. To handle the balloon, they hired the owner and dressed him as Batman.

It proved to be a very harrowing day for Paul. "Again, I'm always up there with the real guy, and Hubie's down below smiling," he lamented. "I'm in the balloon over by Santa Monica with this guy Jay who owned it. I'm up a hundred and fifty, two hundred feet. The prop guys are holding on to this rope while we're up in this balloon, and Jay starts hollering, 'Don't let that rope go!' to the prop guys. I asked him what he was doing, and he says,

'Y'know it's windy today. If they let that rope go, I don't know where we'd end up if we got loose.' I asked him why didn't he tell me that *before* we got up here. So I start yelling to Hubie to pull me down. When we get on the ground, I tell Hubie this guy was telling me if we get loose we'd end up in China. Hubie was just laughing."

Paul pointed out that as Robin, he was often the one hanging upside down, dangling over tiger pits, bouncing along in the Batboat, going up in balloons, or any number of relatively dangerous stunts while Kerns would be on the sideline enjoying every moment. Kerns delighted in Victor Paul's relative torment, and teased him from the very first episode, when they did a stunt drive in the Batmobile. Hubie didn't tell his friend he was an expert driver, and put the old car through some hair-raising turns and spins, much to Paul's chagrin.

"We did a lot of wild and goofy things on *Batman*," said Paul. "We worked around horses, speedboats, motorcycles, you name it. We did it." It was all part of being a Super Hero. They both remember lots of laughter on the set and agreed it was one of the best experiences they ever had as stuntmen. "I loved the work," said Kerns. "I loved the crew. I loved the people. I loved Adam. I loved the whole group. We were one big happy family."

9749-118

9749-119

HUBIE KERNS: ACTING STUNT COORDINATOR
STUNT DOUBLE FOR ADAM WEST

Hubie Kerns (1920-1999) was a collegiate track star. He left USC in 1948 and did stunt work on *Take Me Out to the Ball Game* (1949) and later that same year *Samson and Delilah* (1949). He continued in such movies as *Jim Thorpe—All American* (1951), *The Ten Commandments* (1956, uncredited), *Spartacus* (1960, uncredited), *The Buccaneer* (1958, uncredited), and *Voyage to the Bottom of the Sea* (1964, uncredited). From the 1950s through the 1960s, he worked on TV shows including *Star Trek* (1968), *The Rebel* (1960-1961), *Cimarron Strip* (1968) and *Ironside* (1967). He also took small acting jobs in roles that required physical action. After 1967, he went back to the movies doing stunts for *Conquest of the Planet of the Apes* (1972), *Battle for the Planet of the Apes* (1973), *The Long Goodbye* (1973, uncredited), *The Great Smokey Roadblock* (1977), *52 Pick-Up* (1986) and others. His daughter went into stunt work but had a fire accident on *Airwolf* (1984-1986) and left the industry. His son, Hubie Kerns Jr., became an accomplished stuntman, stunt coordinator, stunt driver and swimmer.

BATCOMPUTER OUTPUT END . . .

FIGHTING CRIME ON LAND, SEA & AIR, BATMAN BRINGS BATCYCLE & MORE TO BEAR

"As an actor, I had the Batcycle, Batboat, Batcopter and the world's most famous car, the Batmobile, at my disposal. Who wouldn't like to portray Batman with those treasures?"

Adam West, 2015 email interview with Bob Garcia

While the Batmobile was the show's biggest attraction, Greenway gave *Batman* an arsenal of vehicles with an eye toward further licensing. In an April 26, 1966 letter to Lou Mindling at the Licensing Corporation of America, Dozier listed television and feature film "props" with licensing potential. The first three items on that list were the Batboat, Batcopter and Batcycle (with separating go-cart) all three of which had appeared in the comics in some form.

The original Batcycle was a rented black 1965 Electra Glide Harley-Davidson with a full sidecar. Fox's prop department created a special scalloped windshield trimmed in red, and painted a small Batman emblem on the sidecar and another on the sidecar fender. It was only used in Episodes #21 and #22, "The Penguin Goes Straight" and 'Not Yet He Ain't.' An April 12, 1966 note from FitzSimons to Fox's director of business affairs Emmet G. Lavery Jr. explained the first Batcycle had "been under continuous rental at $50.00 per week so that it could be used as set dressing in the Batcave and be called upon for use at any time. The deal permitted purchase at any time for $2,500.00 – but rent did not apply against the purchase."

Mechanic Dan Dempski (who would later act under the stage name Dan Magiera) and customizer Richard "Korky" Korke partnered up as Kustomotive and rented an old auto dealership in Burbank to create the Batcycle, though they had yet to receive any permission to do so.

"One day, I was with a friend of mine who raced for Yamaha," said Dempski. "We went down to pick up some parts for his racing motorcycle. When we got there, I asked someone where the advertising department was. I went in and said, 'I want to build the Batcycle.' He looked at me and said, 'That's a good idea, but I don't know who you are.' Luckily enough, I had just written an article for *Motorcyclist* magazine, and they verified who I was. He turned to me and said, 'What color would you like?' I was blown away." At the time he had no connection to the show itself.

Top left: The Batcycle was first seen in Ep#21, being used as Batcave set dressing.
Top right: Burgess Meredith (Penguin) poses for publicity pictures in this setup.
Middle row left: Burt Ward and Adam West are shown "riding" a stationary cycle in this rear projection scene.
Middle row center and right: Batman and Robin first drove the Harley-Davidson Batcycle in Ep#22.

Something's a bit fishy here...

Batcycle number 1,
black 1965 Electra Glide Harley-Davidson

This spread: There are hundreds of reproduction Batmobiles on the road, and possibly dozens of Batcycles and a few Batboats. Since there were only four original Batcycles (one on screen, three that toured), fans have created their own replicas. This reproduction was from the collection of Batman fan Al Wiseman. It's built around a Yamaha Catalina 250 like the originals, and is patterned on the touring cycles done by Dempski and Korkes. The fairing (a shell placed over the frame of some motorcycles), the cart, the back fin and the front wheel cover have the red trim that was absent from the screen-used Batcycle. The Bat insignia on the reproduction fairing is too small and neither it nor the bat on the sidecar have the "face" and "claw" lines that the originals had. The touring car sidecars also had a white outline around their bat insignia. The "S" image on this sidecar is too small, too skinny and doesn't reach as far back as the original touring bikes.

The construction of the sidecar is very different than the original motorcycles (touring or the screen-used) with one pipe at the top of the rear, whereas the touring bikes had none, and the screen-used sidecar had three. The construction of the padding and the handlebars on the non-operational go-cart is different than the originals. The light in the sidecar light post is also different. The control box on the ledge over the handlebars has two rows of lights; the originals had one. Though it's not an original Batcycle, it's certainly clever enough to appeal to any fan.

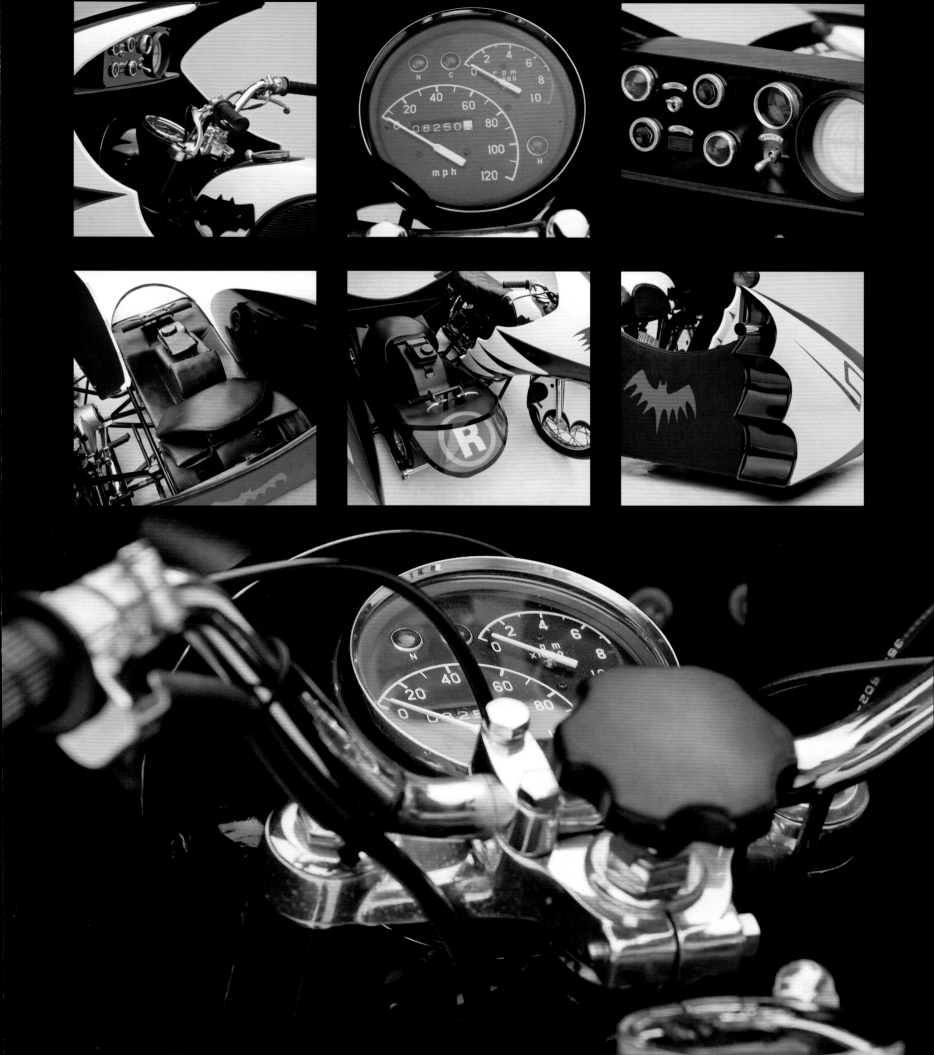

The next day, the company delivered a black Yamaha Catalina 250 to Dempski's home. Before beginning construction, he called his friend Tom Daniel, *Rod & Custom* magazine's famous designer-columnist ("Off the Sketchpad"). Dempski needed a sketch of what he had in mind to pitch the bike to the Filon company for materials. Filon was a fiberglass sheet with integrated nylon generally used for corrugated panels of carports and translucent ceiling panels. Korkes and Dempski used it to build their own handmade front fairing assembly (the part with the scallops on it) and the sidecar. The cycle's long, low Plexiglas® windshield was specially molded and custom blown.

Dempski and Korkes added the sidecar-platform that held Robin's go-cart. Korkes had also received the go-cart free from Yamaha. He narrowed it to fit in the sidecar and altered the carburetor. "The go-cart was built with a 50cc Yamaha electric-start, three-speed engine," said Dempski. "It had a lawnmower-size gas tank and would probably last for ten or fifteen miles. It was a small engine, but would probably go in excess of 50 mph."

While the two were customizing the motorcycle, Dempski acted as the contact man with Greenway and kept calling Charles FitzSimons, who refused to discuss it. Eventually, FitzSimons told him they already had commissioned a cycle. "Well, it's the wrong one," he told him. "You have to see this one first, because if you use that one, you're not going to be happy with it." After a week or so, FitzSimons gave in and met with Dempski and Korkes.

When it was finished, they drove it to the studio. "We pulled our motorcycle onto the lot and showed it to Charles," said Dempski. "He loved it and called [series art director] Serge Krizman, who took one look at it and said, 'This is a Batcycle.'" Before it went into use, Krizman wanted a few modifications. They added a front fender on the bike and a red light at the rear of the sidecar.

Kustomotive signed a contract with Greenway/20th Century Fox and the Batcycle was delivered on April 18, 1966.

Top left: Burt Ward (Robin) and Adam West (Batman) riding the Batcycle on the studio lot.
Top center: Victor Paul (Robin stunt double) and Adam West (Batman) await instructions for the next scene. In background are grips and prop men along with an electrical truck.
Top far right: Rear view of Batcycle built for use in movie and TV series.
Right: Filming the Batcycle at the Van Nuys Airport with Victor Paul and Adam West.

Designer Tom Daniel recalled the delivery day: "My short 'ride' on the Batcycle," said Daniel, "was from the showroom of [the former auto dealership] through a double-door and on outside. The width of the Batcycle with the wide sidecar/go-cart setup made for a very tight clearance. Well, I managed to slightly crease the sidecar wheel fairing on the right doorjamb. The Batcycle was scheduled to be delivered to the studio that day. Fortunately, the crease was popped out and the delivery made."

Dempski and Korkes needed to teach stuntmen Hubie Kerns and Victor Paul how to operate the motorcycle and sidecar. "We as greenhorns would have to [drive] that [cycle] the first thing next morning," said Kerns But we had absolutely no trouble with it."

"When I took the Batcycle down to the studio to demonstrate it," said Korkes, "I was driving the bike and Danny was driving the cart. He's there in a kneeling position, hands between his legs gripping the controls. It had two grips like a motorcycle. He came out of the sidecar and into the parking lot. Then he punched it full throttle, and Danny went flying through the air."

Stuntman Paul explained his problems with the go-cart: "I had to be on my hands and knees [on the go-cart] and they built this platform [attached to] a regular motorcycle. Hubie wasn't that big of a bike man at that time. He drove a motorcycle, but this weirdo thing was different. If Hubie was doing thirty-five I had to really rev [the go-cart] up and gun it to shoot off this platform going the same direction, and that was hard to do."

Designer Daniel remembered the go-cart very well. "Before the machine was fully completed," he said, "I recall Dempski testing the go-cart on the streets of Burbank. Korky may have been on the bike. As I recall, launching the go-cart from the Batcycle sidecar platform – while at speed – was akin to a kamikaze mission."

Almost immediately, FitzSimons started to receive calls about exhibiting the motorcycle. Since the production had gone through this before with the Batmobile, there was already a stipulation in the contract for touring bikes to be made. "After we built one," said Dempski, "[FitzSimons] called and told me that people were calling. They wanted to rent it. So I called Yamaha and told them we need to build more."

Dempski and Korkes didn't have enough Filon to make all the cycles needed, so they contacted the Filon

Corporation again. "It was a relatively small company, so I called this guy up and said, 'Look, we just built Batman's motorcycle out of Filon,'" Dempski said. "'You built it out of Filon? Come on down! Bring a truck down and we'll give you all the Filon you need.'" They were given enough material to build three additional Batcycles and the trailers to haul them.

The screen cycle stayed in the Desilu-Culver transportation garage and the others toured the United States and Canada. Richard Korkes spent two years on tour. The touring Batcycles were very different from the original. The original sidecar's lightning bolt-like motif was turned into a red stylized "S" design. A white "Batface" and highlights were painted onto the red Bat-emblem at the front of the cycles. The go-carts were motorless props. The sidecars' rear-ends did not have the three huge "exhaust" pipes on the side.

Batgirl needed a Batcycle of her own for a 1967 presentation film, an unaired episode made to showcase the character to the ABC executives and introduce her to the series. Yamaha lent a motorcycle to Greenway and Fox to be customized by Kustomotive.

Fox ultimately purchased a red Bonanza 180 model with an electric starter and turned it over to Kustomotive. Before it was delivered on set, someone told Yvonne Craig that she would not be riding the one used in the Batgirl presentation film, but an all-new cycle: "When they said, 'You'll be riding this darling motorcycle, and it'll have this vanity mirror on the front, and it'll have these big Batwings on the front and a bow on the back and it'll look really frilly,' I said, 'Great,' not knowing that in order to customize it in that manner you'd have to take the shocks off. Every time you went over a pebble it was like jumping off a table stiff-legged."

The cycle did have an automatic starter. "[It] was a godsend," said Craig. "All you had to do was punch this button and your bike started. It was great. But they gave me a bike that was really too big for me. Anytime I would get it a little off of its center of gravity, I would have to drop it and pick it up, because I couldn't wrestle back up to a straight-up position. So I used to drop it and kick it and do mean things to it."

On January 23, 1968, Charles FitzSimons wrote to the Fox Prop Department with instructions to return all *Batman* vehicles to their owners. The Batgirl Cycle went back to Kustomotive.

The movie script called for a Batcopter, something

the television series budget would not allow. The costs could be easily assumed into the film's budget, with the added bonus of the producers having stock footage on hand for years to come. "I went to Bell Helicopters in Van Nuys, to see if it could be done," remembered Krizman. "They said they didn't see anything that would be impossible, but they had to get the FAA's approval on flying it. So I designed it and Fox had blueprints made up."

National Helicopter Service provided the 47G-3B-1 Bell helicopter with the FAA Number: N3079G. The retrofit included two Batwings, each twelve feet long with tubular framing made of canvas. Pilot Harry Hauss shed some light on the job: "John Ortega and I flew the Batcopter," he said. "John passed away many years ago. One day John was Batman and I was Robin, and the next day we'd change... I was Batman, etc. The chief of maintenance at NHS was Tom Palmer who made the wings and the phony exhaust stacks, etc. I flew the ship for the FAA examiner at National's facility at Van Nuys airport. The ship performed normally in all respects except when coming to a hover for a landing, at which time with rotor downwash beating on the wings it took a

little more power than normal, nothing critical."

Stuntman Paul was teamed up with pilot John Ortega to do the shots of Robin climbing down the rope ladder to aid Batman, while the copter hovered. It was shot off the California coast, near Marineland of the Pacific on the Palos Verdes Peninsula. "[That] was one of the nightmare shots," Paul explained. "We were in this helicopter about 500 feet over the ocean. It was cold as hell there. There was a regular chopper pilot. I'm on the outside with a forty-foot rope ladder, rolled up in a bundle. I'm hanging on the sled on the outside of the bubble. Then all of a sudden the chopper pilot on the camera chopper gives me the signal to drop the rope ladder. So when I dropped the ladder, that thing went practically straight back. Now I have to climb down very steadily this rope ladder, and hang upside down [to save Batman]. Hubie [Kerns] hung on the bottom of the ladder and I hung above him and we jazzed around in front of a camera boat."

Kerns remembered the scene well, not for anything that happened while it was being filmed, but for what happened afterward. "I was out there on a rope the first time for forty-five minutes over the ocean, then again for fifteen minutes," said Kerns. "I was exhausted. When

Below: The first Batgirl Cycle, shown here, was returned to Yamaha in late February 1967. A different model was used to construct the permanent cycle for the series.

we got back, there were thousands of people. That was the tourist season, and they saw us out there as Batman. When the helicopter landed and I went to the dressing room, you wouldn't believe the mob. When I came back out of there in my own clothes, they stepped aside and let me through and waited for Batman."

NockAir Helicopter Inc. bought the copter in 1996 and restored it sans wings. The company exhibits it at state fairs, air shows, comic conventions, etc.

On January 31, 1966, less than three weeks after *Batman* premiered, C. E. Parson, Manager of Public Relations for Glastron Boat Company, followed up his January 27 phone call to Fox's Public Relations Manager Robert Lee with a letter proposing that the boat company construct a Batboat for *Batman*.

Parson enclosed a possible design based on their Crestflite V-174 Super Sport. The Austin, Texas-based company was experiencing healthy growth at the time, having significantly

Left: So that's how they did it! Batgirl's cycle was firmly locked down and immobilized, but the wheels could spin freely on rollers as the rear-projected background raced past, helping create the illusion of racing along Gotham City's streets. A large fan made Batgirl's hair and cape flow.

Below: Yvonne Craig in front of Gotham City Plaza, an outdoor location used frequently throughout the series.

expanded their plant and added a 45,000 square foot warehouse the previous year. Charles FitzSimons replied on February 4. Greenway was definitely interested and laid out the general terms of a deal.

Glastron employee Mel Whitley made a trip to Los Angeles to meet with FitzSimons and Dozier and brought sketches for the Batboat. Some changes were asked for and Whitley went back to Texas. A second set of sketches, along with vinyl, upholstery and paint samples, were sent to Greenway on March 18. In a March 23 letter, FitzSimons detailed some of the decisions made between department heads at Fox, and suggestions by Serge Krizman:

"...our art director felt that if the tail could have a less symmetrical and more 'ragged' formation in its "Bat-scallops" it might be more visually exciting. Also he felt that if the rear decking could be extended six to ten inches on each side it would enhance the overall design. He believed that if it were possible for you to make a single bubble-type windshield whose center flared back with converging sides to join or almost join the tail, that a sensation of speed and motion would result. He also felt that a streak of flame on the side oval with a forward design would add to the feeling of movement, while also helping to overcome our color problem. He also felt that the "Bat-Eyes" could be given more "character" by placing them less rectangularly."

While the bubble-type windshield was not implemented, other Fox/Greenway requests were met: the Batboat's final scallops were not symmetrical, the flames were painted on the side ovals, and the "Bat-Eyes" angled back. The color problem referred to filming a blue boat in blue water. There was some debate over what color the boat's hull would be to keep it visually separate from the water. At the time of the March 23 letter, the department heads at Fox wanted silver-grey ovals below the deck.

It took thirty-one days for Glastron founder Robert Hammond and Whitley to supervise the final build. Contractors Tony Bell (co-creator of Underground comix character Wonder Wart-Hog) and Rob Robertson actually built the boat, though they had some help from Glastron employees. An illuminated bat-symbol was added to the tail fin. The fin itself made the stern very heavy, which added to the lift from the boat's Aqua-Lift Deep-V design, and it initially caused the builders a bit of trouble. The boat itself was a seventeen-foot ten-inch long powerboat finished in "Bat-Blue and Silver-Gray" with red trim, a beam (width) of seventy-four inches, and a height of seventy-two inches. It weighed 2,000 lbs. Its 150-horsepower MerCruiser Chevrolet V-6 engine brought the boat to a top speed of 40 mph. They installed a water jet on the back to make the boat seem as atomic powered as the Batmobile.

"That thing went like a bat out of hell, something like forty miles per hour on the water," said Krizman. "It wasn't undercranked at all. That was its actual speed." Jim McIlwain, a Glastron-sponsored marathon driver, was the speedboat pilot. He was a co-owner of Anaheim Marine, a Glastron dealership. It took three days to shoot the footage off of Long Beach.

"Hubie and Ward did the close-up shots, but the heavy

Top left: The Batcopter: a reconfigured Bell helicopter from National Helicopter Service.

Top right: Victor Paul (Robin stunt double) and ground crewman (white suit) watch as Adam West races from Batcycle to Batcopter. These sequences were filmed at the Van Nuys Airport.

Below: The Batcopter had two canvas Batwings, each twelve feet long, made with tubular framing.

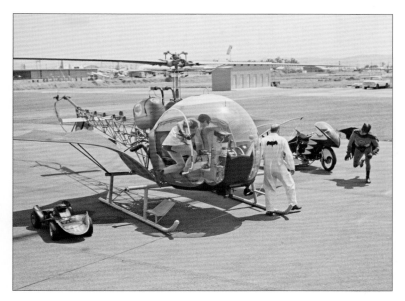

speedboat chases out on the ocean and the long shots were done by the speedboat guy and me," remembered Victor Paul. "This guy almost killed me. We were going about forty miles an hour, and we never did hit water. We were in the air most of the time. It would jar your teeth loose." Aerial photography specialist Nelson Tyler filmed the boat bouncing along the waves from a helicopter using a special rig.

The Batboat was used in the feature film and footage was seen in Episodes #36 and #68: "Walk the Straight and Narrow" and "The Catwoman Goeth." It was kept at the 20th Century Fox prop department and returned in late January 1968 through a local Glastron boat distributor in Culver City.

Opposite, top: Launching the Batboat, as seen in Ep#36. In this sequence, stuntmen Hubie Kerns and Victor Paul are onboard.

Opposite, bottom: The Batboat, piloted by Hubie Kerns (Batman stunt double), with Burt Ward port side holding the "Batzooka."

BATGIRL MAKES COMICS DEBUT, THEN TO TV IN LUMINOUS PURPLE HUE

In June of 1966, National Periodical Publications' (NPP) *Batman* editor Julius Schwartz had Gardner Fox write the story "The Million Dollar Debut of Batgirl!" for *Detective Comics*. Carmine Infantino penciled the story, designing her Batcycle and iconic costume, and Sid Greene inked it. "There wasn't much of a design to draw," said Infantino modestly. "We took

the Batman costume and just adapted it to her." About five months later, *Detective Comics* 359 would be on sale (November 29) with a cover date of January 1967.

Dozier received a proof of the story from Lou Mindling at Licensing Corporation of America around October 11, 1966, which began a series of discussions with Allen Ducovny, VP of Television at NPP. Dozier immediately wanted to know if Batgirl was a permanent addition to the comics (which she was, and enjoys a healthy life at DC Comics even today). Though Dozier did point out in a letter, "Of course, we could put her into the show and keep her there without her staying in the comic books, but we would like to know what your plans are in that direction." Ducovny happened to be in Los Angeles at the time and asked for a meeting with Dozier, which was the beginning of bringing Batgirl to the show. In the next two months, a deal was struck, and Dozier had a script written for a presentation film.

Producer Horwitz invited Yvonne Craig to come in. She had appeared in a number of roles over the years in his *77 Sunset Strip*. "It was really easy, and I don't know whether it should have been or not," she said. "My agent called and said, 'Would you be interested in doing Batgirl on the *Batman* series.' I said, 'Sure.' I went out and talked to Mr. Dozier and Howie Horwitz. I had worked for [both of] them before, because they had done tons of work. They knew I had been a ballet dancer. They knew my work. They simply said, 'We are introducing a new character to appeal to pre-pubescent females and males over forty. She's called Batgirl, and she'll be a good guy and she'll kind of help Batman and Robin, but they won't know who she is. Would you be interested?' I said 'Sure.'"

Pat Barto began working on Craig's costume in December, getting garments to modify from Warner Slimwear-Lingerie. "My costume was very strange," Craig said in a 1993 interview with Bob Garcia. "The first time I put it on, it was made of an almost girdle fabric. So it was not really as thick as neoprene, but was somewhat constricting depending on the cut. And those were in the days of bullet bras, those old pointy things. So Pat cut it on the bias and it was quite comfortable and looked good."

Right: From circa December 1966, Costume Designer Pat Barto's color sketch for Batgirl, based on the character's costume from *Detective Comics* 359.

Below: Pre-production concept paintings by Leslie Thomas, used as a guide during meetings and for set builders. Batgirl's secret lair was not realized precisely as depicted here, although the circular entrance to a secret freight elevator where the Batgirl Cycle was stored appears to be a perfect match.

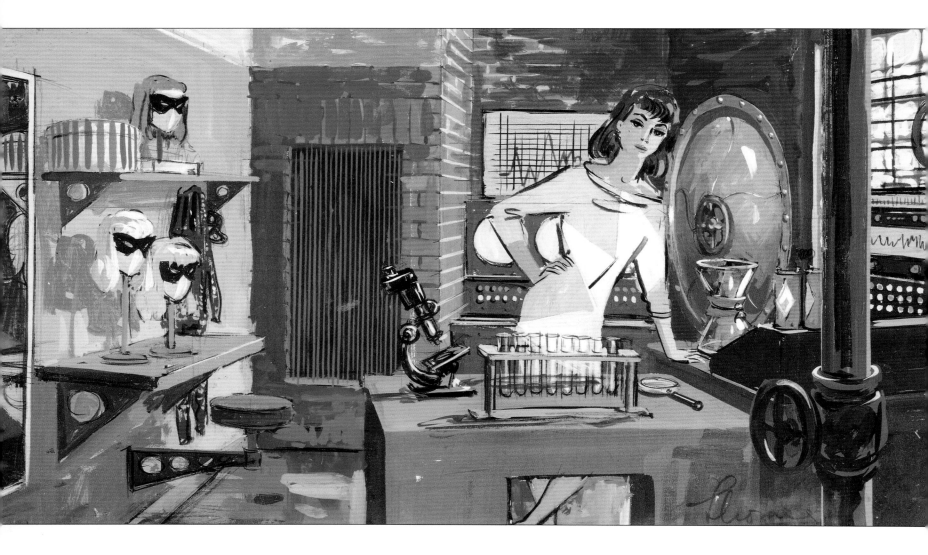

Barto changed Infantino's costume design. His had a red weapons bag on Batgirl's yellow weapons belt, a black costume, a yellow bat chest emblem, gloves and boots, a blue cape, and a blue cowl with v-shaped wedges below the eyes. Barto's version didn't have the weapons bag (though it did appear on her original sketch) and the costume, boots and gloves became violet and blue, while the yellow bat, yellow belt, and pointy cowl design remained the same. Barto also had Richard Korkes at Kustomotive add some of the glittery metallic flakes from Craig's Batcycle to the outside of her boots. He dropped the flakes into a shoebox, sprayed the boots with a contact adhesive and just shook them in the box.

"[The presentation film's] pointy mask was [used] because they thought it looked bat-like," said Craig. "But it turned out that it left dents in my cheek. We realized if we were going to do the show where I would be making quick changes from Batgirl to Barbara Gordon, we wouldn't have time to wait for my cheeks to blow up again."

The script entitled "Presentation of Batgirl" was sent to Ducovny at National in December 1966 for approval. The company approved both the script and the casting of Yvonne Craig as Batgirl on January 17. Final revisions to the script were completed two days before the project was filmed on January 26.

William Self and Dozier flew to New York on February 8 to show the presentation film to VP of network programming Len Goldberg at ABC. They also met with ABC president Thomas Moore to discuss the direction of the series. Dozier must have been confident that Batgirl was a lock, because before leaving for New York, he and Horwitz had a teaser for the character added to the script of "Batman's Waterloo" with revised pages dated February 3. It was a simple bit of dialogue for Commissioner Gordon; "I'm worried about my daughter, Barbara. Well, as Bruce Wayne knows, she's away at college. She'll be graduating shortly and I'd hate to think that some of the dire happenings, which have happened to that fine professor of Egyptology, could also happen to my beloved daughter at her school." Press releases about the character began appearing in April, 1967.

Opposite top far left: Yvonne Craig (Barbara Gordon) with Adam West (Bruce Wayne) at the Gotham City Library.

Below far left: Yvonne Craig and Burgess Meredith (the Penguin) rehearse Ep#95 scene inside the elevator at Batgirl's mid-town apartment house.

Below middle: Yvonne Craig (Batgirl) rehearses a fight with Victor Paul (Robin stunt double) and Roydon Clark (Henchman #3) from Ep#95.

Below right: Typically seen from the front, this view of the opposite side of Batgirl's cowl shows how it fit over her titian wig. Yvonne Craig discusses entering the warehouse at 12 Bannister Street with Alan Napier in this scene from Ep#102.

1) At the Gotham City Library, Tim Herbert (Killer Moth) grabs Yvonne Craig (Barbara Gordon) and locks her up in the Librarian's Lounge, allowing the Mothmen to carry out their plan to kidnap millionaire Roger Montrose. From left: Joey Tata (Mothman #1), Al Wyatt (Mothman #3), Guy Way (Mothman #2) with Murray Roman (Roger Montrose) seated.

The prop for Killer Moth's instant paralyzing cocoon is lowered onto Burt Ward

In the Librarian's Lounge, Craig flips her hat into a cowl as she finishes the costume change to Batgirl.

From left: Sam Bishop (Key Grip), Bruce Hutchinson (Makeup) and Craig in between takes.

Al Bettcher (Camera Operator) films the fight from "*Presentation of Batgirl*."

BRUCE LEE PAID THE SET A VISIT, SHOWED WARD HIS FIGHTING SPIRIT

"The real kick though, was watching Bruce Lee, who was a marvel."

Adam West, *Back to the Batcave*

Late in production of *Batman*'s second season, a crossover with one of Greenway Production's other shows, *The Green Hornet*, brought one of the greatest action stars of all time, Bruce Lee, to the set. Hollywood hair-stylist Jay Sebring had introduced William Dozier to Lee, and the producer jumped at the chance to get him a television show. In 1965, Dozier commissioned Lorenzo Semple Jr. to write a proposal for a spinoff of the Charlie Chan mysteries. The show would have had the martial artist playing Chan's Number One Son, now a butt-kicking Secret Service agent.

Number One Son didn't sell, but Dozier was contacted by *The Green Hornet* owner George Trendle to do a show, and in September 1965, while *Batman* was still in pre-production, the papers were signed between the two parties. When *Batman* proved to be a huge hit, ABC became very interested in *The Green Hornet* as a follow-up, and ordered the series in March of 1966. Dozier cast Lee as Kato.

Dozier's assistant Charles FitzSimons remembered that "[Lee's] kung fu was too fast for the camera. You wouldn't see his arms or legs move. You'd see them in the fixed position, and then they were back in that fixed position before you could see it. We actually had to ask Bruce to slow down his movements so we could film." The two became friends over the years. "He knew that he was the best," said FitzSimons. "There was nobody as good as he was. He was incredible. His body was like marble."

Dozier used *Batman* to promote the Green Hornet and Kato to the national television audience. There was a press conference with Van Williams, Bruce Lee and Adam West, promoting the new show. The Green Hornet and Kato also appeared in a Batclimb in "The Spell of Tut" which aired just before the Green Hornet's fourth episode. The quick scene ended with Robin asking his partner, "Gosh, Batman, what are they dressed like that for?"

Dozier ordered a two-part episode for *Batman* co-starring this new team of heroes, the first Super Hero crossover on television. "A Piece of the Action" and

Opposite, bottom: Bruce Lee (Kato), Van Williams (Green Hornet), Adam West (Batman) and Burt Ward (Robin) discuss the visiting crimefighters' escape from Colonel Gumm's Enlarged Perforation and Coiling Machine in Ep#86. As budgets tightened, complex devices such as this were almost completely eliminated from the show during season three.

Below: Batmobile meets Black Beauty in this publicity picture taken in Gotham City Plaza. Burt Ward, Adam West, Van Williams (Green Hornet) and Bruce Lee (Kato).

"Batman's Satisfaction" was shot in the last week of January/first week of February 1967, and aired March of 1967. The filming turned out to be a blast for the cast and the crew. While the two shows were being produced by Greenway and shared the directors Murray Golden, Larry Peerce, Norman Foster, Leslie Martinson and George Waggner, they had been shot on different lots without much interaction.

The first day of filming was a custom car enthusiast's dream. Both of television's most popular tricked-out automobiles were together on the set of *Batman*. The Batmobile and the Green Hornet's Black Beauty were brought together to do some work on the 40 Acres backlot (location of many Gotham City street scenes). They then "posed" for pictures. The resulting publicity photos have been fan favorites for years.

The main attraction became the fight between Robin and Kato. After months of hearing how good Bruce Lee was, the crew was stoked to see him in action. Lee was friends with Burt Ward and had a trick up his sleeve. The day of the fight, Lee glowered at Ward all day long. Some crew members, in on the joke, told Ward that Lee had heard he was bragging about what a hot-shot martial artist he was, and had decided to teach the Boy Wonder a lesson. Ward got really nervous. Lee prepared for the fight still glaring at him. Finally, just before filming the scene, Lee couldn't contain himself any longer, he jumped back from the fight position, stuck his tongue out at Burt and laughed. He just couldn't resist psyching out his friend. The crew found the whole thing hilarious.

ADDING HIGH HEELS & KICKS TO STUNTS LONG FIXED

"The hardest stunt for me on *Batman* was to run down stairs in that cowl."

Hubie Kerns, Adam West's stunt double and stunt coordinator, 1993 interview with Bob Garcia

Stuntman Paul choreographed Yvonne's fights. He was slighter than Kerns and his action style was more appropriate to someone of Yvonne's build. "I had some dancing background prior to this and she was a dancer," said Paul. "I used to lay out stuff for her that would mix in with our stuff. If you notice, she was always doing a pirouette or kicking a guy and a backhand and we'd pick her up, and we would leap and she would kick two or three guys with both feet.

"I used to put her on top of a table or pedestal," he continued, "and have the villains come to her instead of her going to the villains. I would dream up stuff where I would grab her by the waist and throw her to Hubie, and as she went through the air she'd kick a guy. It was a ballet or adagio [a slow, graceful ballet style] fight."

Craig handled her own motorcycle, though there was one minor incident in "The Ogg Couple." Craig remembered a scene with Price on her cycle that went wrong. "Vincent Price was supposed to ride on the back

of my Batcycle, and I said [to him], 'Oh God, I've never ridden anybody on the back of this thing, and it's heavy enough as it is. So all I can tell you, Vincent, that if it looks like I'm going to lose it, just jump clear.' He said, 'I'm so tall that I could stand up and you could ride it out from under me.' So I thought, that's okay, that's fine. We came roaring into a scene and slammed on the brakes. He's supposed to jump off the bike, run around in front of it. We did it and it looked good.

"The director said the boom mic was in the shot, and normally we would have blown those out, but they said, 'You want to do it again, and try to come in faster this time.' So I came flying in faster the second time, and he jumped off and ran around to the front, and I guess the cycle was still getting gas because it lurched and ran over Vincent's instep. He jumped clear, and it ran over him again. I finally flooded it out, and he straight-armed it, and we stopped it. He was a very good sport about it." He told her that if he had known the scene was going that way, he would have played it as a matador, with a

Above: Batgirl swings into action.

Opposite: From Ep#112. Batgirl is outside of the Perfume Factory, figuring out how to proceed.

loud shout of "Olé!"

Craig had an excellent stunt double, Audrey Saunders. She and her brothers were part of a famous stunt team, The Six DeWaynes, and she herself was inducted into the Stuntmen's Hall of Fame.

Kerns remembered when Saunders clipped him in "The Entrancing Dr. Cassandra" during the fight scene. "The three of us together were fighting these invisible people," said Kerns, "and she had on these spiked heels.

We turn around for the grand finale and as the fight ended, her metal heel got caught in my shin. I'm gritting my teeth, until they yelled, 'Cut!' Then I ran around back, and let out a god-awful yell. Oh man, did that hurt!"

"We all got whacked," said Eddie Hice, Gorshin's stunt double and an occasional henchman, "but with all of the good rehearsals that Hubie and Victor did, we got our scratches, we got our bumps working out routines, but nothing ever serious."

SEASON THREE HAD BEGUN, IT WAS BATMAN'S FINAL RUN

"Burgess always was on a brilliant level with his Penguin character. If you look at season one, two or three, you'll see his character, more than any other, was always the same. That's the true test of a great actor."

Adam West, 2015 email interview with Bob Garcia

The first thirteen episodes of the season would be filmed between July 5 and September 1, 1967. By contrast, on July 5, 1966, the company had completed four half-hour shows and was beginning the third pair. There were three Penguin episodes shot back to back, three Egghead episodes shot back to back, three Londinium episodes, and single episodes for Riddler, Siren, Tut, and Louie the Lilac.

Unit production manager Strangis stepped out from behind the desk to direct. "In the third season I directed [nine] episodes," said Strangis "But it was hard. I had to do both jobs as director and unit manager. I ran it from the stage. [I did it so] I could prove to the other directors we could do it and do it on schedule, because we were running late hours... You can tell people that it's possible to do it on budget, and they say, 'Fine, you say that, but you do it.' If you can, you have a better fight with them."

"Enter Batgirl, Exit Penguin" is one of Yvonne Craig's favorite episodes. "[The Penguin] steals me and is going to marry me so he can do dastardly deeds," she said. "If

he's one of the family, he feels nobody is going to arrest him. As a concept it was my favorite show." And she got to work with one of her favorite actors. "[Burgess] loved doing the Penguin, he had such fun with that."

At the very beginning of "Enter Batgirl, Exit Penguin," Batman had a strange bit of dialogue: "Well, we've managed to clip Catwoman's claws once again. She won't be troubling Gotham City for a long while." It was a June 19 script revision, possibly to leave a romantic opening for Batgirl, an idea that went back to at least January where Dozier intended "to develop a strong romantic interest working both ways between Batman and Batgirl." Such a romance would be problematic considering how Catwoman had been romantically scripted during the second season.

The next Penguin episode, "The Sport of Penguins," began shooting on July 10 with July 11 spent at Los Alamitos Race Track. This episode guest-starred Ethel Merman who asked to be a guest on the series in February. As Lola Lasagne, she teamed up with the Penguin to fix

a race. "Fox didn't think we could do a horse race in a day, but we did," said Strangis. "I used to own horses and race horses, so I knew the owner of the Los Alamitos Race Track and I arranged for us to shoot out there. We surprised them and did all that shooting in a day."

Some of the necessities for that day away from the studio included: two buses, a twelve and a fouteen-passenger stretch-out, one sound truck, a station wagon, a five-unit honey wagon, three walkie-talkies and a bullhorn, 120 hot lunches, ten gallons of coffee, eight dozen donuts, three picture horses with three doubles and two outrider horses.

Craig was pushing to ride one of the racehorses. When they arrived early in the morning at the track, they brought the horse out and invited Craig to give it a try.

Bottom left: Donna Hall (Batgirl riding double) chats with Chloy Cunnington (the Penguin riding double).

Bottom middle: Donna Hall works her way around the track on Waynebeau.

Bottom right: Donna Hall mounts Waynebeau with assistance from wrangler.

Batman and Robin to the rescue

Top right: With Commissioner Gordon a caged prisoner at Olga's hideout, Batman and Robin peek out from inside the huge Brass Samovar of Genghis Khan in this pre-production concept painting for Ep#102 by Leslie Thomas.

"Racehorses are nuts," recalled Craig. "They're so hyper. They're crazy in the morning. And this little thing that you sit on is like a spool of thread... I took a look at this horse that they were having absolute horrors trying to control and I thought 'Are you crazy?'" Horse expert Donna Hall ended up as the riding double for Craig that day. Hall, like Saunders, was an inductee into the Stuntmen's Hall of Fame, and both were founding members of the Stuntwomen's Association of Motion Pictures.

Anne Baxter returned to the show, not as Zelda the Great, but as Olga, Queen of the Bessarovian Cossacks in "The Ogg and I/How to Hatch a Dinosaur" Baxter had a blast learning to swear in Russian. Baxter was teamed with Vincent Price as Egghead. "Anne and Vinnie were marvelous," recalled Strangis, "You wished you could do a regular TV series with those two, they were so good."

Vincent Price was delighted to be co-starring with Baxter. "I knew Anne for a long time," explained Price in a 1993 interview with Bob Garcia. "I had done a couple of movies with her (*The Eve of St. Mark* and *A Royal Scandal*), I knew her very well, but she had retired from the movies and gone to live in Australia."

All three Egghead episodes were directed by Oscar Rudolph filmed as a three-parter from July 17-31. The footage was edited into a two-parter: "The Ogg and I/

How to Hatch a Dinosaur" which aired in early November and a stand-alone episode "The Ogg Couple" which aired on December 21. Yvonne Craig loved Price. "Any day that I worked with Vincent Price was especially wonderful," she said. "He was bright and witty and erudite. I always looked forward to the day he was to be in."

Frank Gorshin returned August 1, 1967 for three days of filming on "Ring Around the Riddler," which introduced Joan Collins as the beautiful Siren. It had been over a year since Gorshin had donned the green and purple gear of the Riddler. The episode had an unforgettable scene of skinny Gorshin wearing his classic leotard under boxing trunks, facing down heavyweight Jerry "The Bellflower Bomber" Quarry in the ring. "Jerry Quarry was in his bathrobe," recalled Craig. "I asked if he was a heavyweight, because I hadn't seen him box. He said, 'Yes,' and I said, 'You don't look big enough.' He said 'When I take off my bathrobe I look bigger.' I walked away and decided not to pursue it."

"It was great to see Frank (Gorshin) back," said Adam West. "He always brought such energy to the set. I recall after one scene with Joan Collins, he did a fantastic impression of her then-current husband, Anthony Newley. [Gorshin] was always spot on. He was a huge talent."

Writer Stanley Ralph Ross, who developed Archer, King Tut, Dr. Cassandra, Cabala, Shame and Calamity

Jan, created the Siren for Joan Collins. "They said, 'We have other guys who can do the comic characters,'" Ross recalled. "'We need you for originals.' So that's why I kept coming up with originals. My favorite original after the Archer, was Shame. I had opera singers named Leonora Sotto Voce and Fortissimo Fra Diavolo. You know, that's the way you cook lobster. Those are just funny names that I would make up."

"Louie, the Lilac" was the "hippy episode" of *Batman* with the lingo, hippies, flower children, music and an opening "flower-in" segment. Who should star as the special guest villain in such a psychedelic landscape but Milton "Uncle Miltie" Berle. It was a surreal bit of casting that reflected the inherent goofiness of 1940s and 1950s television and movie stars cast as villains. Adam West had also appeared on *The Hollywood Palace* and *The Milton Berle Show* during the past year, so this may also

have been Berle returning a favor. "That was a difficult shoot," said Strangis. "We were out in Fox's Rancho Park and almost a thousand kids and adults came crowding around to see Batman and Uncle Miltie. Miltie was quite a ham. He went out and told jokes and signed autographs." They managed to leave Rancho Park at 3 p.m., and return to Stage 16 at Desilu-Culver for more filming.

Cesar Romero returned as the Joker on October 16 with a day at Torrance Beach to film "Surf's Up! Joker's Under!" Cast and crew boarded buses for the forty-five-minute trip from the studio to Via Riviera and Paseo de la Playa streets in Redondo Beach. The day before had been the hottest day of the year in the Los Angeles area.

On October 20, while "The Funny Feline Felonies/The Joke's on Catwoman" was filming and Bill Self was in Europe, Dozier sent a letter to ABC's top execs Moore and Goldberg. The last of the seventeen-episode order was scheduled to

Above: Batman and Robin trapped by the larcenous Louie the Lilac.

Opposite: Batman meets the Riddler in a rigged boxing match.

finish filming October 31. With no word from ABC, Dozier warned that shutting down on October 31, and then having to wait until November 3 before starting to prepare for "Louie's Lethal Lilac Time," could ultimately delay shooting by another ten days. Dozier requested a decision regarding pickup: "Assuming it is your intention to renew, then you could help us a very great deal if we could have word to that effect on Monday or Tuesday."

Dozier must have been devastated by the reply he received the next day: "Renewal of *Batman* extremely doubtful. If you must have answer now it would be negative. Will advise you of conclusion as soon as possible." Filming did end Tuesday, October 31 and without a renewal from ABC, everyone had to be ready for a possible cancellation.

A week later ABC did exercise their option on November 7 for nine additional episodes. Greenway must have been ready to go, because filming began the next day and except for a Thanksgiving break, production went on uninterrupted to the end of the season.

THE FINAL NINE EPS FINISH STRONG, BEFORE CAST & CREW SAY "SO LONG"

"I wanted a show that was fun. That was fun to do and that would be fun to see. And it was great fun to do it. Getting these special villains and villainesses was great fun... Watching them do the show was fun. The anticipation they all had before they did it – they enjoyed doing it, all of them. And it shows in their performances."

Interview with William Dozier, by Kevin Burns

Milton Berle returned to the *Batman* set November 8 as Louie the Lilac in "Louie's Lethal Lilac Time," the first filmed of those last nine episodes. This time the script kept things mostly indoors, far away from any madding crowds.

In "The Joker's Flying Saucer," a time bomb hidden in the Batmobile by one of the Joker's pals exploded in the Batcave (of course the Dynamic Duo survived). To make it look convincing, there was quite a mess, but episodes 114 to 117 as well as 119 and 120 remained to be filmed, so everything had to be cleaned up. The bomb "explosion" was filmed Monday, November 20 and the crew then had about nine days to return the Batcave to its former glory, although time off for Thanksgiving had to be factored in. The next Batcave scenes, with everything back in order, were filmed November 29 for "Penguin's Clean Sweep." This episode was shot over three days by Oscar Rudolph, from November 27–30. In a brilliant lapse of super-villain logic, the Penguin contaminated millions of dollars with a virus to get people to throw away the bills. He vacuums the money up only to find that he can't spend it.

In "The Entrancing Dr. Cassandra," Ida Lupino and Howard Duff starred as Dr. Cassandra and her husband Cabala – an interesting pairing as the couple had been married in real life, but separated in 1966. Lupino had a stunning career as an actress and director, and was the second woman to enter the Directors Guild. Duff was starring as Det. Sgt. Sam Stone on ABC's *Felony Squad*. Lupino once told a method actor, "Darling, we have a three-day schedule. There's no time to do anything, but to *do* it."

The episode sported a gimmick that would have made former *Batman* comic-book editor Jack Schiff proud. Stanley Ralph Ross centered this episode around a supremely silly science fiction idea. "I'd written a weapon," said Ross, "where the characters zap Batman and Robin and took the third dimension out of them and made them into cardboard cutouts. I wanted to name the weapon something interesting so I called it the Ronald-ray gun. They said no. At the time he was our governor.

Right: Pre-production concept painting by Leslie Thomas, used as a guide during meetings and to help prop builders and set decorators visualize the script. This image blocks out the foyer and corridor of Minerva's Mineral Spa. Minerva was played by Zsa Zsa Gabor in "Minerva, Mayhem and Millionaires."

So I changed it to the Alvino-ray gun. Now you gotta know Alvino Rey was an old-time band leader from the 40s. And, you know, [only] four people who played with Tommy Dorsey laughed, but I laughed."

On December 5, the first day of "The Great Escape/The Great Train Robbery," Cliff Robertson hurt his back during a fight rehearsal. Yet Robertson worked for all of his scheduled five days on this six-day shoot.

"I'll Be A Mummy's Uncle" had King Tut blast a mineshaft and unwittingly discover the Batcave, much to his delight. Sam Strangis directed this December 13–15. Episode scribe Ross loved writing King Tut. "Victor Buono could make me laugh with anything he said. I could write delicious eight-syllable words for him and he could always speak them well. Since he was supposed to be a professor of Egyptology, I would refer to these arcane Egyptian phrases."

"One of my favorite King Tut episodes," said West, "was when Tut breaks through the Batcave wall figuring out Bruce Wayne is Batman. Most of that scene was ad-

libbed by Victor. He was such a fantastic actor, who had great fun doing his Tut role."

Lorenzo Semple Jr. suggested Zsa Zsa Gabor back in November of 1965 when he decided to rewrite the part of The Great Carnado as Zelda the Great. Gabor missed out on being Marsha, Queen of Diamonds in the second season when she became ill, but she finally appeared on the last episode "Minerva, Mayhem and Millionaires."

On December 18 they began filming and the next day they revised the script so Dozier and Horwitz could have one final cameo. Both were specifically named in the script but not in the dialogue. Their scenes were filmed on Stage 3, December 20, the final day of filming. Oscar Rudolph, the series' most prolific director, was able to wrap it all up. The show's two stars were dismissed before the final scenes. West went back to his dressing room to gather his things and decided to pack up his Batsuit to take home. The episode aired March 14. ABC had decided not to broadcast any repeats, thus marking an end to Batman's network television run.

Below: Reoccurring villian King Tut, played by Victor Buono.

CULVER CITY SAYS GOODBYE
BATMAN GOES OUT ON A HIGH

"[We'll] go into syndication, and I expect *Batman* will go on playing forever... and there will be a whole new generation of kids coming along who will have never seen the show."
William Dozier in an *Omaha World-Herald* interview by Bob Thomas, February 3, 1968

ABC cancelled *Batman* on January 17, 1968. It was reported in *Daily Variety* January 18 and subsequently in other publications.

Once the cancellation was official, Fox moved quickly to syndicate the series and had twenty-nine markets signed up by July 15, including Boston, Chicago, Denver, Detroit-Windsor, Los Angeles, New York, Philadelphia and San Francisco. A Miami station began broadcasting the shows in April, while most others began in September. Episodes often ran during late afternoons, with some larger independent stations using it in the former timeslot of 7.30 p.m. but five days a week. By June of 1969, Fox was syndicating the series in fifty-five markets.

On January 22, 1968 Dozier sent a letter to Adam West, in which he wrote: "Now that our mutual friend, BATMAN, has apparently hung up his network gloves, I simply want to tell you how much I admire and respect your highly professional approach to your task throughout the many months of production, and thank you for your contribution to the show's success. The atmosphere was often heady and conditions frequently tense, but you handled yourself like a gentleman and a professional from start to finish."

Lorenzo Semple Jr. wrote to William Dozier on January 18, 1968. The letter itself contains the last bit of Batman dialogue ever written by the screenwriter:

> L O R E N Z O   S E M P L E ,   J R.
> 765 KINGMAN AVENUE
> SANTA MONICA 90402
>
> January 18, 1968
>
> Dear Bill:
>
> Heard today that our old Bat has finally been shot down, and that the famous shadow will no longer strike terror into the hearts of criminals throughout the realm.
>
> It has been a long time (or so seems) since you handed me that comic-book in the garden of the Ritz in Madrid, and we plotted our capers with aid of the good Marques de Riscal. (Aristocratic all the way, our project, despite those cigar-smoking syndicate thugs in yr suite at H. House!)
>
> Has been a wonderful ride, which I will remember fondly to my grave, & I thank you for everything most profoundly and sincerely.
>
> BATMAN
> The end of an era, Robin.
>
> ROBIN
> Reminds me of a poem I learnt in school today, Batman. "All, all of a piece/Our chase had a beast in view./ Our wars were all for nought/Our lovers were all untrue./ 'Tis well the old age is out/ 'Tis time to begin a new."
>
> BATMAN
> No, Robin, no! Not those words of the great John Dryden. Far better the sentiment of old Rabbi Ben Ezra, as passed down to us by Mr. Browning... "Grow old along with me, the best is yet to come."
>
> ROBIN
> Gosh, Batman, when you put it that way... Wow! Let's go!!
>
> luv toujours,
>
> Lorenzo

AN INSPIRATION TO MODERN WRITERS AND MOVIE-PRODUCING FIGHTERS

"It was a comic strip come to life, literally. It was a very clever show."

Bob Kane, 1992 Interview with Bob Garcia

 The *Batman* television show was over in 1968. Today older baby-boomers are showing episodes to their grandchildren who love it. Perhaps it's the bright colors, tongue-in-cheek humor and sheer novelty of seeing Batman dance the "Batusi" or chide Robin into wearing his seatbelt. Or maybe they all just love the car. Most likely it's because the show was smarter than anyone expected it would be.

When *Batman* came to television, TV shows were filled with square-jawed, conscientious, good-hearted, moral (very moral) heroes. Scott Mendleson wrote in his November 11, 2014 *Forbes* article: "what made the show work as more than a cheeky put-on was the implicit target of its satire. The show wasn't just gently mocking Batman and his super-heroic ilk, it was mocking the entire mentality that defined 1950s America and presented that same attitude and moral simplicity as something to be mocked and/or laughed at."

But if it had been just a parody, the show wouldn't have worked. First and foremost, *Batman* needed to be a true Super Hero show, and an excellent one at that. William Dozier, Douglas Cramer, and William Self who guided the adaptation understood that basic fact. The stars had to be recognizable as their Super Hero counterparts. The characters' origins had to be true to the source. And the villains had to be as over-the-top and wonderfully outrageous as in the comics. As important, it couldn't look cheap. *Batman* had to be brighter, more colorful and slicker than anything else on the air. The "wow" factor was an important component of the show's success.

When William Dozier realized this was going to be

Below: Holy Cow, Batman, are we going down? No, Robin, not without a fight!

his signature show he called Hollywood stars and top television actors to come and play in his sandbox. He hired one of the hottest jazz talents, Neal Hefti, to create the theme song, and it paid off by winning a Grammy. He hired the incomparable Nelson Riddle from *Route 66* for the weekly score. He even pulled his best guys from his other productions, art director Serge Krizman from *The Tammy Grimes Show* and Sam Strangis from *The Loner*.

So the show was a winner. How could it not be? When it ended, the show went on in syndication to introduce the entire world to Batman and his wonderful Gotham City. *Batman* began a long run not only in the United States but across the globe. Adam West and Burt Ward won the hearts of hundreds of thousands of new *Batman* fans.

Ten years later, the film *Superman* was a raging box office success. It followed the Batman TV show model: the characters were recognizably their comic-book counterparts. Their histories had come directly from the comics. The villains were over-the-top, and wonderfully outrageous, and while it wasn't a satire/comedy, the movie had some very funny dialogue. Plus no expense was spared. It was a model that also made its immediate sequel a success. It was that movie that opened the way for a new *Batman* franchise.

In 1984, 20th Century Fox remastered the original 35mm TV prints for *Batman*, and by 1988 (while Tim Burton was filming the *Batman* movie) Fox decided to spur syndication sales through promoting television marathons of the series. It was a huge success. Fox was proud of pointing out that somewhere in the world on any given day, *Batman* was running on television.

After a few years of development, Warner Bros. gave the film *Batman* the go-ahead in April 1988, helmed by legendary director Tim Burton. The movie premiered June 23, 1989 and was the year's top earner at the U.S. box office. All of the elements were there that made the TV show a success, except that this time it definitely wasn't a comedy. There was, however, a cool car. The studio brought back Michael Keaton as Batman for a sequel, which led to a film dynasty giving Val Kilmer, George Clooney, Christian Bale and Ben Affleck a crack at the Bat. Each new actor brought a new dimension to the role, making the classic character their own, and everyone has their favorite.

Along with the films, Warner Bros. Animation launched *Batman: The Animated Series* in 1992, the first in what has

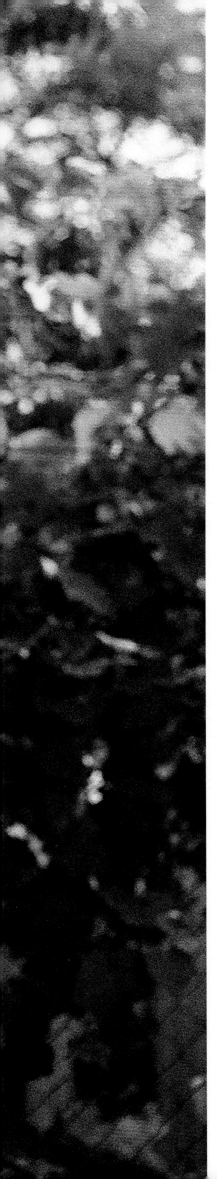

become a powerful spate of animated TV series (*Beware the Batman*, *Teen Titans Go!*) and original DVD films: the DC Universe Original Animated Movies (*Batman: The Killing Joke*, *Batman: The Dark Knight Returns*).

Other popular DC Comics Super Heroes have also made the jump to the big screen. In 2016, *Batman v Superman: Dawn of Justice* made history, bringing the "trinity" of Batman, Superman and Wonder Woman together on the big screen for the first time. Wonder Woman will star in her own film in June 2017, and a *Justice League* film will follow in November 2017.

Meanwhile, television is going through a golden age of Super Hero shows with *Arrow*, *The Flash*, *DC's Legends of Tomorrow* and *Supergirl* all taking up residence on the primetime schedule. Producer Greg Berlanti is making sure our childhood heroes are battling those super-villains we grew up with, just like the *Batman* producers did in 1966.

Batman inspired producers, artists and writers to tell stories of Super Heroes. The show itself garnered a huge audience willing to go along with the fantasy, because it wasn't done cheaply, and was done with respect. Once studio executives understood that the audience loved the source material, today's golden age of Super Hero television and movies began. It all started because William Dozier, Lorenzo Semple Jr. and company laid out the ground rules for success back in 1966. And that's why the show is still loved today.

EPISODE GUIDE:
SEASON ONE

#1   Hi Diddle Riddle

first aired January 12, 1966

#2   Smack In The Middle

first aired January 13, 1966

Batman and Robin are sued for one million bucks' worth of false arrest by the Riddler. Reason: the Riddler anticipates an abbreviated crime-fighting career for Batman since the Gotham Guardian would have to be unmasked in court. At What A Way To Go-Go, a hot and trendy discotheque, Batman showcases the "Batusi" with the Riddler's accomplice, Molly, but succumbs to a drugged glass of Florida sunshine. Molly later masquerades as the Boy Wonder, bamboozling Batman into bringing her to the Batcave.

#3   Fine Feathered Finks

first aired January 19, 1966

#4   The Penguin's A Jinx

first aired January 20, 1966

Fresh out of the slammer, the Penguin and his gang create several disturbances. From atop a giant umbrella which lands in Gotham City, the Caped Crusaders retrieve an umbrella of ordinary dimensions, and quickly return to the Batcave for analysis. In short order, Bruce Wayne visits the Penguin's K.G. Bird Umbrella Factory headquarters, only to be caught attempting to bug the place (with a tiny, spider-shaped surveillance device). Wayne is promptly dispatched onto a conveyor belt for a short trip into a 12,000° furnace.

#5   The Joker Is Wild

first aired January 26, 1966

#6   Batman Is Riled

first aired January 27, 1966

Frustrated and continually conquered because of Batman's Utility Belt, the Joker devises a belt of his own. The Clown Prince of Crime then launches Gotham City's worst-ever crime wave, successfully and regularly eluding Batman and Robin. During a fight in darkness, the Joker manages to switch belts with Batman, who unwittingly assists the Joker's escape by tossing the wrong device at the fleeing villain. Later, after capturing Batman and Robin, the Joker is about to unmask the Dynamic Duo on live TV.

#7 Instant Freeze

first aired February 2, 1966

#8 Rats Like Cheese

first aired February 3, 1966

Mr. Freeze dupes the Dynamic Duo with several decoys of himself, allowing the human icebox and his boys to escape in the ensuing chaos. Batman and Robin later attempt to thwart Mr. Freeze's plans to steal the Circle of Ice Diamond, but find themselves struggling to extinguish drapes which the cool crook set afire. Still hoping to halt Mr. Freeze's escape, Batman and Robin give chase. They quickly intercept him but are frozen in their steps by a deadly ice-gun.

#9 Zelda The Great

first aired February 9, 1966

#10 A Death Worse Than Fate

first aired February 10, 1966

The annual April Fool's Day theft of $100,000 from the First National Bank turns out to be the effort of master escape artist Zelda the Great. The Albanian genius and escape device inventor Eivol Ekdal has demanded payment from Zelda before revealing the secret of his latest novelty, forcing her to steal in order to generate cash and thus afford Ekdal's invention. Believing the stolen funds to be counterfeit, Zelda kidnaps Aunt Harriet, suspends her over a vat of flaming oil and demands a ransom.

#11 A Riddle A Day Keeps The Riddler Away

first aired February 16, 1966

#12 When The Rat's Away The Mice Will Play

first aired February 17, 1966

A riddle leads Batman and Robin to the Miss Galaxy crowning. The Riddler attends the ceremony as well and steals a tiara crown. However, he throws it back at Batman and Robin, tells them he knew it was a planted fake and offers another riddle. Visiting King Boris is then kidnapped by the Riddler, leading Batman and Robin into a trap. They are strapped to a generator drive shaft which the Riddler sets spinning. Believing the Dynamic Duo to be extinct, the Riddler notifies Commissioner Gordon that the Queen of Freedom statue in Gotham City's Museum of Fame has a time bomb which he will gladly deactivate for $1,000,000.

#13 The Thirteenth Hat

first aired February 23, 1966

#14 Batman Stands Pat

first aired February 24, 1966

Using his Super Instant Mesmerizer, paroled Jervis Tetch (alias the Mad Hatter) attempts to capture every member of the jury that originally convicted him. The Mad Hatter is also pursuing Batman who testified against him. Visiting the studio of Octave Marbot, a sculptor working on a statue of the Cowled Crusader, the Dynamic Duo find the Mad Hatter attempting to disguise himself as Marbot. In the ensuing struggle, Robin is knocked out and Batman buried in super-fast hardening plaster.

#19 The Purr-Fect Crime
first aired March 16, 1966

#20 Better Luck Next Time
first aired March 17, 1966

In the series' first Catwoman adventure, the Feline Fury spirits away one of a pair of golden cat statuettes which contain the secret to Captain Manx's lost treasure. Batman and Robin attempt to guard the second cat-clue, but Catwoman manages to heist it as well. Having previously sprayed the second priceless figure with radioactive mist, the Gotham Guardians are able to trace it to Catwoman's lair, but they rush headlong through a trapdoor and into a dungeon. Separating the Dynamic Duo, Catwoman leaves Batman to battle a single ferocious Batman-eating tiger, while the Boy Dinner is balanced over a pit with two hungry tigers.

#15 The Joker Goes To School
first aired March 2, 1966

#16 He Meets His Match, The Grisly Ghoul
first aired March 3, 1966

#21 The Penguin Goes Straight
first aired March 23, 1966

#22 Not Yet, He Ain't
first aired March 24, 1966

The Joker plans to undermine student morale and recruit high school dropouts from Disko Tech for his gang, the Bad Pennies. Fixing vending machines to spew silver dollars, the Clown Prince of Crime also rigs a milk machine that first shackles Batman and Robin and then blasts them with knockout gas. The Dynamic Duo are transferred to the trickster's van where they are wired to a slot machine about to generate 50,000 volts.

The Penguin apparently abandons his criminal past when he routs several robberies and establishes the Penguin's Protective Agency to guard society's wealth. One of the Penguin's first successes as the sentinel of aristocracy is to nab Batman and Robin while they are switching Sophia Starr's real jewelry for fakes. Starr is one of the Penguin's clients and the feathered felon accuses the Dynamic Duo of burglary, thereby making them fugitives from justice. At Gotham City's Amusement Pier, they crash a party being thrown by the abominable avian but are hit by a cement-filled umbrella and strung up behind a balloon shooting gallery. Chief O'Hara and Commissioner Gordon are unknowingly about to take pot shots at the suspended hidden heroes using live ammunition.

#17 True Or False Face
first aired March 9, 1966

#18 Holy Rat Race
first aired March 10, 1966

False Face steals the Mergenberg Crown, replacing it with a replica. From a clue in the false crown, Batman and Robin conclude the devil of disguise is about to hijack an armored truck. Masquerading as a guard, False Face escapes in his Trick-Truck. Later, he again eludes the law's clutches, this time disguised as Chief O'Hara. The Dynamic Duo manage to capture False Face's accomplice, Blaze, and she subsequently leads them to what they believe is the hideout: a shut-down subway station. In reality a trap, the Gotham Guardians are gassed and then stuck to the tracks with quick-setting plastic cement as a train approaches.

#23 **The Ring Of Wax**
first aired March 30, 1966

#24 **Give 'Em The Axe**
first aired March 31, 1966

A figure unveiling at Madame Soleil's Wax Museum goes sour when a supposedly imported Batman statue turns out to be a figure of the Riddler. The statue spouts two riddles and then rudely spray paints attendees. Batman and Robin solve the riddles, leading to the public library. Here, the Riddler manages to attach the duo to the floor (with Dr. Riddler's Instant Forever Stick Invisible Wax Emulsion) and then flees with a rare, old book containing the secret to the Lost Treasure of the Incas. The Caped Crusaders unfasten themselves from the floor and track the Riddler back to the wax museum; however they are drugged, tied up and suspended over a vat of boiling wax by the Remote Control Enormous Candle Dipper. Batman and Robin escape in an explosion but remain motionless on the floor. Believing the duo deceased, the Riddler and his gang rush off to pilfer the Incan treasure.

#25 **The Joker Trumps An Ace**
first aired April 6, 1966

#26 **Batman Sets The Pace**
first aired April 7, 1966

First stealing a hole from a golf course, followed by a hairpin from a woman at a fur salon, the Joker subsequently reveals a plot to pilfer the Maharajah of Nimpah's solid gold golf clubs. The Clown Prince of Crime indeed does that, but also steals the actual Maharajah himself and temporarily eludes the Dynamic Duo. They manage to track him down at his oil refinery hideout but are captured, tied up and locked in a chimney filling with lethal gas.

#27 **The Curse Of Tut**
first aired April 13, 1966

#28 **The Pharaoh's In A Rut**
first aired April 14, 1966

A student riot endows an eminent Yale professor with a head wound. Awaking with a strange double delusion, he now believes himself to be King Tut, Great King of the Nile, and sets up an Egyptian Sphinx in Gotham City's Central Park. Tut hopes to claim Gotham City as his kingdom. As Bruce Wayne conducts a museum exhibit press tour of ancient Egyptian artifacts, a mummified Pharaoh from 1500 BC appears to come alive. Wayne is kidnapped for ransom and although he escapes, he finds himself strapped to a gurney, free-wheeling towards a 300-foot drop-off. Wayne manages to escape again, then devising a plan allowing Batman to be intentionally kidnapped by Tut. Plans go slightly awry and Batman finds himself subjected to the ancient Theban pebble torture which is supposed to render him a mindless slave.

#29 **The Bookworm Turns**
first aired April 20, 1966

#30 **While Gotham City Burns**
first aired April 21, 1966

An apparent assassination attempt on Commissioner Gordon lures Batman and Robin to Police Headquarters. Bookworm's accomplice plants a bomb on the front seat of the parked Batmobile, but Batman safely ejects the device, which lets loose an asbestos bookcover clue: the well-educated master of stolen plots will blow up the Amerigo Columbus Bridge. However, the blow-up is simply a picture enlarged on a warehouse wall. A Batclimb (using the "Batzooka" and a grappling hook, since the walls are too high for a Batrope toss) allows the Dynamic Duo to spot the projector in a nearby bookmobile where they also discover the Bookworm's criminal cohort, Lydia Limpet. Uncovering the Bookworm's plot, Batman knowingly follows Limpet's deceptive clues, leaving Robin behind to guard her. The Boy Wonder is gassed by a trick book, kidnapped and strapped to the clapper of Big Benjamin, the giant bell in the Wayne Memorial Clock Tower… and the clock is about to toll midnight. Although Batman rescues the Boy Wonder at the last second, the Duo is eventually trapped inside a monstrous recipe book filled with billowing steam about to turn our heroes into the Cooked Crusaders.

#31 **Death In Slow Motion**
first aired April 27, 1966

#32 **The Riddler's False Notion**
first aired April 28, 1966

The Riddler first escapes with $200 worth of box office receipts from a silent film festival, and then proceeds to pilfer the payroll from Mother Gotham's Bakery, capturing the event on film in the spirit of a silent movie comedy. "Mr. Van Jones has commissioned me to make him the greatest silent film since the days of immortal Charlie," says the Riddler. The Riddler lenses another epic when he captures the Dynamic Duo on film as they are hit on the head by *A Pictorial History of Silent Films* by Y.Y. Flurch, a 4' x 5' book at a branch library. And the Riddler's cameras continue to roll as he later spikes the lemonade at a temperance party. While Batman attends the no-booze bash, Robin waits in the Batmobile but is kidnapped and taken to the Gotham City Lumber Yard. The Boy Lumber is placed on a conveyor belt and readied to be sawed in two as the Riddler records the event.

#33 **Fine Finny Fiends**
first aired May 4, 1966

#34 **Batman Makes The Scenes**
first aired May 5, 1966

The Penguin and his fiends capture Alfred, forcing him to reveal secrets about Bruce Wayne's upcoming Multimillionaire's Annual Award Dinner. The felons subsequently brainwash Alfred, who returns to Wayne Manor with a twitch and no memory of his absence. But a fish hook which falls from Alfred's coat tips off Batman that the Penguin is up to something. Tracing the man of a thousand umbrellas to his hideout, Batman and Robin are caught in an umbrella field, gassed and then locked inside the Gigantic Reversing Bellows – a vacuum tank. Balloons in the tank burst as Penguin extracts the remaining air.

EPISODE GUIDE: SEASON TWO

#35 Shoot A Crooked Arrow
first aired September 7, 1966

#36 Walk The Straight And Narrow
first aired September 8, 1966

Another successful attempt to pillage stately Wayne Manor, this time by Archer, who distributes his loot to the destitute. Batman and Robin bag Archer but impecunious Gothamites manage to raise bail with $50,000 in milk bottle deposit money. Attempting to search the villain's archery range hideout, the Gotham Guardians are apprehended and tied to stakes. They are later readied to be run through by lances as Archer tries to discover the location of the Batcave. Our heroes escape by using concealed "Batsprings" in their boots, but Archer manages to commandeer an armored truck containing $10,000,000 in cash earmarked by the Wayne Foundation for distribution to Gotham City's poor.

#37 Hot Off The Griddle
first aired September 14, 1966

#38 The Cat And The Fiddle
first aired September 15, 1966

Batman arranges a trap for Catwoman at the Gotham City Natural History Museum, but is caught off guard because the Feline Fury has discovered his plans beforehand. Gotham City's guardians are hit with paralyzing Catatonic cat-darts and tossed out of a twelfth-story window, but land safely on prearranged fishing nets which were set up in case Catwoman tossed a canary cage out of the window. Subsequently tracking down Catwoman at the Pink Sandbox restaurant, the Duo is again surprised when their table suddenly does a 180° spin, tossing them into a metal chamber. Now trapped by Catwoman, Batman breaks a water pipe, hoping to cool the floor Catwoman is super-heating, but the pipe contains liquid Catatonia which knocks out the twin crime fighters. They awaken to find themselves tied to aluminum reflectors and under magnifying glasses… with a bright, midday sun.

#39 The Minstrel's Shakedown
first aired September 21, 1966

#40 Barbecued Batman?
first aired September 22, 1966

The Gotham City Stock Exchange's computerized stock quotations are fouled up thanks to that electronics genius and musician, Minstrel. The lute-playing rogue cuts into a TV newscast to announce his demand for a $1,000 payment per stock exchange member… or face major problems in the market. Batman deduces the Melodic Fiend's hideout, but the Duo is captured and hoisted onto a rotating spit over electronic "super units of a radar-type grill."

#41 **The Spell Of Tut**

first aired September 28, 1966

#42 **Tut's Case Is Shut**

first aired September 29, 1966

Batman and Robin track King Tut to the Apex Apothecary Shop where he is attempting to revive some ancient green bugs (aka scarabs). The fat pharaoh escapes, but fortunately, the Dynamic Duo salvage one scarab. Batcave analysis uncovers Tut's ploy: distill Abu Raubu Simbu Tu, a deadly potion capable of paralyzing the will, and in fact, enough to debilitate Gotham City. Using the sphinx from episodes #27/28, Batman conceals Robin inside. Tut toddles off with the Trojan sphinx but the Boy Blunder gives himself away by dropping his "Batcommunicator" and ends up standing on a receding plank overlooking a crocodile pit. Meanwhile, Commissioner Gordon's pill-crazy summer secretary is a Tut plant and the pharaoh has Chief O'Hara high up on a window ledge performing acrobatics.

#43 **The Greatest Mother Of Them All**

first aired October 5, 1966

#44 **Ma Parker**

first aired October 6, 1966

One by one, Batman and Robin capture Ma Parker's corrupted kids, ultimately apprehending Ma and her daughter at the Gotham City Old Folks Home. But Ma had previously been sneaking sympathetic staff into the pen and immediately takes over the joint, capturing Warden Crichton. A bomb planted in the Batmobile by one of Parker's cronies is set to explode when the speedometer hits 60 mph, but Batman discovers the device in time. Ultimately, the Dynamic Duo learn of what has really happened at the prison. While sneaking in, they are captured and strapped into electric chairs.

#45 **The Clock King's Crazy Crimes**

first aired October 12, 1966

#46 **The Clock King Gets Crowned**

first aired October 13, 1966

Clock King's gang loots a jewelry store and then, joined by their boss who is disguised as a pop artist, crash a pop art gallery opening. Batman and Robin arrive in time to foil Clock King's heist of a time-related surrealist painting, but Clock King and his men flee as the Dynamic Duo are bombarded by giant flying watch springs. Batman tracks down Clock King's hideout but the Duo are stuffed into the bottom of an oversize hourglass and left to be drowned in pink sand. Meanwhile, Clock King plots to filch Bruce Wayne's collection of antique pocket watches.

#47 **An Egg Grows In Gotham**

first aired October 19, 1966

#48 **The Yegg Foes In Gotham**

first aired October 20, 1966

Egghead attempts to wrest ownership (and therefore control) of Gotham City from lease holder Chief Screaming Chicken, the last of the "Mochicans." The egg-squisite crook plans to delay the every-five-years payment of nine raccoon pelts in order to revert ownership of Gotham City to the Chief, and, subsequently, to Egghead himself. Batman and Robin locate Egghead although he egg-scapes in a flourish of laughing gas. As part of the plot, Egghead abducts three descendants of the original Gotham City settlers; one of them is Bruce Wayne and Egghead believes Wayne is Batman. Wayne and Egghead are attached to an Electro-Thought Transferrer which will not only egg-stract Wayne's knowledge but leave him "an empty-headed fop."

#49 **The Devil's Fingers**

first aired October 26, 1966

#50 **The Dead Ringers**

first aired October 27, 1966

Following the robbery of Chandell's jewels and some other goodies from Wayne Manor, the police position guards – complete with machine gun emplacements – at the famed pianist's evening concert at Gotham Town Hall. Batman and Robin are out of town, but while listening to the concert on his portable radio, Bruce notices a false note in the music, contacts Dick and both hightail it back to the Batcave. Chandell, also known as Fingers, puts the make on Aunt Harriet. He hopes to eventually marry her, bump off Bruce and Dick and thereby have access to the Wayne fortunes, allowing him to pay off his blackmailing brother, Harry. Batman and Robin are led into a trap, subdued by three thugs and plopped onto a conveyor belt, about to be perforated into human piano rolls.

#51 **Hizzonner The Penguin**

first aired November 2, 1966

#52 **Dizzonner The Penguin**

first aired November 3, 1966

The polls show overwhelming support for the Penguin in his run for mayor, thanks to his rescue of a baby from a runaway carriage, a contribution of $100,000 to the Gotham City Charity Fund and other equally outstanding efforts. Since the only alternative to the Penguin for Mayor is Batman for Mayor, the Caped Crusader enters the race, but cannot match the Penguin's flair, snappy jingles and willingness to kiss babies. Soon after, Batman and Robin are waylaid and strung up over a vat of sulphuric acid.

#53 **Green Ice**

first aired November 9, 1966

#54 **Deep Freeze**

first aired November 10, 1966

Mr. Freeze is on the rampage. After kidnapping Miss Iceland from Gotham City's Annual Miss Galaxy Contest, the Coldblooded Culprit freezes Commissioner Gordon and Chief O'Hara, robs guests at a poolside reception and then freezes them in the pool, while simultaneously managing to discredit Batman and Robin by routing wimpy doubles of the Dynamic Duo. The genuine Batman and Robin find Mr. Freeze in a seemingly abandoned cold storage plant but are jumped and then placed in giant frozen popsicle containers, soon to be turned into human Frosty Freezies.

#55 **The Impractical Joker**

first aired November 16, 1966

#56 **The Joker's Provokers**

first aired November 17, 1966

The Joker is on a crime spree involving keys and manages to incapacitate Batman and Robin with a mysterious little box. The Grim Jester soon appears on TV, offering clues. The box turns out to be electronic junk, capable of nothing more than blinking lights; in reality, the Duped Duo had been hypnotized. They discover the Joker in an old key factory but when the Gotham Guardians burst in, they are captured. Robin is placed in a Wax Spray Chamber which will spray wax him to death while Batman is strung out on a giant human key duplicator.

#57 Marsha, Queen Of Diamonds
first aired November 23, 1966

#58 Marsha's Scheme Of Diamonds
first aired November 24, 1966

Marsha wants the "Batdiamond," a monstrous gem which provides power to the Batcomputer. In the process, she manages to leave Chief O'Hara, Commissioner Gordon and a roomful of lovesick men in her wake. After obtaining a love potion strong enough to capture Batman, an amazed Marsha discovers he is able to resist its effects. But in an ensuing fight, Robin is hit with one of Marsha's love darts and orders Batman to surrender in order to please Marsha. Batman demands the Boy Lover's freedom, but it can only be gained by marrying Marsha. And so the Caped Crusader proceeds to join Marsha at the altar of the Little Church Around The Corner...

#59 Come Back, Shame
first aired November 30, 1966

#60 It's How You Play The Game
first aired December 1, 1966

Shame and his cohorts are stealing car parts in order to soup up their truck so it can outrun the Batmobile. When Shame hears that Bruce Wayne's limo has some powerful new goodies, Shame decides to steal it as well. This is a setup, naturally, and Batman and Robin are able to track the rustlers to their hideout. However, the Duped Duo end up staked to the ground with stampeding cattle bearing down on them.

#61 The Penguin's Nest
first aired December 7, 1966

#62 The Bird's Last Jest
first aired December 8, 1966

Once again, the Penguin appears to go straight (also see #51/52 and #73) when he opens The Penguin's Nest, a super-swank restaurant catering to the wealthy. In reality, he is collecting handwriting samples (patrons must write out their own order). The Penguin spends much of his time attempting to get back into the State Prison so he can link up with Ballpoint Baxter, a notorious forger. The cagey bird finally gets arrested, but only makes it to Gotham City Jail ("Petty Crooks Only" reads a sign in the jail), and so his cohorts spring him and kidnap Chief O'Hara, keeping the copped cop in a trunk. Batman and Robin come to the rescue but are attacked with machine gun fire as the O'Hara-filled trunk tumbles into a pool which Penguin is about to electrify.

#63 The Cat's Meow
first aired December 14, 1966

#64 The Bat's Kow Tow
first aired December 15, 1966

After stealing the voices of both Commissioner Gordon and a morning TV announcer with a Voice-Eraser she clandestinely fabricated in prison, Catwoman plots to appropriate the voices of Chad and Jeremy. Disguised as Edna Klutz, the Feline Fury visits Wayne Manor (where the singing duo will be staying) to offer Dick Grayson free dance lessons at the Duncan Dance studios. Klutz gives herself away, gassing Grayson, Aunt Harriet and Alfred to aid her escape. The Dynamic Duo later head to the dance studio to nose around. Catwoman drugs the heroes into unconsciousness, locking them inside a huge echo chamber with the sound of a dripping faucet – magnified ten million times – blasting their eardrums.

#65 **The Puzzles Are Coming**
first aired December 21, 1966

#66 **The Duo Is Slumming**
first aired December 22, 1966

Shakespeare-spouting Puzzler appears to be working out an honest, money-making deal with multi-billionaire Artemus Knab. A message on a publicity balloon leads Batman and Robin to Gotham Airport for the christening of Knab's new supersonic plane, Retsoor. Arriving too late, the Dynamic Duo find the gassed guests relieved of their jewelry. Another riddle leads them to the Puzzler's balloon factory where the Duo are rendered unconscious, lashed to the basket of an aerial balloon and sent skyward. The basket holding our heroes will free fall back to earth when the balloon reaches 20,000 feet.

#67 **The Sandman Cometh**
first aired December 28, 1966

#68 **The Catwoman Goeth**
first aired December 29, 1966

Catwoman and Euro-crook Sandman plot to relieve billionaire noodle queen J. Pauline Spaghetti of some of her tremendous wealth. Sandman, disguised as Dr. Somnambula, visits Spaghetti at her request (this insomniac last dozed about seven years ago at a rock and roll concert). Batman and Robin charge in but nothing is found missing and Sandman slips away. The Dynamic Duo track down the alleged sleep expert at his hideout; however, Robin is put into a trance and pushes a button that brings the needle of a giant button-stitching machine down on Batman, who has been tied to a mattress.

#69 **The Contaminated Cowl**
first aired January 4, 1967

#70 **The Mad Hatter Runs Afoul**
first aired January 5, 1967

In order to store his hat collection, Mad Hatter needs hat boxes, so he purloins 700 of the receptacles from Bon Bon's Box Boutique. Then, posing as the Three-Tailed Pasha of Panchagorum, Hatter heists Hattie Hatfield's valuable ruby. Jervis Tetch escapes the clutches of the Dynamic Duo, but not before blasting Batman with radioactive fumes. Batman had taken precautions but his cowl remains contaminated and is now bright pink. While attempting to have it decontaminated, a disguised Tetch appropriates the cowl, and with the help of his henchmen, overcomes the Caped Crime-Busters. Locked inside an X-Ray Accelerator Tube and Fluoroscopic Cabinet, Batman and Robin are about to be obliterated.

#71 **The Zodiac Crimes**
first aired January 11, 1967

#72 **The Joker's Hard Times**
first aired January 12, 1967

#73 **The Penguin Declines**
first aired January 18, 1967

The Joker and the Penguin collaborate in a series of crimes inspired by signs of the Zodiac. Joker initiates the caper by pilfering a Rare Art Map (Aries) from Police Headquarters, then purloining The Twins, a pair of diamonds (Gemini). He then kidnaps opera star Leo Crustash (Leo, Cancer) and steals a museum painting entitled *Virgin Bereaved* (Virgo). During the museum heist, the Daring Duo are tied down with an eight-ton meteorite about to fall on them.

Batman and Robin escape from being crushed thanks to an amazingly accurate Batarang toss; however, the Joker takes the Statue of Justice (Libra) from outside Police Headquarters. Joker's henchgirl, Venus, makes off with a jeweled antique scorpion (Scorpio) as the Joker plots to kidnap millionaire Basil Bowman (Sagittarius). The Crime Clown also steals two rare fish (Pisces). Venus turns from her evil ways to assist Batman and Robin, but all three are chained in a shallow pool by the Joker, about to be eaten by a giant clam.

#74 **That Darn Catwoman**
first aired January 19, 1967

#75 **Scat! Darn Catwoman**
first aired January 25, 1967

Catwoman's aide, Pussycat, attacks Robin with Cataphrenic, turning him to the Feline Fury's side of the law. The first job: relieve Wayne Manor of Bruce Wayne's housekeeping money ($200,000). Catwoman needs a million bucks to buy plans for the Gotham City Mint. She proceeds to nail the Ninth National Bank and empty the cash-filled mattress of inventor Pat Pending. Batman tracks Catwoman to her hideout but is bound to a mousetrap and Robin is cutting the rope...

#76 **Penguin Is A Girl's Best Friend**
first aired January 26, 1967

#77 **Penguin Sets A Trend**
first aired February 1, 1967

#78 **Penguin's Disastrous End**
first aired February 2, 1967

Batman and Robin accidentally break up a movie the Penguin is legally filming and so are coerced into appearing in the production. The Penguin forces Batman and Marsha, Queen of Diamonds to do 100 takes of a kissing scene in retaliation for Batman having encouraged Aunt Harriet and the Gotham City League of Film Decency to raid his set. Later, shooting on location at the Museum of Antiquities, Penguin's gang appropriates the entire collection of 15th-century chain mail armor. Batman discovers the theft and the Penguin again retaliates, this time calling for a scene where the Twin Defenders of Justice are beat up and captured for real. The duo is tied to a giant catapult and readied to be launched across Gotham City, landing like a pair of squashed tomatoes.

#79 **Batman's Anniversary**
first aired February 8, 1967

#80 **A Riddling Controversy**
first aired February 9, 1967

The Dynamic Duo are surprised by a party given in Batman's honor. The Riddler and two of his cohorts are uninvited guests who depart with a golden calf filled with $200,000 intended for charity. Later, the Riddler strikes again when he floods and robs the Gotham City Bank. Returning to his lair to dry out the cache, it is learned that the Riddler is attempting to purchase a destructive De-Molecularizer. Batman and Robin, thinking they are posing for life-size marshmallow figures of themselves atop a giant cake, discover they are sinking into quicksand.

#81 **The Joker's Last Laugh**
first aired February 15, 1967

#82 **The Joker's Epitaph**
first aired February 16, 1967

On the trail of phony funds, Batman discovers that the chief teller at Gotham National Bank is a Joker-controlled robot. By analyzing the robot's apparel, Batman is able to track Joker to Penthouse Publishers, a comic-book company. Feigning bankruptcy, Bruce Wayne attempts to strike up a deal with the Clown Prince of Crime while Robin surprises the Joker and attempts to arrest him. But Robin is captured and about to be pressed flat into a comic book.

#83 **Catwoman Goes To College**

first aired February 22, 1967

#84 **Batman Displays His Knowledge**

first aired February 23, 1967

Upon being paroled, Catwoman registers – with ulterior motives – for a class in elementary criminology at Gotham City University. She steals a life-size statue of Batman, intending to design a Batsuit for use in criminal activity. After her fake Batman robs a supermarket, the real Batman is arrested, although he later escapes thanks to Alfred's assistance. Catwoman then lures the Dynamic Duo to the top of a building where they are dumped into a giant coffee cup. A huge percolator filled with sulfuric acid is about to pour liquid death over our subdued heroes.

#85 **A Piece Of The Action**

first aired March 1, 1967

#86 **Batman's Satisfaction**

first aired March 2, 1967

Batman believes the Pink Chip Stamps Factory is counterfeiting rare stamps. The Gotham Guardians enter the picture when factory owner Pinky Pinkston wants Batman to guard her facility. The Green Hornet and Kato visit the company's foreman, Colonel Gumm, who has been running the counterfeiting scam and is suddenly attempting to depart. Batman and Robin arrive but end up stuck to a glue table, while the Hornet and Kato are being fed into a machine, about to be pressed into stamps.

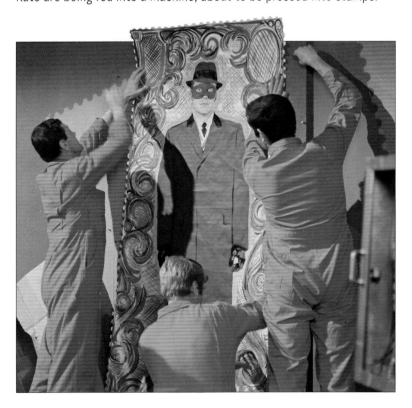

#87 **King Tut's Coup**

first aired March 8, 1967

#88 **Batman's Waterloo**

first aired March 9, 1967

Tut and his Tutlings cop a sarcophagus from the Gotham City Museum. The flaky pharaoh then plots to kidnap Lisa Carson who will be dressed as Cleopatra for the upcoming Egyptian Costume Ball. Batman and Robin trace Tut to his roadhouse hideout, but the Caped Crusader is knocked out, sealed in the royal sarcophagus and dropped into a large vat of water. Robin's fate: to be royally boiled in oil.

#89 **Black Widow Strikes Again**

first aired March 15, 1967

#90 **Caught In The Spider's Den**

first aired March 16, 1967

Black Widow walks out of the American National Bank with a sack of cash, thanks to some help from her Cerebrum Short-Circuitor. After her heists at the Beneficial, Commercial, Diversified, Empire and Federal State Banks, Batman concludes she is conveniently robbing in alphabetical order and so lies in wait at Gotham City General Bank and Trust. Widow escapes but the Dynamic Duo track her on radar to a white-frame bungalow. Black Widow eventually catches the Gotham Guardians in a giant web as two monstrously huge black widow spiders crawl towards them.

#91 Pop Goes The Joker
first aired March 22, 1967

#92 Flop Goes The Joker
first aired March 23, 1967

#93 Ice Spy
first aired March 29, 1967

#94 The Duo Defy
first aired March 30, 1967

The Joker joins the world of pop art when he disfigures paintings at Bernie Park's Artistic Procurers gallery using twin spray-paint guns. The original artist loves the changes! The Joker's next move: enter rich Baby Jane Towser's art contest, which he wins. Using these credentials, he offers an art course exclusively for millionaires. Bruce Wayne is among the budding creatives but the Joker suddenly announces his pupils are now his prisoners. Their ransom: their Renaissance art collections. Robin attempts a rescue but ends up in a giant rotating mobile of deadly palette knives that will slice apart the Boy Wonder.

Mr. Freeze kidnaps Professor Isaacson hoping to obtain an instant ice formula. He moves his headquarters to a location below the Bruce Wayne Ice Arena and sticks Isaacson in the freezer, hoping to force out the formula. Meanwhile, Batman discovers the connection between Freeze and ice-skating star Glacia Glaze. Mr. Freeze demands a ransom for Isaacson but Batman believes he can outwit the frigid felon. The Dynamic Duo surprise Mr. Freeze at the ice arena but are shoved into a Sub-Zero Temperature Vaporizing Cabinet, shortly to become part of the ice rink above them.

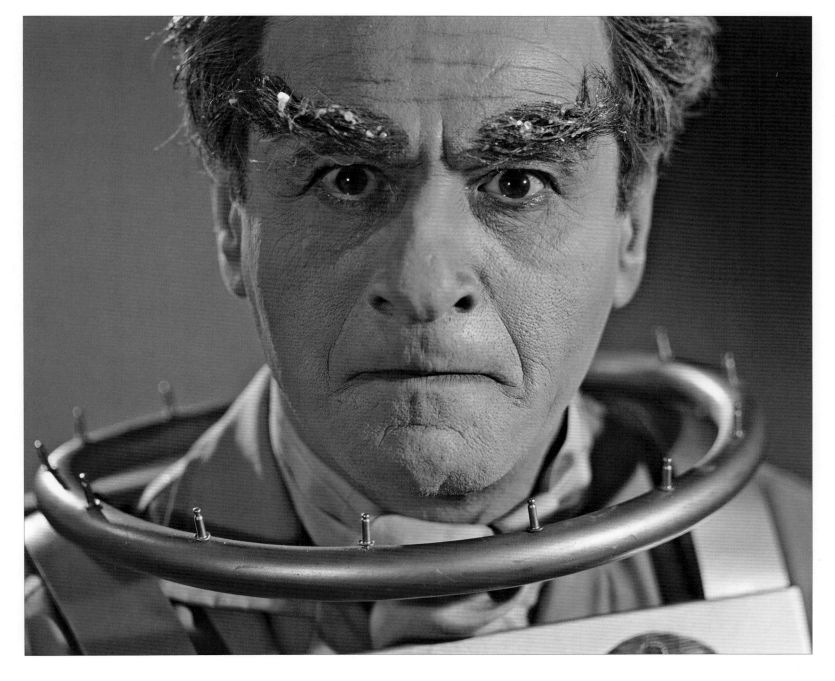

EPISODE GUIDE: SEASON THREE

#95 Enter Batgirl, Exit Penguin

first aired September 14, 1967

Commissioner Gordon discovers that his daughter, Barbara, has been kidnapped by that well-known entrepreneur, the Penguin. The cagey bird shows Barbara a wedding dress he selected and describes his plans to marry her. As the Commissioner's son-in-law, the Penguin would become immune from prosecution. Barbara consents to marriage only after the Penguin threatens to kill her father. Alfred, mistaken for a minister, is kidnapped to perform the ceremony. The alert butler clandestinely switches on a signal in his belt which leads the Dynamic Duo straight to the Penguin. Barbara secretly changes to Batgirl and the fight ensues.

#96 Ring Around The Riddler

first aired September 21, 1967

The Riddler wants to take control of a prize fight in Gotham City. Attempting to persuade the champ to throw a fight, the Riddler tosses him into a steam room. Later, he steals the night's receipts and poses as boxing champion Mushy Nebuchadnezzar. He also calls on Siren for assistance. Batgirl comes to the rescue but gets tossed in the steam room as well.

#97 The Wail Of The Siren

first aired September 28, 1967

With Commissioner Gordon under her spell, Siren initiates a plan to discover Batman's secret identity. She shoves Gordon into the Batmobile's trunk while the Dynamic Duo are occupied. The Commissioner subsequently pops out while Alfred is dusting the Batcave, but a whiff of "Batsleep" temporarily solves that predicament. The real problem is that Siren has now hypnotized Bruce Wayne, had him turn over all the Wayne family jewels and cash and has ordered him to jump off the top of a tall building.

#98 The Sport Of Penguins

first aired October 5, 1967

#99 A Horse Of Another Color

first aired October 12, 1967

Lola Lasagne is nearly broke so she links up with the Penguin in hopes of fixing an upcoming horse race: the Bruce Wayne Foundation Memorial Handicap at Gotham City Park Race Track. The Penguin figures if Lola's horse, Parasol, can be replaced with a lookalike, he can successfully bet the horse to lose. A glue factory filly resembling Parasol is located, but Batman, Robin and Batgirl attempt to break up the potential horse-napping. The Penguin diverts the Gotham Guardians by gluing the Batmobile in place – and our heroes to their seats – using a bucket of Library Glue.

#100 The Unkindest Tut Of All
first aired October 19, 1967

The Nabob of the Nile returns to Tut-ness after being hit on the head by a brick during a love-in. Batman and Robin pay a visit to King Tut who has been successfully predicting crimes, but the Dynamic Duo uncover nothing wrong. Tut later phones Bruce Wayne and accuses him of being Batman. Wayne agrees to appear in public with Batman and indeed does so. Tut has failed but utters a clue that leads Batgirl and Batman to believe he will attempt to pilfer the library's priceless collection of ancient Egyptian scrolls.

#101 Louie, The Lilac
first aired October 26, 1967

Louie plans to control the minds of Gotham City's flower children. He kidnaps Princess Primrose, one of their leaders, as Barbara Gordon watches. Gordon contacts the Dynamic Duo for assistance. But Robin is subdued after sniffing Louie's Alba Vulgaria-poison lilac and Batman is put away by a vase to the face. The caped crime fighters are then left in Louie's Hot House to be devoured by a giant Brazilian man-eating lilac. And Gordon has been followed by one of Louie's henchmen.

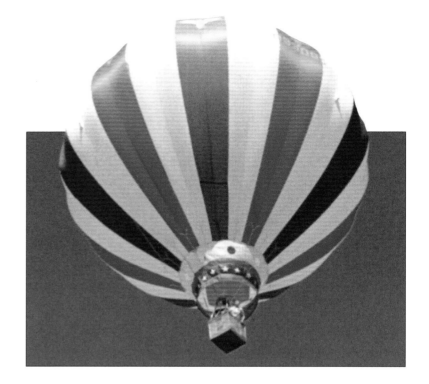

#102 The Ogg And I
first aired November 2, 1967

#103 How To Hatch A Dinosaur
first aired November 9, 1967

Egghead joins with Olga, Queen of the Bessarovian Cossacks to kidnap Commissioner Gordon. The ransom: a 10¢ tax on every egg consumed in Gotham City. Batman, Robin and Batgirl attempt to track the fiends, but they manage to steal the brass samovar of Genghis Khan and Egghead proceeds to collect his taxes. The Dynamic Duo have hidden in the samovar but are gassed while attempting to escape. Robin and the Commissioner are to be made into borscht while Olga plans to marry Batman. Batgirl arrives to save the day but Egghead tosses onion-laced eggs at them, blinding the Super Hero team and the whole evil entourage escapes.

#104 Surf's Up! Joker's Under!
first aired November 16, 1967

The Joker and his men shanghai surf champ Skip Parker from the Hang Five, a surfers' hangout, transporting him to the Ten Toes Surfboard Shop. His beach bunny, Barbara Gordon, sees the Jokermobile driving away and phones the Commissioner. Chief O'Hara and Commissioner Gordon, disguised as surfin' dudes Buzzy and Duke, visit the Hang Five. When Batman and Robin drop in and hang with O'Hara and Gordon, the Joker's spy reports the news using her two-way hot dog. But the Joker is busy with his Surfing Experience and Ability Transferometer and Vigor Reverser, acquiring Skip's surfing abilities for himself so he can become a world champion surfer. Batman and Robin track down the Joker's shop but are poisoned and turned into human surfboards.

#105 The Londinium Larcenies

first aired November 23, 1967

#106 The Foggiest Notion

first aired November 30, 1967

#107 The Bloody Tower

first aired December 7, 1967

Lord Ffogg and his sister, Lady Peasoup, have stolen a collection of snuffboxes from a Londinium museum. Batman, Robin and Barbara Gordon travel by ship to Londinium, the Batmobile and Batcomputer secretly and securely stowed away. There they meet with Ireland Yard Superintendent Watson to discuss the man-made fogs that are masking the thieves' escapes. Batman is suspicious of Lord Ffogg and requests a visit under the pretense of comparing his aftergrass (a form of lawn sometimes called fog) with that of Bruce Wayne's. Robin is taken on a tour of the estate, supposedly a posh girl's finishing school, and learns the students receive shoplifting lessons. Departing in the Batmobile, the Dynamic Duo are attacked by some of Ffogg's servants, but Batgirl arrives in time to help them. As Batman and Robin return to the temporary Batcave – a country manor house dungeon – a deathly fog bomb attached to the Batmobile explodes.

#108 Catwoman's Dressed To Kill

first aired December 14, 1967

Catwoman bursts into a luncheon at La Maison du Chat honoring Gotham City's ten best-dressed women. Setting off a Hair-Raising Bomb which destroys the others' hair-dos, Catwoman indeed remains best-dressed. She then appears at the annual *Fashionation Magazine* fashion show to steal Rudi Gernreich's new dress designs. Batman and Robin show up to foil her attempts but are ensnared in bolts of cloth. Batgirl rescues the trapped Duo and chases after Catwoman through a door, but a sign warns "Models Dressing Room – All Men Keep Out." After a minute, the embarrassed Gotham Guardians enter but discover the Princess of Plunder has nabbed Batgirl. The Feline Fury subsequently ties her to a pattern-cutting machine. Batman is then faced with the dilemma of rescuing Batgirl or, on the other side of town, preventing Catwoman from stealing the Golden Fleece. The Fleece is one million dollars in woven gold and its theft has international repercussions with the small country of Belgravia.

#109 The Ogg Couple

first aired December 21, 1967

Olga, Queen of the Bessarovian Cossacks again teams with Egghead to steal the Silver Scimitar of Taras Bul Bul and the golden Egg of Ogg from the Gotham City Museum. Egghead plans to steal 500 pounds of condensed caviar (at $200 per ounce) which is stored at the Gotham City Bank, but the Cossacks beat him to it. Batgirl gets Egghead to lead her back to Olga. The Dynamic Duo arrive at the bank after everyone has left, but they follow Batgirl. Which is fortunate since Batgirl has been led into a trap.

#110 The Funny Feline Felonies

first aired December 28, 1967

#111 The Joke's On Catwoman

first aired January 4, 1968

The Joker is released from prison early due to good behavior. He immediately links up with Catwoman. After attempting to gun down Chief O'Hara and Commissioner Gordon, the devious duo plot to track down clues to the location of hidden gunpowder so they can break into the Federal Depository and remove the cash. With some help from Batgirl, the Dynamic Duo locate and subdue the villains. While querying the Joker regarding his return to crime, they shake hands with the Grim Jester. A bad move, because they are zapped by the Joker's buzzer which will slowly numb their senses.

#112 **Louie's Lethal Lilac Time**
first aired January 11, 1968

Two of Louie's gang members kidnap Bruce Wayne, Dick Grayson and some ambergris, a waxy substance from whales used in making perfumes. Louie's coconspirator, Lotus, decides that several animal scent pouches are additional necessities and Wayne can remove them from the critters. Wayne will also come in handy for a million dollar ransom, enough for Louie's perfume marketing campaign. Thefts of zoo animals are soon reported. The police are stymied, but Batgirl (with Alfred's assistance) locates the hideout. However, Batgirl is dumped into a vat that Louie orders filled with hot oil.

#113 **Nora Clavicle And The Ladies' Crime Club**
first aired January 18, 1968

Mayor Linseed arrives at a testimonial banquet for Commissioner Gordon. The Civic Luncheon at the Gotham City Astoria is honoring twenty-five years of faithful service by Gordon, and Linseed presents him with a 24-carat gold watch. Immediately afterwards, under pressure from his wife, Linseed discharges Gordon, replacing him with Nora Clavicle, a women's rights advocate. "To prove women can run Gotham City better than men," asserts Clavicle. Commissioner Clavicle dumps the police chief (O'Hara is replaced by Mrs. Linseed) as well as Batman and turns the police department into a women-only force. But Nora is up to no good as her girls later rob the Gotham City National Bank. Batman, Robin and Batgirl hear the robbery report and trace the female crooks to the Dropstitch and Company warehouse. The trio is subdued and tied into a Siamese Human Knot; the slightest move and they will crush each other. Nora and her henchwomen then unleash crates of explosive mechanical mice on Gotham City.

#114 **Penguin's Clean Sweep**
first aired January 25, 1968

After the Penguin's jail break and a report that he was at the U.S. Mint, Batman and Robin corner the villain in an elevator at Police Headquarters. In Gordon's office, the Penguin threatens to sue for false arrest because he did not steal anything. Although he could be charged for breaking and entering, he is set free. But Batman and Robin, joined by Batgirl, discover the Penguin has infected a bin of bucks with Somnophelia Lygeria: Lygerian Sleeping Sickness. The bacteria are normally carried by the Lygerian fruit fly. The Penguin was able to plant a culture of the bacteria in the ink used to print money and some of the funds have already left for the Gotham City National Bank. The dirty bird has also destroyed the only available vaccine (after inoculating himself and his gang). Batgirl discovers $13,000 worth of the funds are in circulation and warnings are broadcast to the public. Citizens begin tossing their currency into the street and the Penguin promptly vacuums up the cash-laden boulevards. Meanwhile, Bruce Wayne telephones his numerous connections advising them that U.S. bills are contaminated. As a result, the Penguin is rich, but cannot do anything with his ill-gotten gains.

#115 **The Great Escape**
first aired February 1, 1968

#116 **The Great Train Robbery**
first aired February 8, 1968

Shame escapes from jail with the help of his girlfriend Calamity Jan, her mother, Frontier Fanny and a Sherman tank. Thanks to Shame's clues, Batman, Robin and Batgirl deduce the crooked cowboy's next criminal move: stealing a diamond and some cash from the Gotham City Opera House. The villains are taking a beating until Fanny and Jan rush in and spray the terrific trio with fear gas. Batman and Robin cower while Shame takes Batgirl with him to his stable.

#117 I'll Be A Mummy's Uncle

first aired February 22, 1968

Tut escapes from Mount Ararat Hospital and is planning to purchase a piece of land adjacent to Wayne Manor so he can mine a vein of Nilanium, the world's hardest metal. After querying the Batcomputer, Batman learns that Tut's slanting mine shaft is aimed at the Batcave. Tut's blasting could pierce the Batanium Shield which protects the Batcave. Batman, Robin and Batgirl catch Tut just as he has struck something too tough to break through – the shield. But Tut hops into a mine car with his four Tutlings and zooms to the bottom of the shaft. Batman and Robin give chase but arrive too late; the pharaoh's crew is already in the Batcave.

#118 The Joker's Flying Saucer

first aired February 29, 1968

Abetted by a mad scientist cell-mate, the Joker's plans are underway for a flying saucer to help take control of the world. Batman discovers the Joker's caper and sends Alfred to check on some lightweight beryllium at the Wayne Foundation. The faithful butler is surprised by the Joker and his men as they make a raid for the beryllium. Believing the butler to be another mad scientist, they take him, along with the metal, to their hideout. Shortly, the Dynamic Duo become trapped in the Batcave due to an explosion from a time bomb previously placed in the Batmobile by one of the Joker's henchmen.

#119 The Entrancing Dr. Cassandra

first aired March 7, 1968

Criminal Dr. Cassandra and her accomplice, Cabala, are capable of camouflaging themselves so they appear invisible, then later using their anti-antidote pill to reappear. They have already been responsible for six thefts. The Dynamic Duo attempt to stop Cassandra from stealing the Mope Diamond at Spiffany's Jewelry Salon on fashionable 15th Avenue, and Batgirl steps out to join them. But the evil doctor fires her Alvino-ray gun, flattening the heroes paper-thin. The evil duo slips the flat trio under Commissioner Gordon's office door and takes off for Gotham City State Prison. Over the prison loudspeakers, Dr. Cassandra announces she is releasing Catwoman, Egghead, the Penguin, the Riddler, the Joker and King Tut.

#120 Minerva, Mayhem And Millionaires

first aired March 14, 1968

The final episode. Minerva's Mineral Spa caters to millionaires, Bruce Wayne among them. Minerva overhears a conversation Wayne has with a friend about some diamonds at the Wayne Foundation vault. Clandestinely palming Wayne's watch gives Minerva an opportunity to later phone the millionaire and verify that the watch has been located. Wayne returns and receives a complimentary Eggplant Jelly Vitamin Scalp massage but unknowingly gives up the combination to the Wayne Foundation vault courtesy of Minerva's Deepest Secret Extractor. Batman and Robin then pay Minerva a visit. Suspecting something is up, she promptly pops the Dynamic Duo into a giant pressure cooker for safekeeping.

ACKNOWLEDGMENTS

This one's for Frederick S. Clarke, who started it all. Thanks. - Bob

To Aunt Mary and her television. Without her, *My Favorite Martian,* *Lost In Space* **and** *Batman* **would not be part of my universe.** - Joe

What the producers, directors, and actors did on Batman looked easy. It was a fun, light-hearted show bringing straight-arrow heroes and colorful villains into the homes of TV viewers. It was so brilliant, fans believe it must have just been a wonderful show to work on. We found that it was, with many interviewees saying that it was a terrific time, and some going so far as describing it as the best professional experience they ever had.

During the course of the interviews, we discovered that these guys and gals have many fond memories of the show, especially of the people they worked with every day. The makeup men and hair stylists were close friends. The car and motorcycle customizers, most of whom worked for Batmobile designer George Barris at some time, enjoyed the camaraderie and competition of the California customizing community. The stuntmen were all pals. And on and on. The interesting thing was that while they knew their own stories, they weren't always familiar with the stories of others in the production.

Back in 1994, we wrote an in-depth feature story about the Batman TV show for *Cinefantastique* magazine. The articles have been used widely on the Internet as a source of information. Some of those interviews appear in this book. Some of the information we were given was wrong and we've corrected those things in this book.

That issue was the first time many of the people who worked on the show discovered what was going on at the network, in the front office, or on the other end of the lot. When we came back to them to do this book, they welcomed us with open arms. It was quite humbling and kind of awesome. We are very grateful for their cooperation and assistance.

We hope, this time, we have provided even more to talk about at conventions, dinner parties, and with friends. We also hope, fellow fans, that we've done the same for you.

BOB & JOE

The authors would like to thank:

The folks of Greenway Productions, 20th Century Fox and ABC: Lorenzo Semple Jr., Harve Bennett, Al Bettcher, Kathryn Blondell, William Bohny, Robert Butler, James B. Clark, Douglas S. Cramer, William D'Angelo, Thomas Del Ruth, Charles FitzSimons, Lee Harman, Harry Hauss, Chuck Hicks, Bruce Hutchinson, Jan Kemp, Hubie Kerns, Serge Krizman, Ivan Martin, Michael McLean, David F. Miller, Robert Mintz, Victor Paul, Charles Picerni, Stanley Ralph Ross, Edgar J. Scherick, William Self, Jack Senter, Milton Stark, Yale Udoff, David Whorf, Ralph Woolsey and with special thanks to Bonnie and Sam Strangis who had great patience with us and made this book infinitely better.

The illustrious cast members who gave us their precious time: Adam West, Vincent Price, John Astin, Yvonne Craig and Julie Newmar.

The professionals of DC Comics: Irwin Donenfeld, Julius Schwartz, and Carmine Infantino.

The comic-book writers and artists: Jeff Parker, Rubén Procopio, Bruce Timm and Matt Wagner.

The vehicle builders: George Barris, Michael "Gale" Black, Bill Cushenbery, Tom Daniel (sketch artist), Dan Dempski, and Richard "Korky" Korkes.

The men who created the whole thing: Bob Kane and Bill Finger.

The fans of the show who supplied us with invaluable assistance and material: Dave Anderson, Kevin Burns, Saul Ferris, Mike Karberg, Mark Racop of Fiberglass Freaks and fiberglassfreaks.com, Eric Seltzer of 1966batmobile.com, and Fred Westbrook. Special thanks to incredible Ivan Tabac whose endless cooperation, patience and superlative enthusiasm made difficult things easier, resulting in a better and even battier book.

The researchers: Oscar Jay Lilley, Abbey Robbins-Lilley and Amanda Stow at American Heritage Center, Klaudia Englund at Thousand Oaks Library, Janine Bailey, Boyd Magers, Martin O'Hearn, and Mike Tiefenbacher.

The image scanners: Scott A. Schutz and Tom Gram at Rode's Camera, Andrew Mueller and Steve Varick at Precision Color Graphics, and Doug Petznick at Sun Printing.

The family members of those that have passed on: Anne Rutherford-Dozier, Deborah Potter-Dozier, Diana Muldaur Dozier, Jodye Horwitz-Bartold, and Paul Hefti.

The staff at Titan: Especially our astoundingly patient editor Bridie Roman, along with Laura Price, Nick Landau, Adam Newell and Simon Ward. And our designer Tim Scrivens, assisted by Cameron Cornelius and Alison Hau, for all their hard work putting the book together.